Creating an Inclusive Social Studies Classroom for Exceptional Learners

Creating an Inclusive Social Studies Classroom for Exceptional Learners

edited by

Darren Minarik
Radford University

Timothy Lintner
University of South Carolina, Aiken

INFORMATION AGE PUBLISHING, INC.
Charlotte, NC • www.infoagepub.com

Library of Congress Cataloging-in-Publication Data

A CIP record for this book is available from the Library of Congress
http://www.loc.gov

ISBN: 979-8-88730-645-2 (Paperback)
    979-8-88730-646-9 (Hardcover)
    979-8-88730-647-6 (E-Book)

Copyright © 2024 Information Age Publishing Inc.

All rights reserved. No part of this publication may be reproduced, stored in a retrieval system, or transmitted, in any form or by any means, electronic, mechanical, photocopying, microfilming, recording or otherwise, without written permission from the publisher.

Printed in the United States of America

CONTENTS

PART I
THE MODEL FOR INCLUSIVE EDUCATION

1 The Social Studies Classroom: Advocating for Inclusive Education 3
  Darren Minarik and Timothy Lintner

2 Integrating Effective Special Education Practices With Best
  Practices in Social Studies 17
  Stephen Ciullo and Justin Garwood

PART II
CREATING AN INCLUSIVE CLASSROOM ENVIRONMENT

3 Inclusive Social Studies Through Collaboration and Co-Teaching 45
  Melissa Lisanti, Elizabeth Altieri, and Karen Douglas

4 Developing the Civic Engagement of Students With
  Disabilities: Inclusive Civic Action Projects 71
  Leah M. Bueso and Richard Cairn

5 Embracing Universal Design for Learning: Planning
  for Inclusive Social Studies Classrooms 97
  Kari A. Muente

PART III
INCLUSIVE INSTRUCTION

6 Addressing the Learning Needs of Students With Disabilities Through Effective Questioning 123
Darren Minarik and Janis A. Bulgren

7 Supporting Inclusion With Higher Order Thinking and Reasoning 135
Janis A. Bulgren and Darren Minarik

8 Active and Engaging Social Studies Instruction for Higher Level Learning 155
Melissa Martin and Alison Puliatte

9 Social Studies Literacy 175
Daniel Wissinger and Susan De La Paz

About the Editors 197
About the Contributors 199

PART I

THE MODEL FOR INCLUSIVE EDUCATION

CHAPTER 1

THE SOCIAL STUDIES CLASSROOM

Advocating for Inclusive Education

Darren Minarik
Radford University

Timothy Lintner
University of South Carolina, Aiken

Today's students come from increasingly diverse cultural backgrounds, possess an array of ability levels, and bring into our classrooms a myriad of exceptionalities. With the continued and concerted push toward inclusion, a growing number of students with disabilities (SWDs), including those with intellectual and developmental disabilities, are participating in general education settings with the expectation that they learn the same content as their peers without disabilities (Mastropieri & Scruggs, 2010; Wehmeyer et al., 2021). Furthermore, teachers who support inclusive education are expected to presume competence in all students regardless of disability label, provide an education that addresses the skills necessary for participatory citizenship and independence later in life, and establish an environment that is welcoming, accessible, and both socially and emotionally supportive for all students (Jorgensen, 2018). The academic and social participation in the general education classroom is provided to the maximum extent possible.

It is estimated that roughly 66% of students aged 5–21 who qualify for special education services spend upwards of 80% or more of their school day in general education classrooms, including social studies (National Center for Education Statistics, 2021). According to the U.S. Department of Education (2021), the most common disability evident in the general education classroom was specific learning disabilities (LD), comprising 33% of learners. Roughly 41% of students with autism, 19% of students with speech and language impairments (SLI) and 18% of students with intellectual disabilities (ID) accessed the general education curriculum as well. Only 12% of students with autism, 8% of students with an intellectual disability and 6% of students with an emotional and/or behavioral disorder (EBD) spent a significant part of their day in the general education classroom. These statistics highlight that a portion of the special education population is not afforded the presumption of competence and the opportunity to receive an education in the general education classroom (Agran et al., 2020; Fitzpatrick & Wehmeyer, 2020; Minarik et al., 2021).

These percentages do not tell us anything about the quality of instruction SWDs are receiving when placed in a general education setting, or if they are fully immersed in the general education curriculum versus receiving a modified curriculum based on perceived abilities. They also do not share the content being taught, so little is known about which subjects are taught more in inclusive settings, although instruction in reading, writing and mathematics tends to receive the more intensive specialized interventions outside of the general education classroom (Smith & Larwin, 2021). Data only shows how much time a student spends in the general education setting but tells us nothing about how truly inclusive those settings are for SWDs. Those who question the value of inclusive education for SWDs use educational progress data to demonstrate limited improvements in areas like reading for SWDs included in general education classrooms, without fully considering how to make inclusive instruction more effective or recognizing the positive postsecondary outcomes of SWDs who experience a more inclusive K-12 education (Barrett et al., 2020; Fuchs et al., 2023; Kauffman et al., 2018; Rojewski et al., 2015).

SPECIAL EDUCATION AND THE MOVE TOWARD INCLUSIVE EDUCATION

With the passage of the Education for all Handicapped Act or Public Law 94-142 in 1975, SWDs were provided with a free appropriate public education in the least restrictive environment, opening the door for SWDs to receive instruction and special education services in public schools (Curtis, 1991; Minarik & Lintner, 2011). An advocacy effort in the 1980s known as the regular education initiative (REI) called for the mainstreaming of students with less complex disabilities in the general education classroom to the maximum extent possible. Continued reauthorizations of PL 94-142 with the Individuals with Disabilities Education Act in 1997 and Individuals with Disabilities Education Improvement Act in 2004 further advanced the idea that SWDs should be placed in the general education classroom before considering more restrictive placements (Hardman & Dawson, 2008). Public education laws like the No Child Left Behind Act in 2001 and the 2015 Every Student Succeed Act continued to push for greater academic accountability for all students, highlighting the needs for teachers to have the qualifications to ensure student success. Finally, laws like section 504 of the Rehabilitation Act of 1973 and the 1991 Americans with Disabilities Act advanced inclusion within society.

MODELS OF DISABILITY AND PERCEPTION

One of the drawbacks to the federal legislation supporting special education was the requirement to identify SWDs by one of 13 disability categories defined as an impairment. This medical model for disability addresses the biology of the disability and "seeks to reduce the complex problems of disabled people to issues of medical prevention, cure or rehabilitation" (Shakespeare, 2006, p. 199). Students are viewed by their perceived deficits rather than their strengths. Classroom instruction in special education is often framed in terms of interventions using specific strategies to improve student academic performance and address social and behavioral issues. With high stakes testing and accountability, the focus is often on what students are failing to do as opposed to what they are doing well.

In response to the medical model is the social model or sociocultural view of disability where disability is framed as a construction created by societal interactions and norms and recognizes disability as a vital contributor in society (Connor, 2013). The linguistic representation of the word "disability" is seen as negatively positioning the ability of an individual and only seeing someone from a limitation perspective, demonstrating how society marginalizes people not considered to be able-bodied (Anastasiou & Kauffman, 2011). This suggests people without disabilities are defining and judging normality and frame much of what is assumed about disability through an ability normative or ableism lens (Foucault, 1977; Wolbring, 2008). The social model challenges these assumptions, encouraging recognition of those who have been excluded in the past (Wolbring, 2008). Table 1.1 provides a side-by-side comparison of the medical and sociocultural views of disability that can both create challenges and support inclusion in our schools.

TABLE 1.1 Medicalized and Sociocultural View of Disability

Medicalized View of Disability	Sociocultural View of Disability
Person has a medically diagnosed disability that is preventable, curable, or improved with rehabilitation.	The person's disability is a complex condition affected by context and largely a consequence of prejudice and marginalization.
Focus on diagnosis, labeling, and the impairment first. When a person struggles or fails, the disability is seen as the primary cause.	Focus is person-centered with an emphasis on strengths, needs, and ways to address challenges. When a person struggles or fails, it is more directly related to the environment. And not utilizing strengths rather than the disability.
Emphasis placed on the educational environment that fixes the impairment, which may mean alternative services and settings instead of inclusive settings.	Emphasis placed on the inclusive educational environment first with consideration of alternative settings only after exhausting inclusive options.
Learning is best achieved in an individual or small group situation where instruction is very teacher directed.	Learning is a social activity requiring active involvement with other students and where the teacher guides instruction with scaffolds that provide for a gradual release of control. Instruction is both teacher and student directed.
Society sees disability as not the norm and sees people with disabilities as needing to adapt and fit in.	Society evolves to question the definition of normal and how society can change to better include people with disabilities.

Source: Connor (2013). Adapted from Minarik & Blevins (2017).

Anastasiou and Kauffman (2011) suggested that these debates about medicalized and sociocultural models of disability have implications for how special education is delivered in public schools. The concern is that special education is in danger of becoming "not-special" if inclusive educational practices stop specializing the instruction for the individual learner or completely transfer the responsibility for SWDs to the general education classroom (Anastasiou & Kauffman, 2011; Singer, 2005). Regardless of where one falls within this discussion, these models raise important questions about inclusion. It is important to consider how these theoretical models connect to perceptions of disability and the relationship between special education and general education in public schooling. How schools position themselves in this discourse impacts the feasibility of implementing fully inclusive schooling for SWDs.

INCLUSION AND THE SOCIAL STUDIES CLASSROOM

Until the last decade, there was relatively little conversation about the intersections between special education and social studies other than strategies to memorize and comprehend content (Martin et al., 2021; Mullins et al., 2020). Since 2014, several meta-analyses were published that highlighted effective strategy instruction in social studies classrooms for SWDs (Ciullo et al., 2020; Garwood et al., 2021; Swanson et al., 2014). Much of this literature appears in special education publications rather than social studies journals, potentially preventing social studies educators from learning about those practices that positively impact academic outcomes for SWDs (Curtis & Green, 2021). In response to the limited research and small number of disability topics in social studies journal publications, Lintner and Schweder (2011) published *Practical Strategies for Teaching K–12 Social Studies in Inclusive Classrooms*, the first book solely addressing SWDs in social studies classrooms. Five years later, the National Council for the Social Studies (NCSS) released *Social Studies and Exceptional Learners*, a comprehensive primer for social studies educators to support inclusive social studies instruction in elementary, middle, and high school classrooms (Minarik & Lintner, 2016; Minarik et al., 2021). These two publications served as early indicators of how the the field of social studies could position itself as a leader in the effort to model and support effective inclusive education for SWDs.

When examining the purpose of social studies education, it fits well in both theory and practice with the belief and practice of inclusion for SWDs. The NCSS curriculum standards, civic mission, and the College, Career, and Civic Life (C3) framework all emphasize the importance of meeting the needs of diverse students and providing meaningful and powerful teaching and learning opportunities that are scaffolded and engaging (NCSS, 2010a; NCSS, 2010b; NCSS, 2013). Similarly, an inclusive classroom for SWDs involves an engaging and meaningful environment that supports the full integration and participation of all students. In our schools, social studies teachers encourage active learning through the promotion of diverse thought and action which enables all students to become informed, participatory citizens (Martin et al., 2021; National Council for the Social Studies, 2016). Schools are charged with teaching the fundamentals of participatory citizenship to all students, including SWDs. It is in the social studies classroom that such rich opportunities for participatory learning for SWDs naturally occur and these spaces serve as a starting point for including students more throughout the school day (Curtis, 1991; Johnson & Busbee, 2015; Minarik & Lintner, 2011; Passe & Beattie, 1994; Patton, 1987; Scruggs et al., 2008).

Inclusive education, and inclusive social studies, is not simply about a seat in the classroom or the provision of accommodations for SWDs. Inclusive social studies is a vision and belief that all students belong in a heterogeneous and socially democratic setting "that fosters the development of a community of learners, attempts to balance the unity and diversity of democratic citizenship, and adopts a curriculum that is flexible, participatory, and accessible to learners of all abilities" (Urban, 2013, p. 10; Villa & Thousand, 2021). Inclusive education is believing that SWDs belong first in the general education setting and have a right to learn the same curriculum as their peers without disabilities in the least restrictive environment to the maximum extent possible (Minarik & Lintner, 2016). Inclusion is less concerned with educational outcomes of attainment (i.e., test scores, class rankings, etc.) but rather the degree and depth of engagement and participation in and through the process of learning (Cummings et al., 2003). Inclusive education and democratic citizenship, evidenced in and through powerful social studies, not only encourages but demands the full acceptance and active participation of all students.

A PATHWAY FOR CREATING AN INCLUSIVE SOCIAL STUDIES CLASSROOM

This publication is a response to the need for our social studies classrooms to be leaders in providing impactful and inclusive instruction for all students. In the book, *Social Studies and Exceptional Learners* (Minarik & Lintner, 2016), social studies educators learned introductory methods for creating a more inclusive social studies classroom and were provided with a basic understanding of special education and where social studies fits in the process (Mullins et al., 2020). This book moves social studies educators to the next level, calling on all of us at the pre-service and in-service level to create social studies classrooms that include, challenge, and purposefully engage all SWDs, regardless of perceived ability attached to a medical label.

Each chapter provides critical components necessary for an inclusive social studies classroom beginning with an introduction to the importance of inclusive education and advocating for the use of social studies as a starting point for inclusion in our schools. In Chapter 2, Ciullo and Garwood take a closer look at intersections between special education and social studies with an examination of what best practice in special education looks like through the lens of High Leverage Practices (HLPs) and how these best practices align with the latest social studies research. Many of the best practices discussed in Ciullo and Garwood's chapter are given additional attention in later chapters.

Collaboration with special education personnel, particularly in the form of co-teaching, is essential in addressing the needs of SWDs and Lisanti, Altieri, and Douglas establish a compelling case for collaborating with special educators and co-teaching. Schools have come to rely more on collaborative models of instructional practice where knowledge and expertise are shared with the common goal of supporting student outcomes. We know co-teaching is an effective instructional model for meeting the needs of all students, particularly SWDs (Cook et al., 2017; Scruggs & Mastropieri, 2017; Strogilos & King-Sears, 2019; Walsh, 2012). Students in co-taught classrooms get the attention (and expertise) of two teachers. The curriculum in co-taught classrooms is often more enriched, layered, engaging, and responsive than in a typical classroom. Both general education and special education teachers report increased levels of academic achievement for students with exceptionalities in their classrooms (Cook & McDuffie-Landrum, 2020; King-Sears et al., 2021; Lochner et al., 2019), including social studies classrooms (van Hover et al., 2012; Young Buckley, 2005; Zgonc, 2007).

Powerful civic education in our schools is one way to support more inclusive practice and Bueso and Cairn's chapter makes a case for including strategies that promote self-determination, social emotional learning, equity, and inclusion in our social studies classrooms to support the knowledge, skills, and dispositions necessary to be engaged in democratic society. Their ideas for including more disability history and developing inclusive civic action projects present opportunities for social studies teachers to create inclusive learning opportunities for all students. Universal Design for Learning (UDL) is the focus of Chapter 5 as teachers learn how to plan social studies instruction using the inquiry design model (IDM) along with multiple means of representation, multiple means of engagement, and multiple means of action and expression. In the next two chapters, Bulgren and Minarik move from the broader planning process into specific questioning techniques and higher order thinking and reasoning strategies to support powerful and effective learning opportunities for SWDs. The Strategic Instruction Model™ content enhancement approach to learning is emphasized. Chapter 8 continues the themes of strategy instruction and the promotion of critical thinking using tools like project-based learning (PBL), simulations, role-play, experiential learning, and kinesthetic strategies. DeLa Paz and Wissinger complete the chapters with a focus on literacy skills and strategies to address writing and comprehension in the inclusive social studies classroom.

Each chapter provides insight for future research and challenges the reader to implement what was shared, either through pre-service methods courses or in K–12 social studies classrooms. What these chapters do not represent is a form of special teaching that is exclusively beneficial to one group of students over another. Instead, the chapter authors provide social studies educators with impactful and research-based inclusive teaching that will support SWDs and enhance learning for any student that might need additional scaffolds or supports to access the content. The pedagogical practices outlined in this publication support opportunities for all students to experience social studies and become informed and participatory citizens. It also creates an opportunity for teachers in social studies to collaborate with their colleagues in special education and advocate for greater inclusion of SWDs in the school community. If our schools are to be laboratories of democracy, they must be accepting of all our students (O'Brien, 2000). People with disabilities are a significant part of our society. Most of us will experience disability at some point in our lives. The social studies classroom and social studies curricula provide the avenue to create inclusive teaching and learning opportunities, educate students about disability, and support full participation and acceptance for people with disabilities as citizens.

TAKING A POSITION ON THE INCLUSION OF STUDENTS WITH DISABILITIES

It is our hope that social studies educators take on a leadership role in improving inclusive opportunities for students with disabilities (SWDs). We still have a long way to go in terms of research, publications, professional development, and there needs to be a continued cultural shift in how we think about disability and social studies education. We do not want to discount the progress made in the last decade and this book is testimony to the fact that social studies and special education is finally receiving more attention. However, we feel that it is critical to keep this forward momentum and recommend that the National Council for the Social Studies (NCSS) consider ways to expand support for teaching SWDs and learning about the history of disability. The 2016 NCSS publication, *Social Studies and Exceptional Learners* was a great first step in recognizing the importance of this topic. The next step should be the creation of a position statement that affirms a commitment to creating more fully inclusive social studies classrooms for SWDs and supporting a larger effort to use social studies education as the catalyst for more inclusive school community. Several professional education organizations in other content areas have clear statements about working with SWDs and it is time for NCSS to do the same. Below is a suggested statement for NCSS to consider. It is our hope that NCSS will adopt a statement, whether it is the one we provide here or a similar document that positions a clear message that all SWDs deserve to receive a high-quality social studies education in an inclusive setting.

Position Statement: Promoting Inclusion for Students With Disabilities in Social Studies

The National Council for the Social Studies (NCSS) recognizes that social studies educators can lead the effort in supporting better inclusive practice for SWDs in K–12 education by encouraging full inclusion in social studies classrooms. In 2016, NCSS demonstrated support for better inclusive practice in social studies through the publication of *Social Studies and Exceptional Learners*. This was an essential introductory step in educating teachers about disability, special education, and the importance of including SWDs in social studies instruction.

The National Council for the Social Studies strongly encourages all social studies educators to take an active role in promoting inclusive education for SWDs. It is important to recognize how inclusive education aligns with the principles of equity, diversity, and social justice, fostering the belief that all students belong, regardless of a disability label or perception of ability (Cole et al., 2023; Minarik et al., 2021; Villa & Thousand, 2021). Thus, it is our official position that all teachers, especially social studies teachers, become advocates for the inclusion of SWDs in the general curriculum to the maximum extent possible. To foster inclusive practice, the National Council for the Social Studies supports the following principles:

- It is important to presume competence in all students and hold high expectations for academic, social, and emotional success regardless of labels or perceived abilities (Agran et al., 2020; Biklen & Burke, 2006). Every student, including those with disabilities, possesses unique strengths, skills, and perspectives that contribute to the learning community. By presuming competence, social studies educators create inclusive classrooms that provide meaningful opportunities for all students to engage in active learning, higher-order thinking, reasoning, and civic participation.
- Social studies educators should both be advocates for SWDs and promote the skills of self-determination and civic engagement. When SWDs are empowered with the skills and dispositions associated with self-determination and civic engagement, they become more independent and empowered citizens who can advocate for themselves and for others (Mann et al., 2015; Minarik et al., 2021; Wehmeyer & Shogren, 2016).
- Effective inclusion is not possible without collaboration between social studies educators, special education professionals, families, and other stakeholders who support SWDs. Collaborative efforts lead to the development and implementation of effective instructional practices that meet the diverse needs of all learners. Co-teaching, Universal Design for Learning, and differentiation strategies are valuable methods for promoting the full inclusion of SWDs in social studies classrooms (Jenkins & Murawski, 2024). These approaches empower educators to provide multiple means of representation, engagement, and action and expression, ensuring that all students can access and actively participate in social studies content (Minarik & Lintner, 2016).

- Inquiry-based learning is an approach that benefits all students, including those with more complex developmental or multiple disabilities (Ryan et al., 2019). Inquiry-based learning promotes curiosity, critical thinking, and problem-solving while addressing different learning preferences and abilities. Social studies educators should employ inclusive instructional methodologies and strategies, such as UDL and differentiated instruction, to ensure that every student has full access to content and can actively participate in the process of inquiry and exploration.
- The inclusion of disability history is essential when promoting a more inclusive social studies classroom. Organizations like Emerging America are leading the effort to provide curriculum resources for teachers to incorporate disability history into social studies curricula. States are passing laws recognizing disability history and awareness weeks or months and adding disability history to their standards. These efforts foster empathy and challenge stigmas and stereotypes, thereby promoting a deeper understanding of the experiences and contributions of individuals with disabilities throughout history. Including disability history in social studies curricula reinforces the principle of inclusivity, teaches students to explore marginalized histories, and prepares students to become informed, compassionate, and socially responsible citizens (Minarik et al., 2016).

We support the full inclusion of SWDs in K–12 social studies classrooms. By presuming competence in all students, supporting self-determination and civic engagement, collaborating with special education professionals, embracing inquiry-based learning, and incorporating disability history, social studies educators can create inclusive learning environments that support diversity and self-determination and promote the development of an informed and engaged citizenry. We encourage schools, districts, policymakers, higher education institutions, and professional organizations to provide the necessary support, resources, and professional development opportunities to ensure the successful implementation of inclusive practices in social studies education. With this assistance, educators will create equitable and inclusive social studies classrooms that empower SWDs to reach their full potential.

REFERENCES

Agran, M., Jackson, L., Kurth, J. A., Ryndak, D., Burnette, K., Jameson, M., Zagona, A., Fitzpatrick, H., & Wehmeyer, M. (2020). Why aren't students with severe disabilities being placed in general education classrooms: Examining the relations among classroom placement, learner outcomes, and other factors. *Research and Practice for Persons With Severe Disabilities, 45*(1), 4–13.

Anastasiou D., & Kauffman, J. M. (2011). A social constructionist approach to disability: Implications for special education. *Exceptional Children, 77*(3), 367–384.

Barrett, C., Stevenson, N. A., & Burns, M. K. (2020). Relationship between disability category, time spent in general education and academic achievement. *Educational Studies, 46*(4), 497512. https://doi.org/10.1080/03055698.2019.1614433

Biklen, D., & Burke, J. (2006). Presuming competence. *Equity and Excellence in Education, 39*(2), 166–176.

Ciullo, S., Collins, A., Wissinger, D. R., McKenna, J. W., Lo, Y. L., & Osman, D. (2020). Students with learning disabilities in the social studies: A meta-analysis of intervention research. *Exceptional Children, 86*(4), 393–412.

Cole, S. M., Murphy, H. R., Frisby, M. B., & Robinson, J. (2023). The relationship between special education placement and high school outcomes. *The Journal of Special Education, 57*(1), 13–23. https://doi.org/10.1177/00224669221097945

Connor, D. J. (2013). Who "owns" dis/ability? The cultural work of critical special educators as insider-outsiders. *Theory & Research in Social Education, 41*(4), 494–513.

Cook, S. C., & McDuffie-Landrum, K. (2020). Integrating effective practices into co-teaching: Increasing outcomes for students with disabilities. *Intervention in School and Clinic, 55*(4), 221–229.

Cook, S. C., Mcduffie-Landrum, K. A., Oshita, L., & Cook, B. G. (2017). Co-teaching for students with disabilities: A critical and updated analysis of the empirical literature. In J. M. Kauffman, D. P. Hallahan, & P. C. Pullen (Eds.), *Handbook of special education* (pp. 233–248). Routledge.

Cummings, C., Dyson, A., & Millward, A. (2003). Participation and democracy: What's inclusion got to do with it? In J. Allan (Ed.), *Inclusion, participation, and democracy: What's the purpose?* (pp. 49–64). Kluwer Academic Press.

Curtis, C. K. (1991). Social studies for students at risk and with disabilities. In J. P. Shaver (Ed.), *Handbook of research on social studies teaching and learning* (pp. 157–174). MacMillan.

Curtis, M. D., & Green, A. L. (2021). A systematic review of evidence-based practices for students with learning disabilities in social studies classrooms. *The Social Studies, 112*(3), 105–119. https://doi.org/10.1080/00377996.2020.1841715

Fitzpatrick, H., & Wehmeyer, M. (2020). Why aren't students with severe disabilities being placed in general education classrooms: Examining the relations among classroom placement, learner outcomes, and other factors. *Research and Practice for Persons with Severe Disabilities, 45*(1), 4–13.

Foucault, M. (1977). *Discipline and punish: The birth of the prison* (A. Sheridan, Trans.). Pantheon.

Fuchs, D., Mirowitz, H. C., & Gilbert, J. K. (2023). Exploring the truth of Michael Yudin's claim: The more time students with disabilities spend in general classrooms, the better they do academically. *Journal of Disability Policy Studies, 33*(4), 236–252. https://doi.org/10.1177/10442073221097713

Garwood, J. D., McKenna, J. W., Roberts, G. J., Ciullo, S., & Shin, M. (2021). Social studies content knowledge interventions for students with emotional and behavioral disorders: A meta-analysis. *Behavior Modification, 45*(1), 147–176.

Hardman, M. L., & Dawson, S. (2008). The impact of federal public policy on curriculum and instruction for students with disabilities in the general classroom. *Preventing School Failure, 52*(2), 5–11.

Jenkins, M. C., & Murawski, W. W. (2024). *Connecting high-leverage practices to student success: Collaboration in inclusive classrooms.* Corwin Press.

Johnson, J., & Busby, R. (2015). Including young learners with special needs in social studies classrooms. *Social Studies Research & Practice, 10*(3), 98–108.

Jorgensen, C. M. (2018). *It's more than "just being in."* Paul Brookes Publishing.

Kauffman, J. M., Felder, M., Ahrbeck, B., Badar, J., & Schneiders, K. (2018). Inclusion of all students in general education? International appeal for a more temperate approach to inclusion. *Journal of International Special Needs Education, 21*(2), 1–10. https://doi.org/10.1080/09362835.2020.1727326

King-Sears, M. E., Stefanidis, A., Berkeley, S., & Strogilos, V. (2021). Does co-teaching improve academic achievement for students with disabilities? A meta-analysis. *Educational Research Review, 34*, 100405.

Lintner, T., & Schweder, W. (Eds.). (2011). *Practical strategies for teaching K–12 social studies in inclusive classrooms.* Information Age Publishing.

Lochner, W. W., Murawski, W. W., & Daley, J. T. (2019). The effect of co-teaching on student cognitive engagement. *Theory & Practice in Rural Education, 9*(2), 6–19.

Mann, J. A., Dymond, S. K., Bonati, M. L., & Neeper, L. S. (2015). Restrictive citizenship: Civic-oriented service-learning opportunities for all students. *Journal of Experiential Education, 38*, 56–72.

Martin, M., Minarik, D., & Lintner, T. (2021). Inclusive practices in social studies classrooms: Including all students in all aspects of learning. In A. Samuels & G. Samuels (Eds.), *Fostering diversity and inclusion in the social sciences* (pp. 69–84). Information Age Publishing.

Mastropieri, M. A., & Scruggs, T. E. (2010). *The inclusive classroom: Strategies for effective differentiation instruction* (4th ed.). Merrill.

Minarik, D., & Blevins, M. (2017). Going "full retard": Teaching about disability through film. In W. Russell & S. Waters (Eds.), *Cinematic social studies: A resource for teaching and learning social studies with film* (pp. 101–128). Information Age Publishing.

Minarik, D., Carroll, M., & Sheridan, K. (2016). A compelling history worth mentioning. *Oregon Journal of the Social Studies 4*(1), 58–69.

Minarik, D., Grooten, R., & Lintner, T. (2021). A justice-oriented approach to addressing disability. In Ronald W. Evans (Ed.), *Handbook on teaching social issues* (2nd ed.; pp. 339–348). Information Age Publishing.

Minarik, D. W., & Lintner, T. (2011). The push for inclusive classrooms and the impact on social studies design and delivery. *Social Studies Review, 50*(1), 52–55.

Minarik, D., & Lintner, T. (2016). *Social studies and exceptional learners.* National Council for the Social Studies.

Mullins, R. D., Jr., Williams, T., Hicks, D., & Mullins, S. B. (2020). Can we meet our mission? Examining the professional development of social studies teachers to support students with disabilities and emergent bilingual learners. *The Journal of Social Studies Research, 44*(1), 195–208.

National Center for Education Statistics. (2021). *Percentage distribution of school-aged students served under Individuals with Disabilities Education Act (IDEA).*

National Council for the Social Studies. (2010a). *National curriculum standards for social studies: A framework for teaching, learning, and assessment.*

National Council for the Social Studies. (2010b). *A vision of powerful teaching and learning in the social studies: Building social understanding and civic efficacy national curriculum standards for social studies: A framework for teaching, learning, and assessment.*

National Council for the Social Studies. (2013). *College, career, and civic life (C3) framework for Social Studies State Standards.* https://www.socialstudies.org/system/files/2022/c3-framework-for-social-studies-rev0617.2.pdf

National Council for the Social Studies. (2016). A vision of powerful teaching and learning in the social studies. *Social Education, 80*(3), 180–182.

O'Brien, J. (2000). Enabling all students to learn in the laboratory of democracy. *Intervention in School and Clinic, 35*(4), 195–205.

Passe, J., & Beattie, J. (1994). Social studies instruction for students with mild disabilities: A progress report. *Remedial and Special Education, 15*(4), 227–233.

Patton, J. R., (1987). Social studies instruction for handicapped instruction. *Social Studies, 78*(3), 131–135.

Rojewski, J. W., Lee, I. H., & Gregg, N. (2015). Causal effects of inclusion on postsecondary education outcomes of individuals with high-incidence disabilities. *Journal of Disability Policy Studies, 25*(4), 210–219.

Ryan, J., Jameson, J. M., Coleman, O. F., Eichelberger, C., Bowman, J. A., Conradi, L. A., . . . & McDonnell, J. (2019). Inclusive social studies content instruction for students with significant intellectual disability using structured inquiry-based instruction. *Education and Training in Autism and Developmental Disabilities, 54*(4), 420–436.

Scruggs, T. E., & Mastropieri, M. A. (2017). Making inclusion work with co-teaching. *Teaching Exceptional Children, 49*(4), 284–293.

Scruggs, T. E., Mastropieri, M. A., & Okolo, C. M. (2008). Science and social studies for students with disabilities. *Focus on Exceptional Children, 41*(2), 1–24.

Shakespeare, T. (2006). The social model of disability. In L. J. Davis (Ed.), *The disability studies reader* (2nd ed.; pp. 197–204). Routledge.

Singer, J. D. (2005). Should special education merge with regular education? In J. M. Kauffmann & D. P. Hallahan (Eds.), *The illusion of full inclusion: A comprehensive critique of a current special education bandwagon* (pp. 7–24). Pro-Ed.

Smith, E., & Larwin, K. H. (2021). Will they be welcomed in? The impact of K–12 teachers' and principals' perceptions of inclusion of students with disabilities. *Journal of Organizational and Educational Leadership, 6*(3), 1. https://files.eric.ed.gov/fulltext/EJ1315495.pdf

Strogilos, V., & King-Sears, M. E. (2019). Co-teaching is extra help and fun: Perspectives on co-teaching from middle school students and co-teachers. *Journal of Research in Special Educational Needs, 19*(2), 92–102.

Swanson, E., Hairrell, A., Kent, S., Ciullo, S., Wanzek, J. A., & Vaughn, S. (2014). A synthesis and meta-analysis of reading interventions using social studies content for students with learning disabilities. *Journal of Learning Disabilities, 47*(2), 178–195.

United States Department of Education. (2021). *Forty-third annual report to Congress on the Implementation of the Individuals with Disabilities Act.* Washington, DC.

Urban, D. J., Jr. (2013). *Toward a framework of inclusive social studies: Obstacles and opportunities in a preservice teacher education program* [Doctoral dissertation, Columbia University]. https://doi.org/10.7916/D83F4WVX

van Hover, S., Hicks, D., & Sayeski, K. (2012). A case study of co-teaching in an inclusive secondary high-stakes World History I classroom. *Theory & Research in Social Education, 40*(3), 260–291.

Villa, R. A., & Thousand, J. S. (2021). *The inclusive education checklist: A self-assessment of best practices.* National Professional Resources.

Walsh, J. M. (2012). Co-teaching as a school system strategy for continuous improvement. *Preventing School Failure: Alternative Education for Children and Youth, 56*(1), 29–36.

Wehmeyer M. L., & Shogren K. A. (2016). Self-determination and choice. In N. Singh (Ed.), *Handbook of evidence-based practices in intellectual and developmental disabilities. Evidence-based practices in behavioral health* (pp. 561–584). Springer International Publishing.

Wehmeyer, M. L., Shogren, K. A., & Kurth, J. (2021). The state of inclusion with students with intellectual and developmental disabilities in the United States. *Journal of Policy and Practice in Intellectual Disabilities, 18*(1), 36–43.

Wolbring, G. (2008). The politics of ableism. *Development, 51*, 252–258.

Young Buckley, C. (2005). Establishing and maintaining collaborative relationships between regular and special education teachers in middle school social studies inclusive classrooms. In T. E. Scruggs & M. A. Mastropieri (Eds.), *Cognition and learning in diverse settings* (pp. 153–198). Emerald Group Publishing Limited.

Zgonc, K. C. (2007). *The impact of co-teaching on student learning outcomes in secondary social studies classrooms implementing content enhancement routines.* University of Central Florida.

CHAPTER 2

INTEGRATING EFFECTIVE SPECIAL EDUCATION PRACTICES WITH BEST PRACTICES IN SOCIAL STUDIES

Stephen Ciullo
Texas State University

Justin Garwood
The University of Vermont

BEST PRACTICES IN SOCIAL STUDIES

Students who receive special education services can be successful and engaged learners in the social studies classroom. Social studies teachers have expressed a need for more specific suggestions and classroom strategies that can be used to boost learning and literacy for students with disabilities (Mason et al., 2022). Fortunately, there are effective instructional practices that can be applied across subject areas (e.g., high-leverage practices from

Creating an Inclusive Social Studies Classroom for Exceptional Learners, pages 17–41
Copyright © 2024 by Information Age Publishing
www.infoagepub.com
All rights of reproduction in any form reserved.

the Council for Exceptional Children) as well as specific social studies interventions that are helpful for students with disabilities (SWDs) (Ciullo et al., 2021; Swanson et al., 2014). In this chapter, we describe strategies that can be used within inclusive social studies classrooms (i.e., SWDs served in general education, sometimes with the support of a special education teacher) to promote curriculum access, content learning, and active participation in enriching activities such as those suggested by the National Council for Social Studies (NCSS).

This chapter includes three sections that we hope will equip readers with strategies, techniques, and resources that can be immediately used for SWDs in social studies. First, we provide a "Review of Literature" to highlight research-supported learning strategies and instructional theories that are beneficial for SWDs. This review of research is the foundation for the instructional practices and strategies discussed in this chapter. The second section—"How Do I Plan to Teach Effective Strategies?"—includes six high-leverage practices for effective special education instruction. Each high-leverage practice includes examples depicting how to apply this practice while teaching a social studies learning strategy (e.g., a concept map, graphic organizer, cognitive strategy instruction). The chapter's final section is called "Looking Ahead." Here, we provide a roadmap for readers to practice implementing the strategies presented in this chapter. Thus, the central aim of this chapter is to provide readers with techniques that can be immediately practiced and implemented with SWDs to improve curriculum access, learning of important information, and learner engagement in social studies classrooms.

Why is this chapter relevant to current and/or future teachers? To begin with, social studies teachers in Grades 6–12 are sometimes at an instructional disadvantage due to social studies marginalization that has occurred at the elementary-school level (Fitchett & Haefner, 2010; Fitchett et al., 2014). Standardized testing in other disciplines has been associated with less time allocated for social studies. These discrepancies in access to the curriculum are more pronounced in low-socio-economic schools, and for students receiving special education services who may be removed from social studies instruction for other special services (Fitchett & Heafner, 2010; Heafner, 2018). Thus, teachers and students can benefit from strategies that can improve learning outcomes for SWDs to address previous instructional gaps. Second, concepts in social studies and civics empower SWDs who have historically been less involved in community and civic engagement relative to students without a disability (Garwood et al., 2021). Students benefit from domain knowledge such as identifying their civil rights, comprehending governmental processes (local, state, national), and learning about individuals who have affected instrumental historical progress (e.g., Fannie Lou Hamer, Nelson Mandela). In sum, concepts included in expert recommendations such as the College, Career, and Civic Life (C3) Framework can promote improved academic as well as community-based outcomes for a broad range of learners (National Council for the Social Studies, 2013). We are enthusiastic that the strategies, suggestions, and resources in this chapter can be utilized by educators to provide SWDs the opportunity to thrive in their social studies classrooms.

REVIEW OF LITERATURE

Research studies have identified instructional strategies and interventions in social studies that are effective for SWDs. This section provides information describing the research base for teaching SWDs in the social studies. First, we present instructional theories and practices associated with improved achievement. This includes literature about high-leverage practices (HLPs) in special education. While there are numerous practices designated as "high-leverage," six practices will be highlighted because they are relevant for inclusive social studies instruction. Next, we review findings from social studies intervention studies to illustrate successful strategies to accelerate student learning.

For the duration of this chapter, students with disabilities are abbreviated as SWDs. We also refer to specific special education categories when discussing research studies. For instance, we sometimes refer to students with learning disabilities (LDs) as well as students with emotional or behavior disorders (E/BD). The recommendations in this chapter are based on research for a broad range of SWDs, including LD and E/BD. Readers are encouraged to apply the strategies included in this chapter when instructing students who receive special education services within general education inclusive-social studies classrooms.

High-Leverage Practices in Special Education

The Council for Exceptional Children (CEC) commissioned a panel of educational scholars to develop a list of practices that *all* teachers should implement to support SWDs. The purpose of these practices (along with the associated resources including videos, guidebooks, etc. included in Table 2.1) is to provide teacher-education faculty, professional development providers, and teachers with techniques that can be used across subject areas. The expert panel (McLeskey et al., 2017) formulated the High-Leverage Practice list by consulting with teachers, educational leaders, and by reviewing extensive special education research to identify essential practices. The list contains 22 high-leverage practices (HLPs) than span four

TABLE 2.1 High-Leverage Practices in Special Education Relevant to Social Studies

High-Leverage Practice	Description	Resource
HLP 12: Systematically design instruction toward a specific learning goal.	Teachers help students to develop important concepts and skills that provide the foundation for more complex learning. Teachers sequence lessons that build on each other and make connections explicit, in both planning and delivery. They activate students' prior knowledge and show how each lesson "fits" with previous ones. Planning involves careful consideration of learning goals, what is involved in reaching the goals, and allocating time accordingly. Ongoing changes (e.g., pacing, examples) occur throughout the sequence based on student performance. https://highleveragepractices.org/four-areas-practice-k-12/instruction	HLP 12 Video https://highleveragepractices.org/hlp-12-systematically-design-instruction-toward-specific-learning-goal
HLP 14: Teach cognitive and metacognitive strategies to support learning and independence.	Teachers explicitly teach cognitive and metacognitive processing strategies to support memory, attention, and self-regulation of learning. Learning involves not only understanding content but also using cognitive processes to solve problems, regulate attention, organize thoughts and materials, and monitor one's own thinking. https://highleveragepractices.org/four-areas-practice-k-12/instruction	HLP 14 Video https://highleveragepractices.org/hlp-14-use-cognitive-and-metacognitive-strategies
HLP 15: Provide scaffolded supports	Scaffolded supports provide temporary assistance to students so they can successfully complete tasks that they cannot yet do independently and with a high rate of success. Teachers select powerful visual, verbal, and written supports; carefully calibrate them to students' performance and understanding in relation to learning tasks; use them flexibly; evaluate their effectiveness; and gradually remove them once they are no longer needed. Some supports are planned prior to lessons and some are provided responsively during instruction. https://highleveragepractices.org/four-areas-practice-k-12/instruction	HLP Video https://highleveragepractices.org/hlp-15-use-scaffolded-supports

(continued)

TABLE 2.1 High-Leverage Practices in Special Education Relevant to Social Studies (continued)

High-Leverage Practice	Description	Resource
HLP 16: Use explicit instruction	Teachers make content, skills, and concepts explicit by showing and telling students what to do or think while solving problems, enacting strategies, completing tasks, and classifying concepts. Teachers use explicit instruction when students are learning new material and complex concepts and skills. They strategically choose examples and non-examples and language to facilitate student understanding, anticipate common misconceptions, highlight essential content, and remove distracting information. They model and scaffold steps or processes needed to understand content and concepts, apply skills, and complete tasks successfully and independently. https://highleveragepractices.org/four-areas-practice-k-12/instruction	HLP 16 Video https://highleveragepractices.org/hlp-16-use-explicit-instruction
HLP 18: Use strategies to promote active student engagement	Teachers use a variety of instructional strategies that result in active student responding. They promote engagement by connecting learning to students' lives (e.g., knowing students' academic and cultural backgrounds) and using a variety of teacher-led (e.g., choral responding and response cards), peer-assisted (e.g., cooperative learning and peer tutoring), student-regulated (e.g., self-management), and technology-supported strategies shown empirically to increase student engagement. https://highleveragepractices.org/four-areas-practice-k-12/instruction	HLP 18 Video https://highleveragepractices.org/hlp-18-use-strategies-promote-active-student-engagement

Note: The High-Leverage Practice Guidebook and online toolkit is located here: https://highleveragepractices.org/

categories: (a) assessment, (b) collaboration, (c) instructional, and (d) social/emotional/behavioral. Each of the 22 HLPs are important and we encourage readers to utilize the materials linked in Table 2.1 to explore each Practice. This chapter emphasizes six HLPs from the "instructional" category that are salient for social studies. These practices are defined in the following section. The abbreviation HLP is used for HLPs.

HLP 12: Systematically Design Instruction Toward a Specific Learning Goal

This HLP is defined as:

> Teachers help students to develop important concepts and skills that provide the foundation for more complex learning. Teachers sequence lessons that build on each other and make connections explicit, in both planning and delivery. They activate students' prior knowledge and show how each lesson "fits" with previous ones. Planning involves careful consideration of learning goals, what is involved in reaching the goals, and allocating time accordingly. Ongoing changes (e.g., pacing, examples) occur throughout the sequence based on student performance.

HLP 12 suggests that boosting students' foundational knowledge (i.e., learning key concepts in social studies) lays the groundwork for complex learning tasks presented in the future. SWDs will benefit from systematic instruction to reinforce concepts (e.g., the role of the Judicial Branch of government) along with details about those concepts (e.g., how many Justices serve on the Supreme Court) in order to demonstrate their knowledge of these topics and to apply knowledge to sophisticated activities including written argumentation or historical inquiry activities. Relatedly, Alexander's (2003, 2005) model of domain learning also suggests that foundational knowledge (e.g., key people, events) helps students to eventually apply this conceptual knowledge to increasingly sophisticated learning tasks as students become an expert in a given domain.

HLP 13: Adapt Curriculum Tasks and Materials for Specific Learning Goals

This HLP is defined as:

> Teachers assess individual student needs and adapt curriculum materials and tasks so that students can meet instructional goals. Teachers select materials and tasks based on student needs; use relevant technology; and make modifications by highlighting relevant information, changing task directions, and decreasing amounts of material. Teachers make strategic decisions on content coverage (i.e., essential curriculum elements), meaningfulness of tasks to meet stated goals, and criteria for student success."

Adapting assignments and materials is an aspect of differentiated instruction that helps students access to information. There are numerous ways that materials can be adapted within the inclusive social-studies classroom including providing audio or electronic versions of text, using short videos or historical images, or using a guided note-taking system.

HLP 14: Teach Cognitive and Metacognitive Strategies to Support Learning and Independence

This HLP is defined as

> Teachers explicitly teach cognitive and metacognitive processing strategies to support memory, attention, and self-regulation of learning. Learning involves not only understanding content but also using cognitive processes to solve problems, regulate attention, organize thoughts and materials, and monitor one's own thinking.

Research for students with LD suggests that teaching students to implement a cognitive strategy to complete a learning task can enhance students' learning (Jitendra et al., 2011; Swanson et al., 2013). These strategies, such as a strategy for paraphrasing a paragraph, are explicitly taught (modeling, guided practice, etc.), consistent with years of effective instruction for SWDs (Hughes et al., 2017).

HLP 15: Provide Scaffolded Supports

This HLP is defined as:

> Scaffolded supports provide temporary assistance to students so they can successfully complete tasks that they cannot yet do independently and with a high rate of success. Teachers select powerful visual, verbal, and written supports; carefully calibrate them to students' performance and understanding in relation to learning tasks; use them flexibly; evaluate their effectiveness; and gradually remove them once they are no longer needed. Some supports are planned prior to lessons and some are provided responsively during instruction.

Scaffolded instruction is characterized as providing students with temporary supports that enhance student proficiency before gradually removing the support to strengthen student independent learning (Applebee & Langer, 1983; Vygotsky, 1987; Wood et al., 1976). Scaffolded support in social studies may include temporary study guides, graphic organizers generated by teachers (initially) prior to student-generated graphic organizers, or a guided note-taking system.

HLP 16: Use Explicit Instruction
This HLP is defined as:

> Teachers make content, skills, and concepts explicit by showing and telling students what to do or think while solving problems, enacting strategies, completing tasks, and classifying concepts. Teachers use explicit instruction when students are learning new material and complex concepts and skills. They strategically choose examples and non-examples and language to facilitate student understanding, anticipate common misconceptions, highlight essential content, and remove distracting information. They model and scaffold steps or processes needed to understand content and concepts, apply skills, and complete tasks successfully and independently.

Explicit instruction has a robust corpus of research supporting its use for SWDs (Adams & Carnine, 2003; Hughes et al., 2017). In part two of this chapter, we illustrate examples of how explicit instruction can be used to promote student engagement, learning of key information, and to increase knowledge of how to complete advanced tasks such as historical reasoning or classroom debates. Simple, (but purposeful) techniques such as setting clear goals for learning activities, providing examples and non-examples of a concept, and scaffolding activities can boost student independence.

HLP 18: Use Strategies to Promote Active Student Engagement
This HLP is defined as:

> Teachers use a variety of instructional strategies that result in active student responding. Active student engagement is critical to academic success. Teachers must initially build positive student–teacher relationships to foster engagement and motivate reluctant learners. They promote engagement by connecting learning to students' lives (e. g., knowing students' academic and cultural backgrounds) and using a variety of teacher-led (e.g., choral responding and response cards), peer-assisted (e.g., cooperative learning and peer tutoring), student-regulated (e.g., self-management), and technology-supported strategies shown empirically to increase student engagement. They monitor student engagement and provide positive and constructive feedback to sustain performance.

There are many opportunities to promote student engagement while teaching interesting social studies topics. For instance, linking critical content to students' lives or cultures, as well as working collaboratively with peers on a research project or document-based question, are examples of how teachers can boost enthusiasm and active engagement.

Intervention Research in Social Studies for Students With Disabilities

Systematic reviews of research have helped teachers to identify effective social studies practices for SWDs. Systematic reviews of research are articles that synthesize all prior studies on a topic, such as the topic of improving social studies outcomes. A meta-analysis is a type of systematic literature review that is rigorous because it provides information about *all* previous studies for a population of learners. Findings from meta-analyses allow educators to identify what interventions were used, what learning outcomes were measured, and how effective the interventions were (Therrien et al., 2020). Several meta-analyses focusing on social studies for SWDs have been published (Ciullo et al., 2021; Garwood et al., 2021; Swanson et al., 2014), revealing findings that can guide classroom instruction. The following section summarizes these findings. Several of the research-supported strategies introduced in the following paragraphs are described in greater detail in the next part of this chapter which focuses on how to implement these effective strategies using HLPs.

Content-Enhancement Tools

Content-enhancement tools are materials and strategies that highlight important content to enable students to access information from the curriculum in a clear, organized, and cohesive way (Bulgren et al., 2013 Gajria et al., 2007). The aforementioned systematic reviews of research for SWDs (Swanson et al., 2014) reported high-effect sizes in research studies where SWDs used content enhancement tools. To illustrate, the two following content enhancement tools appeared in numerous research studies for students with LD and E/BD.

- *Graphic organizers:* Visual aids that make abstract information (like a series of events, or supporting details about a broader concept such as the structure of the Supreme Court) more comprehensible and organized (Ausubel, 1963; Darch & Eaves, 1986). There are numerous types of graphic organizers such as Venn diagrams, concept maps, sequencing charts, or timelines, that are useful for social studies.
- *Mnemonics:* A technique used to remember important information. Although social studies is not a discipline that simply involves memorizing information, there are circumstances when mnemonic memory techniques are useful, such as remembering the Great Lakes, or recalling Civil Rights bills signed into law by U.S Presidents. Different types of mnemonics can be used such as mnemonic keywords with illustrations, or acronyms and acrostics, also referred to as letter naming strategies (Fontana et al., 2007).

Cognitive Strategies and Multi-Component Interventions

Researchers reported large effect sizes on social studies interventions that include cognitive strategies (e.g., a strategy for reading an article and locating the main ideas), as well as multi-component interventions (i.e., several strategies and activities combined into one intervention [Swanson et al., 2015]). The following two examples include (a) a cognitive strategy to support understanding social studies text, as well as; (b) an example of a multi-component intervention that has been associated with improved reading comprehension and social studies content learning.

- *"TRAP"*: A strategy taught via explicit instruction (e.g., modeling the strategy, thinking aloud, demonstrating) to assist with comprehending and paraphrasing of text (Hagaman et al., 2016). TRAP stands for "*think* before reading, *read, ask* myself: 'What is this paragraph mostly about?' and *put* (paraphrase) it into my own words." Studies using TRAP to support content-area text comprehension in Grades 4–8 have reported improved student ability to write about the topic (Ciullo et al., 2021) and to recall and comprehend information from a text (Hagaman et al., 2016).
- *PACT multi-component intervention:* PACT stands for promoting accelerated reading comprehension of text. PACT has been implemented with a broad range of learners to promote increased engagement in social studies, and to enhance conceptual understanding (Swanson et al., 2015; Vaughn et al., 2013). Teachers guide students through different learning strategies during PACT including: (a) comprehension canopy instruction, (b) essential words/vocabulary, (c) critical reading, (d) student team-based learning comprehension checks, and (e) knowledge application activities. PACT, a detailed multi-component intervention, unfortunately cannot be described in this chapter in abundant detail. However, readers can access Table 2.2 for PACT resources (e.g., lesson plans, videos, etc.) to learn more about implementing PACT during inclusive social studies instruction.

Scaffolded Instruction

Interventions using scaffolded instruction can accelerate the achievement and active engagement of SWDs in the social studies. Scaffolding (which is also HLP 15) includes embedded supports teachers provide for students to access the curriculum in a way that addresses individual learning needs (McLeskey et al., 2017). Scaffolding is sometimes characterized as temporary support that is modeled and practiced (i.e., guided practice with students) before being faded or reduced to promote student

TABLE 2.2 Additional Resources for Effective Social Studies Strategies and Interventions

Topic	Resource	Description
Content Enhancement Tools in Social Studies	Hall, C., Kent, S. C., McCulley, L., Davis, A., & Wanzek, J. (2013). A new look at mnemonics and graphic organizers in the secondary social studies classroom. *Teaching Exceptional Children, 46*(1), 47–55.	Article with helpful resources and examples of how to apply graphic organizers as well as mnemonics in social studies classrooms for students with learning disabilities (LDs).
Elementary-level social studies intervention for students with learning disabilities (LD)	Ciullo, S. (2015). Improving access to elementary school social studies instruction: Strategies to support students with learning disabilities. *Teaching Exceptional Children, 48*(2), 102–109.	This article describes various strategies and techniques for helping students with learning disabilities to learn important social studies content in Grades K–5.
Multi-Component Intervention in Social Studies: Promoting Adolescents' Comprehension of Text	Capin, P., & Vaughn, S. (2017). Improving reading and social studies learning for secondary students with reading disabilities. *Teaching Exceptional Children, 49*(4), 249–261.	Article that describes an overview of the PACT intervention, which includes peer-mediated learning, reading comprehension, and vocabulary routines for improving reading and social studies outcomes.
Promoting Adolescents' Comprehension of Text: Online Resources	Online Resource Toolkit: https://meadowscenter.org/project/promoting-adolescents-comprehension-of-text/	Includes lesson plans, materials to print, and videos of implementation.
Peer-Mediated Learning in Social Studies	Harper, G. F., & Maheady, L. (2007). Peer-mediated teaching and students with learning disabilities. *Intervention in School and Clinic, 43*(2), 101–107.	This article summarizes several different types of peer-mediated learning for the inclusive classroom.
TRAP Reading Strategy for Paraphrasing Text	Hagaman, J. L., & Casey, K. J. (2017). Paraphrasing strategy instruction in content area text. *Intervention in School and Clinic, 52*(4), 210–217.	Provides a description of the TRAP strategy and classroom examples

independence. Scaffolded supports in social studies can include some of the following techniques.

- *Guided notes:* Guided notes (and other structured note-taking supports) are helpful in content-area classrooms for SWDs (Konrad et al., 2009). Guided notes include handouts, or technologically presented notes, with a structure that guides students through an activity where notes are required, making the process easy-to-follow.
- *Text access and technology:* Students with LD and E/BD have benefited from scaffolded instruction in the social studies. Key examples include the use of digital and audio text (Lintner, 2013) and video segments to support conceptual learning. Further, tech-based interventions such as the Virtual History Museum have increased students' understanding of key historical events and figures (Okolo et al., 2011). Gersten and colleagues (2006) also strategically used a video documentary series (*Eyes on the Prize*) to enhance social studies learning about the U.S. civil rights movement within a multi-component intervention that also included text reading and graphic organizers.
- *Peer-mediated learning:* There are numerous opportunities within social studies to employ peer-mediated learning, which scaffolds students' learning by providing built-in support. Structured and organized peer-mediated instruction (including peer tutoring) has been effective for enhancing social studies content knowledge for students with LD and for learners with E/BD (Scruggs et al., 2012). Importantly, studies with encouraging results for peer-mediated learning focused on assigning structured student roles for reading and tutoring that included the use of direct feedback, encouragement/praise, and a tutoring checklist for students to follow to promote on-task behavior and active engagement (Scruggs et al., 2012; Spencer et al., 2003). Examples of peer mediated learning will be provided in the following section of this chapter to describe how this social studies intervention and HLP can be utilized with students.

HOW DO I PLAN TO TEACH EFFECTIVE STRATEGIES?

This section will help readers to begin their journey with using the effective instructional strategies that were introduced in the previous review of literature. Four strategies will be presented: (a) content enhancement tools (specifically, graphic organizers), (b) a cognitive reading strategy (TRAP) for finding key information from text, (c) guided notes, and (d) peer-mediated learning with active engagement strategies. We will describe *how to teach* the strategies (i.e., what to say and do) to expedite lesson planning. Additional resources including articles with more information about each strategy as well as online links to lesson plans and materials are included in Table 2.1 (HLPs) and Table 2.2 (social studies resources).

Graphic Organizers: Content-Enhancement Tools in Action

Students must acquire foundational domain knowledge about topics that will be covered in the future to enable them to apply this knowledge to writing, classroom discussion/debates, etc. ([Alexander, 2003] "HLP 12: Systematically Design Instruction Toward a Specific Learning Goal"). Graphic organizers are evidence-based content-enhancement tools that teachers use to build background knowledge about a concept or to cultivate deeper conceptual understanding. Graphic organizers are visual aids (paper or technology-based) that make abstract information from text, a lecture, or another learning medium (e.g., video or online resource) clear and organized (Ausubel, 1963; Darch & Eaves, 1986). There are different graphic organizers (see Table 2.2) including Venn diagrams (used for comparing and contrasting concepts), sequencing charts (depicting details in a series of events), timelines, as well as other graphic organizers that teachers can select based on the concept being explored. For example, a unit about events preceding the Civil Rights Act of 1964 could be studied using a sequence chart or an event timeline. A concept map is used in the following example because this tool is helpful for illustrating supporting details about broad concepts, such as the structure of the Supreme Court.

A concept map is a visual aid where the concept being examined is centered in the middle of a page, with lines connecting the concept (e.g., Supreme Court) to various boxes where supporting details about that concept are written. Figure 2.1 depicts a concept map of the U.S. Supreme Court. The following example and instructional steps align with the C3 Civics Standard for Grades 6–8 (D2.Civ.4.6-8), requiring students to describe branches of the U.S. government.

Teaching Steps

Teachers use HLP 16 (explicit instruction) for concept map instruction. Importantly, while explicit instruction is an effective way to demonstrate, model, and build proficiency with a strategy, this teacher-guided support is gradually reduced as students become confident and independent using the strategy (HLP 15 [scaffolded instruction]). The following teaching steps are used.

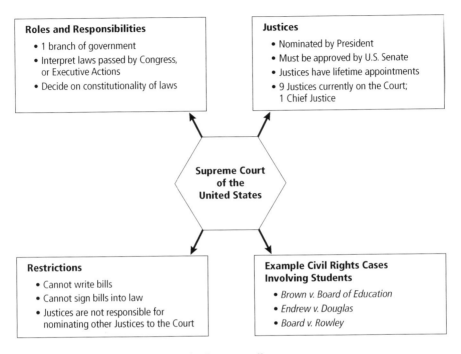

Figure 2.1 Concept map example: Supreme Court.

- *Set purpose:* Teachers describe why a concept map is a helpful learning strategy. Teachers explain that big concepts in history (e.g., Industrial Revolution, Westward Expansion, or people such as Medgar Evers) have supporting details that make the concept (or person) interesting; a concept map helps to us organize those details. Teachers use student-friendly examples (HLP 16 [explicit instruction]) such as:

    > An example concept with extensive detail is soccer's World Cup. The concept, the World Cup, has details that are important for understanding it such as: (a) how soccer venues are chosen, (b) how teams qualify for the tournament, (c) the game structure of the tournament, such as how to advance to the finals, and (d) historical origins of the World Cup.

- *Model:* Modeling *any strategy* or tool includes two steps: (a) thinking aloud while completing the task, and (b) demonstrating the task (step by step) for students. Teachers typically model a new strategy two or three times prior to initiating guided practice. For example, when modeling how to complete the concept map in Figure 2.1, teachers demonstrate how to label the supporting detail box headings such as:

Okay, now I will label my boxes to help me remember what information I need to locate when I read the article later. Let's see... my first box is called "Role of the Supreme Court." This will remind me to write notes about the role of the Supreme Court and what these Justices do. My next box is called, "Information about Justices." This should be interesting! I'm curious to learn how Supreme Court Justices are selected to serve on the court.

- Teachers model how to write brief notes. For example, if the class learns that 9 Justices currently sit on the Supreme Court, the teacher models making notes such as: "Ok, now I'm going to write that 9 Justices sit on the Supreme Court and decide on cases that are argued before the court. You know what? That is a lot of words. Instead, I'll write '9 Justices currently on court.' I shortened my notes while keeping the important information!"

- *Supporting learning and reducing support:* HLP 15 (scaffolded instruction) recommends that teachers fade support when students become proficient with using a strategy. Teachers fade concept mapping support by increasing the amount of information (or notes) that students locate and record independently. For example, teachers may initially complete three important detail boxes (see Figure 2.1) with students, while assigning students to complete the fourth box independently. During the following week, teachers continue to increase the amount of information that students must complete independently after teachers review students' work samples and confirm that SWDs are recording accurate information in their notes. Some teachers also remove the graphic organizer "frame" or design that is given to students (i.e., the concept map template shown in Figure 2.1). To accomplish this, teachers model how to draw (or create on the computer) their own concept map. Student's practice in order to generalize the strategy to implement it in other learning situations, such as when taking a test.

- *Final tips:* The learning goal, content, and curricular activity should guide teachers' selection of an appropriate graphic organizer type. For example, teachers would probably utilize a flow chart, or sequencing chart (showing events or steps in a sequential order) for teaching events leading to the 1964 Voting Rights Law. Table 2.1 includes resources about graphic organizers for SWDs in social studies.

TRAP: A Cognitive Paraphrasing Strategy

The TRAP strategy can assist with paraphrasing social studies text. TRAP stands for "*Think* before reading, *read, ask* myself: 'What is this paragraph mostly about?' and *put* (paraphrase) it into my own words" (Hagaman & Caset, 2017). As described in the aforementioned literature review section, this reading strategy has been successful in research studies for SWDs.

Teaching Steps

TRAP is taught using explicit instruction (HLP 16) and is a cognitive learning strategy. Strategies such as TRAP (HLP 14 [cognitive and metacognitive learning strategies]) are also temporary student supports that teachers spend less time discussing as students learn to independently implement the strategy. Teachers can teach reading strategies such as TRAP while also integrating other helpful techniques such as highlighting key vocabulary or building background knowledge before reading.

- *Set purpose:* Teachers articulate why TRAP can be a simple, yet useful strategy. Specifically, teachers explain that learners must (a) understand what they read, and (b) paraphrase information to write about what has been learned, or to describe the information for others. Teachers promote active-student engagement by having students share examples (with the class or a partner) of other instances when reading for understanding and paraphrasing information are necessary.
- *Model:* Teachers model TRAP by thinking aloud as well as demonstrating the process two or three times using different text passages (e.g., online article aligned with curriculum, history textbook) such as while reading an article about the 1954 *Brown vs. Board of Education* Supreme Court case. Teachers begin by stating,

> The first step of the strategy is "T," which means *think* about what I already know about this topic. I remember reading last week and watching a video in class that some schools were segregated because states were using a rule referred to as "separate but equal" in order to segregate students by race. Many people understood that racial segregation in schools was unjust, so this doctrine was challenged in court.

The teacher and students continue to discuss other background information related to the topic, as well as reviewing highlighted vocabulary words, sub-headings and pictures.

The next step is "R," which means to *read*. Here, the teacher models orally reading the passage twice for students. Students eventually read independently or with a partner (based on student and / or classroom need), but teachers read the passage orally during the modeling stage to demonstrate the entire TRAP process.

Third, teachers complete the *"A"* step, which is to *ask* ourselves what the passage is mostly about, along with locating two or three supporting details about the central idea. "After reading, I *ask* myself what was the passage was mostly about, or what was the central idea? I learned that the passage described how the Supreme Court agreed with lawyer Thurgood Marshall's argument that separate schools were not equal and that separate schools violated the 14th Amendment." Modeling the *ask* stage is an application of HLP 16 (explicit instruction) because the teacher models the metacognitive process of thinking through this strategy out loud to learn important content. Next, the teacher asks herself what three important details were from the passage that supported the central idea. This step is modeled: "I'll revisit the passage to find evidence that supports the idea that separate schools were not equal." The teacher may use examples and non-examples to demonstrate that certain information from the passage is more relevant to the central idea than other details.

Finally, teachers *paraphrase.* This step of TRAP requires teachers to model how to write the paraphrased central idea in a sentence or two, with supporting details included. "Next, I will write: Thurgood Marshal, his colleagues, and clients won the Brown vs. Board case at the Supreme Court by a unanimous (9–0) decision. Winning this case meant that separate schools in public education based on race was unconstitutional and that this practice must stop immediately." Teachers repeat modeling the entire TRAP strategy with different reading passages before transitioning to guided practice.

- *Supporting learning and reducing support:* Teachers fade their support to promote independent student proficiency with TRAP. This stage of guided practice and scaffolded learning includes two options that can be implemented based on student and classroom needs. Option 1 is to reduce support for all phases of TRAP by alternating responsibility between the teacher and the students. For example, students would read the passage once alone (or with a partner) while the teacher reads the passage the second time. Further, the teacher provides one supporting detail from the passage (and models writing it), while students locate the other details without teacher support. The second option is to differentiate the guided practice phase within the classroom. This means that some students may be ready to implement TRAP sooner than others. Teachers provide small group support to students still requiring assistance, while other students work independently. The decision to fade instructional support should be guided by analyzing students' written responses for accuracy (i.e., paraphrased sentences). Teachers provide individual or whole-group re-teaching as needed. For instance, teachers may need to re-teach how to remove less relevant information from paraphrased sentences, or how to use our own words when writing.

Two final instructional tips will benefit teachers who are beginning to use cognitive strategies such as TRAP. First, it is important to remember not to overload students with too many different cognitive learning strategies. There are other cognitive strategies for understanding text besides TRAP that can be used, but selecting one strategy and teaching it until students master it is helpful to avoid the confusion of having too many cognitive strategies. Second, teachers should remember that any learning strategy is simply a tool to promote conceptual knowledge so that students can use this historical information to complete more advanced learning tasks such as writing, debate, or other historical inquiry activities.

Guided Notes

Guided notes can be an effective strategy to assist with acquiring content knowledge, or serving as a study guide, in content-area classrooms such as social studies. Guided notes have been associated with improved learning outcomes for SWDs (Boyle et al., 2015). Guided notes may include handouts, or technologically-presented notes, with an organized structure that guides students through an activity where note-taking is required, making the process easy-to-follow by reducing cognitive burdens and enhancing student engagement (Meltzer & Krishnan, 2007).

Teaching Steps
Explicit instruction (HLP 16) is utilized for guided notes instruction. Importantly, guided notes are an intervention that serve as a learning scaffold (HLP 15) because guided notes may gradually be removed as students become proficient note takers and writers.

- *Set purpose:* Teachers introduce this learning tool by explaining its purpose, which includes two parts. First, the class would discuss why note-taking is a helpful skill. Students provide examples of when notes (handwritten or digital) are beneficial. Second, students learn that guided notes allow them to concentrate on the information they are learning about. Students spend less time writing, while having more time for active engagement in the learning activity.
- *Model:* There are two steps for planning guided notes instruction. First, teachers identify the structure (format) and the length of notes required for an upcoming lesson. Teachers review the curriculum for the upcoming series of lessons and choose a guided notes format based on

learning goals. For instance, the following format could be used for a lesson about child labor during the Industrial Revolution that includes a documentary movie as well as primary and secondary-source reading passages. This lesson would require a structure that lists a subheading provided by the teacher (e.g., exploitation) followed by bullets (or blank spaces) where students list details about that issue such as "children were paid _____ than adults" and "these children often did not attend _____ because they were working." Second, teachers will demonstrate while thinking aloud (HLP 14) to illustrate the teacher's decision-making process for determining which words or phrases should be written in their notes. Table 2.2 includes guided notes resources for additional examples that can be used in content-area classrooms such as social studies for SWDs.

- *Supporting learning and reducing support:* Some students may continue to benefit from guided notes for months, or even years. For instance, if teachers observe that SWDs are improving classroom grades, becoming more engaged in discussions, and are using more accurate information when speaking and writing about historical topics, students may benefit from continuing to utilize this practice. Fading, or gradually reducing how much text in the notes is provided by the teacher versus text that students are responsible for producing, is a technique for reducing support. For example, teachers may shorten the length of their sentence stems on the note-taking form, requiring students to write more. Another option is to alternate who provides the information (e.g., one note/idea provided by teachers, the next idea provided by the student). The goal is for students to eventually take notes independently, but using a note-taking structure that was learned during a guided notes intervention.

There are additional benefits to keeping students actively engaged during social studies instruction. Guided notes serve as an active engagement technique (HLP 18) because students spend more time involved in a learning activity, potentially reducing time for off-task behavior. Additionally, guided notes can be re-used with different students or classrooms, so time devoted to creating a lesson using guided notes can result in more efficient instructional planning in the future. Table 2.2 includes resources where guided notes strategies are explained with additional detail.

Peer-Mediated Learning

Peer mediated learning interventions allow SWD's to be actively involved within the social studies classroom. Previous studies have evaluated various peer-mediated learning frameworks such as class-wide peer tutoring, as well as peer-mediated completion of key learning activities, such as reading for understanding, discussing, and answering critical questions (Scruggs et al., 2012). Several articles cited in Table 2.2 offer in-depth guidance about ways to initiate peer mediated learning in the classroom, including how peer-mediated learning formats are included in multi-component interventions such as PACT.

Teaching Steps

The following example includes peer mediated learning in groups of two students, who read an article from a web-based source to answer questions before completing a graphic organizer. Importantly, any format of peer-based learning requires considerable time to effectively model the procedures. Peer-mediated learning addresses HLP 18 (active engagement) because students are actively involved in the learning process, often providing and receiving feedback from classmates on their work, and responding to historical questions.

- *Model:* Demonstration is integral to the success of peer mediated learning. The duration of modeling depends upon on the students' grade level as well as individual learning needs. The modeling process for the following example would be implemented across six class sessions (15 minutes per modeling session). First, teachers develop a checklist with necessary procedures to implement during peer learning time. To illustrate, a teacher may want partners to use the aforementioned TRAP strategy subsequent to reading, but before completing a graphic organizer. Teachers outline the procedures and provide a visual representation (e.g., classroom poster, tech-based slide) of the learning-step checklist. For example, the first procedure may be for a student to read the passage while her partner provides encouragement and support with difficult to pronounce words. Students then complete TRAP together after the first student reads the passage. Finally, the checklist may specify that students complete a graphic organizer that would eventually be used as a study guide after partner two reads.
  - Teachers model the entire process with a co-teacher (e.g., a special educator with a general education teacher), a paraprofessional, or with a student. Examples and non-examples of positive peer interactions should be included. Importantly, teachers model each step, including modeling the learning strategy that students will be using, even if it has already been acquired.
- *Supporting learning and reducing support:* Teachers promote independence among the student partners, or small groups. One inde-

pendence-building technique is to scaffold peer mediated learning instruction by having students practice one new step on the checklist during each successive class. For example, if the previous day students practiced reading the passage and providing encouragement, the second day of guided practice consists of students reading and then completing the TRAP paraphrasing strategy. Teachers provide feedback and individual practice for small groups of students as needed.
- As with any academic or behavioral intervention, parts of the process will be retaught, or revised. For example, teachers may observe that while students adhere to the agreed-upon procedures for reading and completing TRAP, students were not working collaboratively to complete the graphic organizer. Thus, the teacher may provide several groups with feedback and specific recommendations for improving their collaboration.

Two final suggestions will support readers with peer mediated learning intervention. First, peer mediated learning can be utilized for a broad range of learning activities. While the previous examples focused on reading text to access information, teachers can also use peer mediated learning for more advanced activities such as planning and drafting a persuasive or argumentative essay, completing research projects using historical artifacts, answering document-based questions (DBQ), or preparing for a debate on a historical controversy. Peer-mediated learning can be used for any activity with the understanding that students benefit from an organized series of steps to reduce off-task behavior, and boost time allocated to learning. Finally, readers are encouraged to familiarize themselves with the numerous options of peer-mediated instruction that can be applied within content-area subjects including social studies. Resources with this information are found in Table 2.2.

LOOKING AHEAD: INSTRUCTIONAL GUIDANCE AND NEXT STEPS

The primary aim of this chapter was to describe instructional strategies that could be immediately implemented to improve curriculum access, learning of key information, and active engagement in social studies for SWDs. The final section of this chapter includes some parting guidance for readers to practice implementing the strategies and techniques that were summarized. We also provide considerations for professional development to boost teachers' capacity to support SWDs in social studies and conclude with recommendations for future research.

Next Steps for Educators

Educators can use the following three steps to build their capacity to become more familiar with the procedures described in this chapter, and to begin implementing these strategies. The steps for continuing to learn about the techniques used to support SWDs in social studies can be helpful for undergraduate education students, masters-level students, student teachers, practicing teachers, or school-based professional development providers (e.g., professional learning community teams).

Locate Resources and Begin Planning

Readers will use Tables 2.1 and 2.2 to quickly locate a variety of resources that are designed to enhance their understanding of HLPs and research-supported social studies interventions. The selection of which resources to access is based on the goals of the individual, or group of learners. For example, teachers who already have access to engaging lesson plans and materials would likely explore HLPs in greater depth to ensure that students are getting the most out of these learning activities. Thus, the HLP videos and the HLP guidebook linked in Table 2.1 would be helpful for integrating one or more HLPs into their lesson plans. Additionally, teachers interested in beginning to use one of the specific interventions, or strategies (e.g., concept map) within their curriculum, will benefit from Table 2.2 to locate teacher-friendly articles as well as free materials and lesson plans to download and begin practicing with students!

Practice

The next step is to prepare a lesson (or mini lesson). The planning and practice phase should always include modeling the strategy or technique. As described in this chapter, modeling a new strategy using explicit instruction (HLP 16) includes two parts: (a) demonstrating the strategy and (b) thinking out loud during the process to model the cognitive process. Learning to integrate new instructional techniques (e.g., HLPs) or new learning strategies (e.g., TRAP) can transform your instruction by providing students with a cohesive learning strategy. Further, increasing access to the curriculum will help SWDs become more engaged and motivated to learn.

Future Research

There is an urgent need for research focused on improving teachers' capacity to provide effective instruction in the social studies to accelerate the learning of SWDs. Three specific aspects of research should be considered. First, there is a need for intensive professional development intervention studies that focus on equipping both special educators and general education co-teachers with HLPs. Specifically, we must investigate innovative ways to strategically integrate professional development and instructional coaching within intervention studies. These professional development and coaching-based studies should also emphasize writing instruction for SWDs in social studies, as many content-area teachers perceive themselves as unprepared to do so (Mason et al., 2022).

Second, additional surveys and descriptive-exploration studies are necessary to improve our understanding of teachers' needs (or malleable factors such as self-efficacy) with respect to teaching SWDs in inclusive settings. Researchers and school-based professional development providers will be equipped to provide responsive support if they understand the needs and perceptions of teachers with increased precision. In sum, interventions developed and recommended by researchers and higher-education faculty must be socially valid, acceptable, and responsive to teachers' current needs.

Finally, more research that targets students in Grades K–5 is warranted to promote middle school readiness, fortify content-area domain knowledge, and to begin preparing students for the expansive critical-thinking tasks expected in Grades 6–12. New interventions at the elementary level should be developed and conducted collaboratively with experts in history education, classroom social studies teachers, as well as special educators who work directly with SWDs.

REFERENCES

Adams, G., & Carnine, D. (2003). Direct instruction. In H. L. Swanson, K. R. Harris, & S. Graham (Eds.), *Handbook of learning disabilities* (pp. 403–416). Guilford Press.

Alexander, P. A. (2003). The development of expertise: The journey from acclimation to proficiency. *Educational Researcher, 32,* 10–14.

Alexander, P. A. (2005). Teaching towards expertise. In P. Tomlinson, J. Dockrell, & P. Winne (Eds.), *Pedagogy—Teaching for learning* (pp. 29–45). British Psychological Society.

Applebee, A. N., & Langer, J. A. (1983). Instructional scaffolding: Reading and writing as natural language activities. *Language Arts, 60*(2), 168–175.

Ausubel, D. G. (1963). Cognitive structure and the facilitation of meaningful verbal learning. *Journal of Teacher Education, 14*(2), 217–222.

Boyle, J. R., Forchelli, G. A., & Cariss, K. (2015). Note-taking interventions to assist students with disabilities in content area classes. *Preventing School Failure: Alternative Education for Children and Youth, 59*(3), 186–195.

Bulgren, J. A., Sampson Graner, P., & Deshler, D. D. (2013). Literacy challenges and opportunities for students with learning disabilities in social studies and history. *Learning Disabilities Research & Practice, 28*(1), 17–27.

Capin, P., & Vaughn, S. (2017). Improving reading and social studies learning for secondary students with reading disabilities. *Teaching Exceptional Children, 49*(4), 249–261.

Ciullo, S. (2015). Improving access to elementary school social studies instruction: Strategies to support students with learning disabilities. *Teaching Exceptional Children, 48*(2), 102–109.

Ciullo, S., Mason, L. H., & Judd, L. (2021). Persuasive quick-writing about text: Intervention for students with learning disabilities. *Behavior Modification, 45*(1), 122–146.

Darch, C., & Eaves, R. C. (1986). Visual displays to increase comprehension of high school learning-disabled students. *The Journal of Special Education, 20*(3), 309–318.

Fitchett, P. G., & Heafner, T. L. (2010). A national perspective on the effects of high-stakes testing and standardization on elementary social studies marginalization. *Theory & Research in Social Education, 38*(1), 114–130.

Fitchett, P. G., Heafner, T. L., & Lambert, R. G. (2014). Examining elementary social studies marginalization: A multilevel model. *Educational Policy, 28*(1), 40–68.

Fontana, J. L., Scruggs, T., & Mastropieri, M. A. (2007). Mnemonic strategy instruction in inclusive secondary social studies classes. *Remedial and Special Education, 28*(6), 345–355.

Gajria, M., Jitendra, A. K., Sood, S., & Sacks, G. (2007). Improving comprehension of expository text in students with LD: A research synthesis. *Journal of Learning Disabilities, 40*(3), 210–225.

Garwood, J. D., McKenna, J. W., Roberts, G. J., Ciullo, S., & Shin, M. (2021). Social studies content knowledge interventions for students with emotional and behavioral disorders: A meta-analysis. *Behavior Modification, 45*(1), 147–176.

Gersten, R., Baker, S. K., Smith-Johnson, J., Dimino, J., & Peterson, A. (2006). Eyes on the prize: Teaching complex historical content to middle school students with learning disabilities. *Exceptional Children, 72*(3), 264–280.

Hagaman, J. L., & Casey, K. J. (2017). Paraphrasing strategy instruction in content area text. *Intervention in School and Clinic, 52*(4), 210–217.

Hagaman, J. L., Casey, K. J., & Reid, R. (2016). Paraphrasing strategy instruction for struggling readers. *Preventing School Failure: Alternative Education for Children and Youth, 60*(1), 43–52.

Hall, C., Kent, S. C., McCulley, L., Davis, A., & Wanzek, J. (2013). A new look at mnemonics and graphic organizers in the secondary social studies classroom. *Teaching Exceptional Children, 46*(1), 47–55.

Harper, G. F., & Maheady, L. (2007). Peer-mediated teaching and students with learning disabilities. *Intervention in School and Clinic, 43*(2), 101–107.

Heafner, T. L. (2018). Elementary ELA/social studies integration: Challenges and limitations. *The Social Studies, 109*(1), 1–12.

Hughes, C. A., Morris, J. R., Therrien, W. J., & Benson, S. K. (2017). Explicit instruction: Historical and contemporary contexts. *Learning Disabilities Research & Practice, 32*(3), 140–148.

Jitendra, A. K., Burgess, C., & Gajria, M. (2011). Cognitive strategy instruction for improving expository text comprehension of students with learning disabilities: The quality of evidence. *Exceptional children, 77*(2), 135–159.

Konrad, M., Joseph, L. M., & Eveleigh, E. (2009). A meta-analytic review of guided notes. *Education and Treatment of Children, 32*(3), 421–444.

Lintner, T. (2013). Digital resources in the social studies classroom for students with learning disabilities. In W. Russell (Ed.), *Digital social studies* (pp. 61–74). Information Age Publishing.

Mason, L. M., Ciullo, S., Collins, A. A., Brady, S., Elcock, L., & Sanborn Owen, L. (2022). Exploring inclusive middle-school content teachers' training, perceptions, and classroom practice for writing. *Learning Disabilities: A Contemporary Journal, 20*(2), 111–128.

McLeskey, J., Barringer, M.-D., Billingsley, B., Brownell, M., Jackson, D., Kennedy, M., Lewis, T., Maheady, L., Rodriguez, J., Scheeler, M. C., Winn, J., & Ziegler, D. (2017, January). *High-leverage practices in special education*. Council for Exceptional Children & CEEDAR Center.

Meltzer, L., & Krishnan, K. (2007). Executive function difficulties and learning disabilities: Understandings and misunderstandings. In L. Meltzer (Ed.), *Executive function in education: From theory to practice* (pp. 77–105). The Guilford Press.

National Council for the Social Studies. (2013). *The college, career, and civic life (C3) framework for social studies state standards: Guidance for enhancing the rigor of K–12 civics, economics, geography, and history*.

Okolo, C. M., Englert, C. S., Bouck, E. C., Heutsche, A., & Wang, H. (2011). The virtual history museum: Learning US history in diverse eighth grade classrooms. *Remedial and Special Education, 32*(5), 417–428.

Scruggs, T. E., Mastropieri, M. A., & Marshak, L. (2012). Peer-mediated instruction in inclusive secondary social studies learning: Direct and indirect learning effects. *Learning Disabilities Research & Practice, 27*(1), 12–20.

Spencer, V. G., Scruggs, T. E., & Mastropieri, M. A. (2003). Content area learning in middle school social studies classrooms and students with emotional or behavioral disorders: A comparison of strategies. *Behavioral Disorders, 28*(2), 77–93.

Swanson, E., Hairrell, A., Kent, S., Ciullo, S., Wanzek, J. A., & Vaughn, S. (2014). A synthesis and meta-analysis of reading interventions using social studies content for students with learning disabilities. *Journal of Learning Disabilities, 47*(2), 178–195.

Swanson, H. L., Harris, K. R., & Graham, S. (Eds.). (2013). *Handbook of learning disabilities*. The Guilford Press.

Swanson, E., Wanzek, J., Vaughn, S., Roberts, G., & Fall, A. M. (2015). Improving reading comprehension and social studies knowledge among middle school students with disabilities. *Exceptional Children, 81*(4), 426–442.

Therrien, W. J., Cook, B. G., & Cook, L. (2020). Utilizing meta-analyses to guide practice: A primer. *Learning Disabilities Research & Practice, 35*(3), 111–117.

Vaughn, S., Swanson, E. A., Roberts, G., Wanzek, J., Stillman-Spisak, S. J., Solis, M., & Simmons, D. (2013). Improving reading comprehension and social studies knowledge in middle school. *Reading Research Quarterly, 48*(1), 77–93.

Vygotsky, L. (1987). Zone of proximal development. *Mind in society: The development of higher psychological processes, 5291*, 157.

Wood, D., Bruner, J. S., & Ross, G. (1976). The role of tutoring in problem solving. *The Journal of Child Psychology & Psychiatry 17*(2), 89–100.

PART II

CREATING AN INCLUSIVE CLASSROOM ENVIRONMENT

CHAPTER 3

INCLUSIVE SOCIAL STUDIES THROUGH COLLABORATION AND CO-TEACHING

Melissa Lisanti
Radford University

Elizabeth Altieri
Radford University

Karen Douglas
Radford University

In their introduction to this book, Minarik and Lintner present the 2021 U.S. Department of Education figures for inclusion of students with disabilities, the slow progress we've made nationally, and the goal of having 90% of students with disabilities fully included for most of the school day (Villa & Thousand, 2016). Inclusion is not just social inclusion at lunch and specials. We define inclusion as meaningful inclusion in academic learning in the general education classroom, and we can use IDEA Indicator 5 data of 80% or more of the school day as a reasonable assessment that students with disabilities are at least present in general education classrooms for academic instruction.

Students with complex disabilities lag well behind in inclusion. Data reported for the 2021 Report to Congress on IDEA reveals the following: Only 41% of students with autism, 18% of students with intellectual disability, and 15% of students with multiple disabilities are included for 80% or more of the school day. The range of inclusion by the states is quite startling. For example, only 10% or less of students with intellectual disabilities are included for 80% or more of the school day in California, DC, Illinois, Maine, Minnesota, Missouri, Montana, Nevada, New Jersey, New York, Pennsylvania, South Carolina, Utah, and Washington (U.S. Department of Education, 2022). Vermont leads the way with 55% of their students with intellectual disabilities included for 80% of the school day. Lack of presence in core content academic classes means lack of access to the content as taught by a content specialist, and lack of access to rich academic learning with peers.

We can make the case that social studies is the ideal vehicle for meaningful academic inclusion for all students, but especially for students with complex disabilities. As has been described by almost all the authors in this text, the goal of social studies is to develop civic competence, which aligns perfectly with the important areas of skill development for students with complex disabilities—to expand cultural and social competence. Wood (2020) identified three potential benefits of social studies instruction for these students: "to gain knowledge of the world, to increase aware of self and others, and to develop self-determination and self-advocacy skills" (p. 78).

Given the complexities of learner needs in fully inclusive classrooms, social studies would ideally be co-taught with a social studies educator and a special educator. However, this chapter is for ALL social studies educators and their collaborators in special education, even if co-teaching is not currently an option. We acknowledge that co-taught social studies classrooms are not the norm, but we believe that there is unrealized potential for social studies classrooms to be a vehicle for more meaningful collaboration among professionals and more authentic learning for all students.

In this chapter, we will explain how the social studies classroom offers especially relevant opportunities to make general curriculum equally accessible to every learner. What better place than social studies to begin modeling an inclusive, equitable, diverse society? Other authors have made the case for this and we hope the tools included here will support existing collaborations that are currently consultative rather than co-teaching models and can open conversations around expanding collaboration and co-teaching in the social studies. Then we will elaborate on the co-planning, co-instructing, and co-assessing elements that make this possible.

Students With Disabilities and Social Studies

Social studies receives little attention in the literature when it comes to research that supports rigorous instruction in the general education social studies classroom for students with disabilities, but the tide is turning.

Curtis and Green (2021) did a systematic review of research studies from 2008–2018 that investigated the effectiveness of strategies for students with learning disabilities in inclusive social studies instruction and found 218 articles. Of those 218 articles, only 17 met all criteria. Regrettably, not a single study was found in social studies or disciplinary journals. Almost all the investigations focused on the secondary level. The studies primarily investigated specific vocabulary and reading comprehension strategies. Ciullo and colleagues (2020) completed a meta-analysis of 40 years of research of social studies and students with learning disabilities and distilled this down to 42 empirical studies that met all criteria. The most significant finding was the effectiveness of interventions that included graphic organizers, mnemonics, and reading comprehension strategies. However, the setting for instruction was not a variable and not discussed.

One extensive long-term study being conducted by Vaughn et al. is looking at the use of a text and inquiry-based approach to reading comprehension and content learning in eighth grade social studies classes (The Meadows Center, 2022). The strategies used in the study are also described by Capin and Vaughn (2017).

It is of note that much of the research in this area has been conducted solely around students with learning disabilities, but studies have been done with other populations with more complex disabilities. Spencer et al. (2014) completed an analysis of intervention studies in content area learning for students with autism from 2000–2012 and found only one study related to social studies which taught geography skills in an experimental setting. Schenning et al. (2013) investigated the effectiveness of explicit instruction and graphic organizers in the learning of social studies content for students with autism, but all students in the study were in self-contained settings. Zakas et al. (2013) showed the effectiveness of adapted text and a graphic organizer for social studies learners for three students with autism, also in segregated classrooms. In a more recent study, Reeves and Santoli (2018) identified strategies with strong potential to support learners with autism in the social studies classroom including (a) structured work systems that provide explicit directions and details for class assignments or activities, and (b) visual supports including visual schedules, visual instructions, graphic organizers, charts and diagrams, and adding visual clarity to text in the form of numbers or bullets, color coding, underlining, or pictures.

Research in the area of social studies and students with intellectual disabilities has been limited to single-subject design studies with very limited numbers of subjects in self-contained or resource settings (Karakus & Varalan, 2021; Wood et al., 2015). One recent study was conducted in an inclusive setting with three middle-school aged students, but direct instruction was only provided by the paraprofessional (Ryan et al., 2019). Ryan noted that there are no literature reviews of social studies content instruction for students with significant intellectual disabilities. In her dissertation research study, Ryan (2020) used embedded instruction, inquiry-based instruction, and peer-supported instruction to teach three students with significant intellectual disabilities to answer social studies content questions and to be more independent learners in the inclusive social studies classroom.

Special Education and Social Studies

Today in many schools we are seeing the majority of co-teaching occurring during reading and writing, and mathematics instruction. But we can make a strong case for co-teaching during social studies. Many students with disabilities are receiving reading and writing and math intervention and specially designed instruction (SDI) around specific skills during English or math class or resource time, but there is no follow through on how to use those strategies within social studies classes. The strategies they are learning related to essential reading, writing, and applied math skills should be incorporated into the social studies curriculum. The past twenty years in which reading and math scores have barely budged for students with disabilities make the case for integration of intervention and SDI across the school day. Without this approach, students with disabilities are marginalized in content area classes and their participation is often minimal.

CO-TEACHING OVERVIEW: CO-PLANNING, CO-INSTRUCTING, AND CO-ASSESSING

Co-teaching is a service delivery model where general and special educators effectively collaborate to provide students with disabilities access to the general education curriculum and specially designed instruction. In their model of co-teaching as a method for continuous improvement, Murawski and Lochner (2017) make clear that co-teaching is a process that includes co-planning, co-instruction, and co-assessment. A shared partnership is developed where the general educator offers expertise in content instruction and the special educator provides expertise in adapting differentiated lessons and incorporating specially designed instruction. *Specially designed instruction* (SDI) is intentional and explicit instruction tied to the learning standards, IEP goals, and needs of individual students such as lacking prerequisite skills or needing more opportunities to practice. Appropriate adaptations to the content, methodology, or delivery of instruction may be needed.

Ultimately, both teachers deliver instruction to meet the needs of all students. Students with and without disabilities benefit from learning alongside their peers academically, socially, and behaviorally (Scruggs et al., 2007). Within co-taught classes, there are more opportunities for students to respond and teachers to provide feedback as there are more teachers' eyes and opportunities for small group instruction (Hurd & Weilbacher, 2017). To achieve these outcomes, careful attention must be paid to developing effective and efficient co-planning routines, using instructional models that make space for individualized and small group delivery, and developing consensus on how to assess students equitably and meaningfully. After a brief overview of existing literature pertinent specifically to co-teaching in social studies, this chapter will explore each of these phases of co-teaching in further detail.

CO-TEACHING AND SOCIAL STUDIES

Shaffer and Thomas-Brown (2015) make the case that co-teaching with embedded support can serve as a form of professional development for teachers that enhances their professional competency including gains in content knowledge and teaching strategies, and has the potential to support the teachers as well as the students. The editors of this book, Lintner and Minarik, have authored the two most definitive texts on teaching students with disability in inclusive social studies classroom (Lintner & Schweder, 2011; Minarik & Lintner, 2016) but the sections on collaboration and co-teaching were fairly general. Minarik and Coughlin (2013) suggested that co-planning and co-teaching is an effective way to support interdisciplinary social studies instruction. Little specific guidance exists for co-teaching and bringing SDI into the social studies classroom. For example, in a very recent practical and useful guide for teachers on co-teaching (Goeke, 2021), there are specific chapters for all content areas with the exception of social studies. This chapter hopes to close that gap.

CO-PLANNING: A PIVOTAL PHASE
OF EFFECTIVE COLLABORATION

Effective co-teaching begins with co-planning and, in some situations, co-planning is the only direct support special educators can offer secondary social studies teachers. Depending on available resources, instructional needs, and scheduling, special educators are often supporting the literacy or math instruction of some students with disabilities while others are participating in content-area instruction. When that happens, an instructional assistant or paraprofessional may or may not be available in an inclusive classroom to provide support for students under the direction of the special educator who is required elsewhere. Secondary social studies teachers may well find themselves teaching their students with disabilities with only co-planning and consultative support. While certainly not ideal, even in these contexts, students with disabilities must receive high-quality instruction that is well designed to meet their needs. To ensure that happens, collaborative planning must be consistent, efficient, and thoughtful in order to maximize both outcomes for students and a healthy partnership among the adults.

Scholarship and strategies for developing strong co-planning routines across disciplines are becoming well-documented and include a variety of ways to build vision, identify talents, analyze risk, establish trust, use templates, manage logistics, as well as key talking points, options for supplementing asynchronous activities, and both broad and specific questions for consideration. Further, additional chapters in this text bring into view ways to leverage planning and how to design instruction so that they facilitate the success of all students including those who have disabilities. We will focus our examples specifically on the intersection of collaboration, co-planning, and social studies as we attempt to illuminate a few of the possibilities that could inspire co-teachers who have the privilege of sharing an inclusive classroom.

Holding a broad view of the goals embedded in most IEPs will be pivotal for establishing value for co-teaching in the social studies curriculum. It is rare to find a goal that speaks specifically to social studies, nor do we frequently identify service needs explicitly for content-area instruction. However, when both professionals and school leadership embrace the mindset that literacy and numeracy goals are most meaningful when they empower students to learn about the world around them, we find the extraordinary potential of coaching these goals in the context of the content areas. When students are learning how to read closely and persist through challenging vocabulary and text so that they can better understand the rights they are guaranteed in the Bill of Rights, motivation for literacy work deepens. When students are learning how to construct an argument solid enough to win a debate or change someone's perspective, writing instruction carries with it a new kind of power. When students are developing questioning skills so that they can analyze historical sources and uncover more complex versions of the past, that practice can feel much more novel and intriguing. Finally, when students are learning numeracy skills so that they can study population trends or election data, they are not doing math, they are using it. These kinds of intersections are more fully explored in other chapters in this text. We mention a few here simply to set the stage for co-teaching. Realizing the power of these intersections

Inclusive Social Studies Through Collaboration and Co-Teaching • 51

requires the expertise of both special educators and general educators who work well together both outside and inside the classroom.

It is important that the social studies general educator and the special educator have the opportunity to engage in high-level planning activities prior to the start of the semester or academic year, both those in co-teaching arrangements and those with a consultative model. The focus of these conversations is to establish key goals and infrastructure that will serve as the foundation for the year or semester's work. Teachers already have more to do than they have time to do it, so identifying a few significant goals and a plan for achieving them will be instrumental in maintaining priorities and managing time. Table 3.1 provides a sample timeline of those meetings and what they might include.

TABLE 3.1 Sample Timeline and Activities

Time	Activity
Before the school year begins	This is when we get a head start…
	Identify protected co-planning time.
	Gather a list of students who are collaboratively taught and supported with IEPs.
	Create a graphic organizer of non-negotiables for supporting students in compliance with accommodations or modifications.
	Review goals together and identify potential areas to integrate specially designed instruction or inclusive evidence-based practices.
	Plan three weeks of low-risk and universally designed instruction with accommodations already identified in the IEPs.
At week 3	Now we have some working knowledge of the students based on our own observations and data.
	Revisit IEP goals and potential areas to target for specially designed instruction.
	Create brief action plans for each goal identified, noting what evidence-based practices and assessment evidence will be integrated into what units.
	Identify human resources available to support implementation during classroom instruction—classroom teacher, special educator, paraprofessional(s) with frequency and amount of time.
	Note: For specially designed instruction to be most effective, in-classroom collaboration between special educator and general educator is critically important.
Weekly: Going forward	Create unit snapshots that align general education goals with IEP goals.
	Collaborate on big picture instructional decisions—reflect on proposed activities and assign preparation tasks
	As assessment data is collected, analyze together to determine adjustments, needs for supplemental instruction or practice, etc.

TABLE 3.2 Focus of Student Learning and Contributions by Collaboration Partner

Focus of Student Learning	The general educator might contribute…	The special educator might contribute…
1st grade students are learning about maps, globes, and how to use cardinal directions. *Unit Question:* How do maps help us explore big and small places both near and far?	A large labeled and annotated map and an anchor chart on why we need maps to be posted in the classroom. Large labels of the cardinal directions in multiple languages posted on the appropriate walls of the classroom and a compass rose for the classroom. Instructional activities that involve students analyzing, using, and drawing maps. Classroom scavenger hunt using cardinal directions.	Vocabulary sets that include words, simple definitions, and visuals that students can manipulate. Instructional activities that engage students in practicing and using vocabulary. A map of the current classroom and two other spaces in the school (ex: music room, art room, cafeteria) and the child's bedroom or kitchen completed in partnership with a family of a student whose curriculum is adapted for significant learning complexities—an instructional assistant is trained in using them with the student and peers during class.
4th grade students are learning about the economic specializations of their state and how they trade with others. *Project-based unit question:* How do people who live in our state make money and trade for what they want and need?	A project that organizes students into small groups to create industry profile presentations on several key economic specializations—directions, rubric, research activities, group member roles, presentation template. A collection of student-friendly resources and lessons to build content knowledge needed to complete the project. Three small group lessons will focus on economic specializations and source analysis. Students will rotate through stations with their teammates.	Planning checklists to support students in organizing and accomplishing the work. Strategic groupings for students who are supported by IEPs. Three groups will include one or two students who are simultaneously working on related English/language arts IEP goals. So, three small group lessons will focus on explicit instruction on reading, writing, and oral presentation. All students will receive this useful instruction from the special educator. (Should the special educator not be available during content time, this instruction could happen during ELA time because it is aligned to literacy services. If needed that time can be recovered during social studies when the general educator provides content area literacy instruction.)

(continued)

Inclusive Social Studies Through Collaboration and Co-Teaching ▪ 53

TABLE 3.2 Focus of Student Learning and Contributions by Collaboration Partner (continued)

Focus of Student Learning	The general educator might contribute...	The special educator might contribute...
Middle school students are learning about how the U.S. Constitution reflects principles of government found in previous documents. *Lesson Question:* How does the U.S. Constitution borrow ideas from other important documents?	Small cards with excerpts from a variety of key founding documents that illustrate principles of democratic government—passage on one side, name of document on the reverse side. Slide with instructions for activity. Discussion Frame with essential and recommended questions for discussion. Opening hook—where do ideas come from?	Explicit vocabulary instruction on key words found in the passages students will be reading. Family tree graphic organizer for the Constitution. A self-assessment and reminders for working well with a partner—specific feedback will be provided to a student working on social skills.

Table 3.2 provides examples of student learning by sample units by grade level and what each of the collaborating partners might focus on and contribute to the unit. As you consider the examples below, reflect on the asynchronous collaboration tools that are available in your professional context. Shared drives and documents make the kinds of collaboration detailed below much easier to organize and coordinate even with limited planning and co-teaching time.

Weekly co-planning is also essential but often that co-planning time is hard to find. We have adapted a one-hour co-planning guide by Friend et al. (2014) to fit a more reasonable 30-minute weekly planning time (see Table 3.3). This co-planning can and should occur even if co-teaching is not occurring for all or any of the social studies period to ensure that IEP

TABLE 3.3 30-Minute Weekly Co-Planning Guide for Co-Teachers and Consulting Teachers

General Educator: Prepares by reviewing Pacing Guide, bringing samples of student work and assessments given, and an outline for the week.

Special Educator: Prepares by reviewing Pacing Guide, bringing IEP matrices or IEPs at a Glance, and ideas for differentiation and modifications.

Time	Task	Notes/Plans
1 minute	Review successes and challenges in the past week.	
2 minutes	Review curriculum goals, standards, and outcomes for the coming week.	
8 minutes	Develop differentiated lesson objectives for each day (all, most, some). Review IEP Matrices/Objectives for each student with disability. Both teachers review student data to identify learning gaps for all students. Identify students for remediation, reteaching, and pre-teaching.	
17 minutes	Plan the week by each day. Include grouping decisions and co-teaching models to be used for each component of the lesson. • Opener (hooks or grabbers) • Middle—Core Instruction • Closer—Students engage in summarizing (e.g., exit slips) Identify differentiation of activities including adaptations and modifications.	
2 minutes	Partnership discussion- communication and housekeeping	

goals are being met and effective instructional strategies are embedded for students with disabilities within weekly and daily lesson plans. Even without the presence of the special educator during the social studies block, effective instruction can be provided by the general educator or an instructional assistant (if a detailed step-by-step instructional plan is provided) and if a strong co-planning process is in place.

CO-INSTRUCTION: MODELS FOR SHARING CLASSROOM IMPLEMENTATION

Co-Teaching Models

When co-planning for each daily lesson, consider how to best engage and instruct the students using all available personnel. The following co-teaching approaches are effective instructional strategies: (a) parallel teaching, (b) station teaching, (c) alternative teaching, and (d) team teaching (Friend, 2018). One teach, one observe and one teach, one assist are also approaches; however they should only be implemented occasionally when individualized data collection is warranted. We will focus on the four approaches that, when implemented with fidelity, are most likely to result in positive student outcomes. Co-teachers should not be intimidated to work together, share students and responsibilities, or discuss academic content but the use of the co-teaching models should bring teachers together to enhance their instructional skills and effectiveness as a teacher.

Parallel Teaching
With parallel teaching, the class is divided in half and each teacher instructs half of the class using the same lesson and materials. This model provides the opportunity for more individual attention and participation in a smaller group format. Both groups can meet in the classroom, or one group could move into another classroom, conference room, or the media center. This model does require each teacher to be knowledgeable and well-versed on the content being presented. Timing can be a challenge and takes practice and communication. The parallel model depends on the availability of two licensed professionals who are providing the instruction because the intent is to ensure the same rigor and quality across both groups.

Station Teaching
Station teaching, also called rotational teaching or centers, allows the teachers to divide the content into three or more different segments or activities and the student groups rotate through each station. If there are two teachers in the classroom, each teacher could lead a group and the third

group would be for independent or computer-based work. Both teachers would monitor the third group for on-task behaviors. Either the students or teachers could physically travel from group to group ensuring that all students have the opportunity to participate in each group. Students could be grouped in a variety of ways (heterogeneously or homogenously) depending on the lesson objectives and differentiation within each station. In carefully designed circumstances, paraprofessionals can be trained to supervise a station, especially if it is an opportunity for review or guided practice of skills that have already been introduced. Those skills should have been initially taught by the general educator in the social studies classroom or the special educator in another classroom.

Alternative Teaching

After all students have received the core instruction on a topic then alternative teaching may occur if a smaller group of students would benefit from enrichment, remediation, or pre-teaching activities. In alternative teaching, one teacher works with a larger group of students while the other teacher works with a small group on a specific skill. It is important to ensure that the special education teacher is not always working with the small group and the student composition in the small group is not always the same students nor only the students with disabilities. The key to alternative teaching is that students in the small group are not missing instruction on the general education content, they are only receiving opportunities for pre-teaching, enrichment, or remediation.

Team Teaching

When both teachers are delivering instruction together with equal responsibilities, they are implementing the team-teaching model. The teachers must have mutual respect, rapport, and parity for each other as demonstrated through their collaborative instructional style. They visibly have a shared partnership based on their individual strengths, and effectively provide whole class instruction with engagement activities to facilitate student learning. This model should be used occasionally and for only short periods of time as whole class instruction is not optimal in promoting student success.

Selecting a Co-Teaching Model

There are many considerations when selecting an appropriate co-teaching model that will most effectively and efficiently promote student learning. Co-teachers should address the following in their decision-making:

- What are your students' characteristics and learning needs or supports?

- What are the lesson objectives and how can they best be taught using engaging instructional activities?
- What is the staff availability during the instructional time and their experience/knowledge with the topic?
- How much co-planning time is available and needed to effectively implement the lesson?
- Where will the lesson occur? What physical space is available within the classroom, hall, conference room, library, etc.?

Co-Teaching Examples in the Social Studies Classroom

Merging SDI into the social studies classrooms means intentional and systematic designs that privilege both the social studies learning outcomes for all students and the IEP goals of students with disabilities who are included in the classroom. Table 3.4 shows a few examples of what that might look like.

Co-teaching models are especially instrumental in creating classroom environments that support flexible grouping, individualized support, and space to work in different ways with different students. To really explore the practicalities of what this would look like and how to accomplish it, we have provided a more detailed scenario. Imagine a secondary social studies United States history classroom. Seven students who are supported by IEPs participate in this inclusive classroom and are working on significant IEP goals related to literacy. Accelerated growth is important for all of them, but especially for four students who have gaps in skills that could present barriers to achieving course credits and on-time progress toward graduation. A special educator is assigned to the social studies classroom for one period each day as a co-teaching partner so that reading and writing instruction can be integrated systematically across a larger share of the students' instructional day. If that is not possible, consider creating collaborative teams of language arts, social studies, and special educators so that special educators can align their literacy services to instructional experiences versus class periods. If rich literacy SDI can be made more authentic in the content area classroom, we can create short-term co-teaching opportunities with the special educator more flexibly focused on the SDI and where and when that needs to occur within instructional units rather than at daily fixed times.

Consider this example of an IEP goal that merits SDI for Marcus this school year.

> Sample IEP Goal: By May 20##, when responding to prompts for essays in core content areas, Marcus will construct a multi-paragraph essay that maintains a clear focus on a central topic with only minimal errors in mechanics (which do not impact meaning), as assessed with a rubric for which the final score is 80% or better on 4 out of 5 essays.

58 ▪ M. LISANTI, E. ALTIERI, and K. DOUGLAS

TABLE 3.4 Co-Teaching Examples

	While the social studies teacher is…	The special education teacher is…
Station Teaching		
Core Instruction	Teaching a station with historical sources and focusing on inquiry and analytical skills.	Teaching a station with a nonfiction text (website, textbook, passage, tradebook, etc.) and focusing on comprehension skills.
Differentiated Core Instruction	In some rotations, students are continuing to use an illustrated checklist prompting them through the process of analyzing a source. At this point in the fading process, the teacher is challenging them to recall a good next step and then they refer to the checklist to self-assess their ideas.	While all rotations are working with the same text, in one rotation the graphic organizer is modified to narrow its focus and provide additional time for explicit modeling and guided practice on determining cause and effect for the two key content points that all students need to master.
w/SDI		The graphic organizer and explicit instruction have been designed intentionally to align with one student's IEP goals in literacy. A few additional students who would benefit from the instruction and can provide peer modeling are grouped together for the rotations.

Pulling It Together: Upon returning to whole group instruction, students and teachers (team teaching) can make connections across their stations to develop a sense of what patterns and differences emerged in the sources.

(continued)

Inclusive Social Studies Through Collaboration and Co-Teaching ▪ 59

TABLE 3.4 Co-Teaching Examples (continued)

	While the social studies teacher is...	The special education teacher is...
Parallel Teaching		
Core Instruction	Students are reading Article 2 of the US Constitution and relevant Amendments as an introduction to a mini-unit on the Executive Branch. They are collecting information using a frame (graphic organizer) on what it says about eligibility to hold office, the election process, and the responsibilities of the role.	Students are reading Article 2 of the US Constitution and relevant Amendments as an introduction to a mini-unit on the Executive Branch. They are collecting information using a frame (graphic organizer) on what it says about eligibility to hold office, the election process, and the responsibilities of the role.
Differentiated Core Instruction	The students are paired (4 pairs and one trio). The teacher guides silent reading and partner talk with chunks of the text. Then the group adds notes to the chart together.	Students are paired strategically (5 pairs) and work with a small chunk of text specifically chosen for them. Two of the passages have a small visual support attached to them. After partner work, the full group will work together to share answers and complete the whole chart under the teacher's direction.
w/SDI	One student is working toward independence on a behavior goal. During bell work, the teacher will conference with the student on two ways to interact with a partner successfully and provide specific positive feedback throughout the work time.	One student is mastering using text to make inferences and answer questions. A passage and scaffolded response sheet are chosen and designed specifically for the student and partner. The other pairs are chosen strategically for this group so that the special education teacher will have ample time and attention to teach this pair during partner time.

At the beginning of the year, the social studies teacher reviewed IEPs-at-a-Glance and recognized this goal was well-matched to some of the writing assignments included in the course syllabus. The general educator added this idea to a beginning of the year co-planning session with the special educator. They decided that two of the essays to help measure this goal would be completed in social studies by the end of March. That allowed time for a third trial in April if needed to demonstrate mastery. Two practice opportunities would be built into the fall semester to collect additional baseline data on specific strengths and needs to determine what instruction would be most helpful.

After working with Marcus through the first month of school, the teachers collaboratively determine that Marcus will receive explicit instruction and coaching support throughout the planning, composing, and revising phases of writing in the first semester of the school year. By the second semester, the goal is to leverage instruction in the planning phase with content-area writing and metacognition strategy instruction while fading support in the composing phase. The teachers hypothesize that Marcus will be able to construct a successful multi-paragraph response on his own with a solid plan for writing and, by the final assessment, the teachers' instruction during the planning phase will be focused and brief. The lesson snapshot (see Table 3.5) includes the second assessment in the spring semester. (If the school is on a semester

TABLE 3.5 Sample Lesson Snapshot for Social Studies

Objectives:	Assessment:
Students will be able to synthesize key strategies and events to explain how the Civil Rights Movement shaped public opinion and secured better access to and protection of equal rights.	A written assignment will respond to the prompt: "How did participants in the Civil Right Movement during the 1950s and 1960s shape public opinion to secure better access to and protection of equal rights?"
Compose a multi-paragraph essay to answer a question and provide evidence to support it.	A rubric will score the writing in these categories: • Organization around central idea/thesis • Accuracy of content • Relevance and depth of supporting examples/evidence • Mechanics and polish

Instructional Resources/Materials/Technology	
Teacher: Slide deck with purpose of assignment, directions, rubric, and two annotated/scored student samples from previous year	**Student:** Post-it notes and/or graphic organizer for planning essay; personal device (laptop/Chromebook); lesson resources from Civil Rights unit posted on google classroom; two exit slips completed during the unit that laid foundation for this assignment

(continued)

TABLE 3.5 Sample Lesson Snapshot for Social Studies (continued)

Co-Teaching Model(S)
Team Teaching: To open the lesson, both teachers will help set the stage for the assignment as they team teach the slide deck with directions, rubric, models. **Alternative Group:** Writing time will be organized using a workshop structure in which students have time to plan and write independently as well as opportunities to conference with the teachers in small groups around specific skills.

Instruction

Opening The Lesson (about 5 minutes)

Team Teaching Model:

During the opening, the social studies teacher will introduce the lesson hook that's posted on a slide. "If you could make one big change in the world what would it be?" Both teachers will circulate and talk softly with students and the special education teacher plans to check in with Marcus, Serena, and Tariq to see what they are thinking. After a minute of quiet time, one of the teachers will offer students a scaffold. If you are drawing a blank, raise your hand to get a quick list of choices. One teacher will distribute sheets with three ideas on it—these aren't posted so that students are encouraged to find their own original ideas at first. Students share their ideas with a partner. Both teachers facilitate sharing out with the class and commenting on responses.

To transition into today's lesson, the social studies teacher explains that people who want to change the world can learn a lot from the Civil Rights Movement. The teacher will review the inquiry question that has guided the unit and is now the writing prompt for a final assignment. How did participants in the Civil Rights Movement during the 1950s and 1960s shape public opinion to secure better access to and protection of equal rights?" The special education teacher will follow up with a career connection and remind students that even if you don't want to change the world, being able to answer a complex question with a clear idea and reasons to support it will make us more effective communicators in any career choice. It can even lead to leadership opportunities.

Implementing the New Instruction (about 35 minutes)

Team Teaching Model

Uses a slide deck to introduce the writing assignment and the directions/minimum expectations. Students read the slides to themselves first and identify key words/phrases to discuss. Invite students to ask any initial questions. During this mini-lesson, the special educator thinks out loud about how to use the directions to answer their own questions.

Next, the social studies teacher shows two responses from previous years. In the first one, each teacher notes a strength, and the classroom teacher makes a recommendation for improving it. In the second example, the social studies teacher asks the students to notice strengths and the special education teacher identifies one way to make it better. One example is provided in both Spanish and English to three multilingual learners.

Alternative Groups Model

Post the workshop schedule on the board. One column shows meeting times and teachers. (Both teachers take an alternate group rotation with a small group of students.) A second column shows activities/tasks (a writing process checklist) on which students focus if and when they are *not* in a small group.

(continued)

TABLE 3.5 Sample Lesson Snapshot for Social Studies (continued)

Social Studies Teacher:	Special Education Teacher:
Small Group 1—Marcus (w/IEP), Serena (w/IEP), August (struggles with writing, motivation, & attendance), Hope (needs support with critical thinking), and Javier (w/IEP & multilingual learner) This group will get explicit construction on the planning phase of writing (Troia, 2014) on what they want to include in their graphic organizer to get off to a strong start. Each person will generate one example of how the participants in the Civil Rights Movement shaped public opinion and won better protection for equal rights. They will write a couple of key phrases on an index card. The teacher will guide discussion and add new ideas as they arise. Students will choose which points they think are most important. Then the teacher will think aloud and guide practice as students determine how these ideas are connected to each other to generate a thesis for answering the question. Students will use speech-to-text software to record their planning ideas on a document outline/template.	Circulates and provides planning support to writers who are completing their graphic organizers. Students have the option of filling out a brief outline using speech to text OR filling out a graphic organizer using text boxes OR on paper. The special educator has file cards with some key points on them that can be shared with students as needed when an example can provide useful coaching.
After releasing these students to draft their opening paragraph, the social studies teacher assumes the role of circulating around the room and providing coaching. The goal of this time is to quickly review planning documents and make sure significant content-related errors or oversights are corrected before students begin writing. The teacher collects data on both mastery and misconceptions while conferencing with students and looking over shoulders.	Marcus and the special education teacher have 10 minutes for a one-on-one conference. The teacher has been using the Self-Regulated Strategy Development approach (Troia, 2014) to support Marcus in goal-setting to achieve better organization and elaboration in his writing. They take his planning ideas and begin to organize his opening paragraph and topic sentences.
The social studies teacher now leads a class discussion on reminders for strong opening paragraphs. The students start working on their opening paragraphs and thesis statements. They have the option of speech to text or typing and spread out around the room accordingly. Marcus is now ready to write and moves into the whole class group.	Small Group 2—Serena, August, and Javier, along with Terence and Chris, work on their opening paragraphs using a sentence frame to support their thinking and composing. It is useful to note that Javier, Terence, and Serena have IEP accommodations for writing that include sentence frames. They also have IEP goals connected to idea generation and organization. So, their

(continued)

TABLE 3.5 Sample Lesson Snapshot for Social Studies (continued)	
	frames are designed intentionally to cue a logical order and sufficient elaboration—the special education teacher provides explicit instruction on these cues to support the internalization of text structure. The special education teacher monitors closely and then uses a self-assessment checklist to have them monitor their own progress on the quality of their opening.
Closing The Lesson (about 6 minutes)	
The social studies teacher invites students to share their thesis statements with a partner. The partner is instructed to listen carefully and give feedback on its clarity. Did they understand the main idea the writer wanted to communicate?	
Students share planning documents and opening paragraphs with both teachers for formative feedback before tomorrow's writing session. The teachers will share the assessment responsibility—for the most part a quick review is all that is necessary. They are looking for any serious errors in thinking or oversights. Additional feedback will be provided as students write and revise in tomorrow's lesson.	

block schedule, these opportunities would be compacted appropriately and the practice opportunities would be shorter so they can also occur more frequently without overwhelming students and teachers.)

Using an alternative groups co-teaching model embedded in a writer's workshop environment, the social studies teacher and the special educator both provide SDI. They use the evidence-based practices of explicit writing instruction and self-regulated strategy development to support skill development in using evidence to answer a question with appropriate elaboration and organization. These skills are developed simultaneously with higher-level synthesis of the main ideas of a unit on the civil rights movement. Marcus gets explicit instruction on planning his essay from the social studies educator in one alternative group and then has a short individual coaching session with the special educator who is using self-regulated strategy development to help him set goals and progress monitor the organization and mechanics of his writing. Taken together, Marcus is getting access to instruction using two evidence-based practices that support the writing success of students with disabilities—this instruction is in direct service to an ambitious goal in his IEP.

Incorporating PBS and MTSS

While co-planning and co-teaching, teachers will also need to use positive behavior supports (PBS) and multi-tiered system of supports (MTSS). Both are data-driven, tiered systems that use evidence-based practices to support all students academically and behaviorally. The majority of the time students will demonstrate progress with effective and purposeful implementation of Tier 1 strategies.

PBS

Teachers will build relationships with students, greet them at the door, post and teach classroom rules, reinforce students often with specific positive praise, teach using engaging lessons tied to students' interests, provide choices, be in proximity to students, consider the grouping of students, model expectations, and create a safe and welcoming learning environment—all to proactively prevent problem behaviors. These are universal supports (Tier 1) that benefit all students (Center on PBIS, 2022). However, some students will need targeted supports with more frequent and explicit instruction on a specific skill or problem behavior in a small group setting (Tier 2). Examples include teaching specific social or self-regulation skills, using peer supports, providing additional academic supports, increasing the daily structure, and more frequent praise and feedback on appropriate behaviors. If a problem behavior continues after implementing Tier 1 and 2 strategies or intensifies in nature or frequency, then intensive, individualized supports are warranted (Tier 3). At this time, a functional behavior assessment is needed to determine the function of the behavior and to inform the behavioral intervention plan. This is typically conducted and monitored by the IEP or MTSS team. The general educator plays a key role in collecting important assessment data on in-class behaviors and implementing the prevention, teaching, and response strategies outlined in the plan.

MTSS

Similar to response to PBIS as a system of intervention and support for behavior, MTSS is a tiered system of academic, behavioral, and social-emotional supports to maximize student achievement for all students. It includes the following essential components: a multi-level prevention-based instruction and intervention system, data collection for student screening and progress monitoring, and data-based decision-making (Center on Multi-Tiered Systems of Support, 2022). High-quality evidence-based practices should be implemented with fidelity. With MTSS, teachers make changes to their instruction as opposed to students changing the way they learn. Approximately 80% of students benefit from differentiated instructional strategies (Tier 1—universal supports) that are proactive in meeting the needs of all students. However, some students need more targeted support with an appropriate duration and frequency to promote learning oftentimes in smaller groups (Tier 2—intensified supports). These smaller groups provide increased opportunities for practice and corrective feedback. A minority of students require more specialized interventions (Tier

3—individualized supports). Effective collaborating teachers can seamlessly integrate these different levels of supports as they work to help all students learn in inclusive settings.

Courses in the content area offer powerful opportunities to support supplemental and intensive interventions provided in advanced tiers of support for learners who need accelerated growth. While an interventionist or other highly skilled implementer provides the intervention directly, opportunities to generalize the skills in authentic and real-world learning situations can increase the opportunities for rehearsal, better space and balance practice over shorter and longer periods of time, and deepen the value and motivation for learners. For example, suppose a math interventionist is emphasizing metacognitive strategies like self-talk or self-monitoring checklists in solving problems. Social studies curriculum offers all kinds of real-world problems for students' consideration. If the social studies teacher knows the metacognitive routine and language cues for how and when to prompt it, then it can be embedded in another context. Such opportunities to generalize learning to new situations deepens connections for students; maximizing transfer and generalization is an evidence-based checkpoint for multiple means of representation in the *Universal Design for Learning Guidelines* (CAST, 2018).

CO-ASSESSING

As newly collaborating teachers are getting to know each other and building their collaborative partnership, they should share their assessment philosophies (Conderman & Hedin, 2012). A discussion on the importance of using multiple differentiated opportunities to assess student learning and how the data should guide future instruction needs to occur early on. Grading preferences, styles, systems, and timeliness should be discussed in order to build on each other's strengths (Conderman & Hedin, 2012) and find areas in need of compromise. During co-planning, the two teachers should agree on their shared responsibilities in co-assessing (i.e., developing assessments and rubrics, grading, maintaining a shared gradebook, implementing testing accommodations, and adjusting instruction based on the data). Assignments should be reviewed by both teachers for clarity in directions and organization, appropriate reading and difficulty levels, and opportunities for choice or differentiation to reflect best practices in assessment (Conderman & Hedin, 2012). Both teachers should be actively involved in the assessment process and knowledgeable of the evaluation results to monitor progress of students with and without disabilities. The key to assessment is to accurately evaluate what a student has learned without penalizing them for the barriers posed by their disability.

Grading

Quality grading systems should be accurate, meaningful, consistent, and support the learning process (O'Connor, 2009). Student products, student processes, and students' progress over time should be used to determine grades (Guskey, 2015; Jung & Guskey, 2012). Consequently, students with disabilities should have access to the same grading procedures as those provided to students without disabilities (Jung & Guskey, 2012) unless otherwise noted in their IEP. If students with disability can achieve the learning standard without adaptations or supports or only need accommodations to participate in the lesson or assessment which do not alter the standard, then standard grading procedures should be followed, and no grading changes are needed. It is important that all assessment accommodations in the student's IEP be followed by all teachers for all assessments of progress. However, if a student needs modifications that change the learning outcome, then a modified grading process should occur. This modification should be noted on report cards and in the IEP. Wakeman et al. (2022) provide extensive guidance for grading in inclusive classrooms using four criteria: (a) all grades are an accurate reflection of student performance, (b) all grades are meaningful to students and families as well as the school, (c) grading is consistent, and (d) grading is supportive of learning.

Collaborating general and special educators should share in the grading responsibilities of their students. Clear expectations should be established for consistent grading with fidelity. The teachers should also debrief on weekly testing and assignment results to ensure that both teachers are informed of student progress and can plan next instructional steps based on the data.

Data Collection on IEP Goals

Any adult in the general education classroom can collect data on IEP annual goals and objectives. During co-planning, it should be established who is collecting data on which days and goals and this information should be clearly communicated ahead of time with the respective person. The data collection method needs specific directions and labels to ensure consistency when different individuals are physically collecting the data. For best results, the data collection sheet should include the following: (a) student name, (b) goal/objective, (c) data collectors' initials, (d) data, (e) key for markings, (f) total, and (g) comment section.

IEP progress monitoring reports should supplement report cards. The IEP progress reports will specifically address progress on IEP goals. If the student is not making sufficient progress on an IEP goal, then the IEP team should meet to consider adjustments to supports or services to enhance learning outcomes and access to the general education curriculum.

SUMMARY

Social studies offers rich opportunities for co-planning, co-instructing, and co-assessing. The on-going engagement of general educators and special educators in these collaborative processes ensures that the key elements needed for effective instruction in today's complex classrooms are in place and implemented with fidelity. These include universal design for learning, differentiation, high levels of active engagement, tiered instruction, and SDI.

REFERENCES

Capin, P., & Vaughn, S. (2017). Improving reading and social studies learning for secondary students with reading disabilities. *TEACHING Exceptional Children, 49*(4), 249–261.

CAST. (2018). *Universal design for learning guidelines version 2.2.* Retrieved from http://udlguidelines.cast.org

Center on Multi-Tiered Systems of Support. (2022). *Essential components of MTSS.* National Institutes of Research. Retrieved from https://mtss4success.org/essential-components

Center on PBIS. (2022). *Positive behavioral interventions & supports.* Retrieved from www.pbis.org.

Ciullo, S., Collins, A., Wissinger, D. R., McKenna, J. W., Lo, Y.-L., & Osman, D. (2020). Students with learning disabilities in the social studies: A meta-analysis of intervention research. *Exceptional Children, 86*(4), 393–412.

Conderman, G., & Hedin, L. (2012). Purposeful assessment practices for co-teachers. *TEACHING Exceptional Children, 44*(4), 18–27.

Curtis, M., & Green, A. (2021). A systematic review of evidence-based practices for students with learning disabilities in social studies classrooms. *The Social Studies, 112*, 1–15.

Friend, M. (2018). *Co-Teach! Building and sustaining effective classroom partnerships in inclusive schools* (3rd ed.). National Professional Resources.

Friend, M., Hamby, L., & McAdams, D. (2014). *Scheduling for co-teaching and other inclusive practices.* CEC Convention. https://education.wm.edu/centers/ttac/documents/newsletters/cotschedulingfriend.pdf

Goeke, J. L. (2021). *The co-teacher's guide: Intensifying instruction beyond one teach, one support.* Routledge.

Guskey, T. R. (2015). *On your mark: Challenging the conventions of grading and reporting.* Solution Tree Press.

Hurd, E., & Weilbacher, G. (2017). "You want me to do what?" The benefits of co-teaching in the middle level. *Middle Grades Review, 3*(1), 1–14.

Jung, L. A., & Guskey, T. R. (2012). *Grading exceptional and struggling learners.* SAGE Publications.

Karakus, U., & Varalan, E. I. (2021). Developing the skills of students with mild intellectual disabilities using interactive map applications in a social studies course: An action research. *Participatory Educational Research, 8*(4), 198–214.

Lintner, T., & Schweder, W. (2011). *Practical strategies for teaching K–12 social studies in inclusive classrooms.* Information Age Publishing.

Minarik, D., & Coughlin, D. (2013). Don't forget me! Using special educators to support interdisciplinary teaching and learning. In T. Lintner (Ed.), *Integrative strategies for the K–12 social studies classroom* (pp. 167–190). Information Age Publishing.

Minarik, D., & Lintner, T. (2016). *Social studies & exceptional learners.* National Council for the Social Studies.

Murawski, W. W., & Lochner, W. W. (2017). *Beyond co-teaching basics: A data-driven, no-fail model for continuous improvement.* ASCD.

O'Connor, K. (2009). *How to grade for learning K–12.* Corwin Press.

Reeves, L. M., & Santoli, S. (2018). Involving students with autism in social studies. *Social Studies Research and Practice, 13*(1), 59–71.

Ryan, J. H. (2020). Inclusive structured inquiry-based social studies content instruction for students with significant intellectual and developmental disabilities [ProQuest Information & Learning]. *Dissertation Abstracts International Section A: Humanities and Social Sciences, 82*(10–A).

Ryan, J., Jameson, J. M., Coleman, O. F., Eichelberger, C., Bowman, J. A., Conradi, L. A., Johnston, S. S., & McDonnell, J. (2019). Inclusive social studies content instruction for students with significant intellectual disability using structured inquiry-based instruction. *Education and Training in Autism and Developmental Disabilities, 54*(4), 420–436.

Schenning, H., Knight, V., & Spooner, F. (2013). Effects of structured inquiry and graphic organizers on social studies comprehension by students with autism spectrum disorders. *Research in Autism Spectrum Disorders, 7*(4), 526–540.

Scruggs, T. E., Mastropieri, M. A., & McDuffie, K. A. (2007). Co-teaching in inclusive classrooms: A meta-synthesis of qualitative research. *Exceptional Children, 73*(4), 392–416.

Shaffer, L., & Thomas-Brown, K. (2015). Enhancing teacher competency through co-teaching and embedded professional development. *Journal of Education and Training Studies, 3*(3), 117–125.

Spencer, V. G., Evmenova, A. S., Boon, R. T., & Hayes-Harris, L. (2014). Review of research-based interventions for students with autism spectrum disorders in content area instruction: Implications and considerations for classroom practice. *Education and Training in Autism and Developmental Disabilities, 49*(3), 331–353.

The Meadows Center. (2022). *Promoting comprehension and content acquisition for students with disabilities.* https://meadowscenter.org/project/promoting-comprehension-and-content-acquisition-for-students-with-disabilities/

Troia, G. (2014). *Evidence-based practices for writing instruction.* Ideas That Work: Office of Special Education Programs, U.S. Department of Education. https://ceedar.education.ufl.edu/wp-content/uploads/2014/09/IC-5_FINAL_08-31-14.pdf

U.S. Department of Education. (2022). *IDEA section 618 data products: Static tables, Table 18, Part B child count and educational environments* [data set]. Retrieved from https://data.ed.gov/dataset/5df3e2a2-2500-472a-8f00-3d432d309687/resource/dcea91f1-bf95-4927-bbcf-c3a1e56575e2/download/2021-bchildcountandedenvironment-13.xlsx

Villa, R. A., & Thousand, J. S. (2016). *The inclusive education checklist: A self-assessment of best practices.* Dude Publishing.

Wakeman, S. Y., Thurlow, M., Reyes, E., & Kearns, J. (2022). Fair and equitable grading for ALL students in inclusive settings. *Inclusive Practices, 1*(4), 127–131.

Wood, L. (2020). Expanding cultural and social competence through social studies. In D. M. Browder, F. Spooner, & G. R. Courtade (Eds.), *Teaching students with moderate and severe disabilities* (pp. 276–298). The Guilford Press.

Wood, L., Browder, D. M., & Flynn, L. (2015). Teaching students with intellectual disability to use a self-questioning strategy to comprehend social studies text for an inclusive setting. *Research and Practice for Persons With Severe Disabilities, 40*(4), 275–293.

Zakas, T. L., Browder, D. M., Ahlgrim-Delzell, L., & Heafner, T. (2013). Teaching social studies content to students with autism using a graphic organizer intervention. *Research in Autism Spectrum Disorders, 7*(9), 1075–1086.

CHAPTER 4

DEVELOPING THE CIVIC ENGAGEMENT OF STUDENTS WITH DISABILITIES

Inclusive Civic Action Projects

Leah M. Bueso
University of Illinois Springfield

Richard Cairn
Emerging America, Collaborative for Educational Services

Civic engagement is paramount to establish an inclusive, equitable, and representative democracy. But people with disabilities, especially people of color with disabilities, experience systemic barriers and challenges to existing pathways to participation (Ho et al., 2020). For example, just one in 10 elected officials have a disability and only 2.4% of elected officials with disabilities are people of color (Schur & Kruse, 2019). Moreover, 1.95 million voters with disabilities (11%) reported difficulty casting a ballot in the 2020 election with Black and Latinx voters with disabilities reporting greater wait times and difficulty levels at polling places than their White counterparts

Creating an Inclusive Social Studies Classroom for Exceptional Learners, pages 71–96
Copyright © 2024 by Information Age Publishing
www.infoagepub.com
All rights of reproduction in any form reserved.

(Schur & Kruse, 2021). Although civic engagement is practiced through a wide range of actions beyond voting and running for office, these examples demonstrate how marginalized groups are underrepresented in civic life. And without opportunities for meaningful civic engagement in democratic society, people with disabilities and people of color with disabilities will continue to hold disproportionately little influence and power over their social, economic, and political progress (Ho et al., 2020).

One promising solution is to provide robust civic education to students with disabilities in K–12 schools. Indeed, when students are provided with high-quality civic learning opportunities, studies show increases in the degree to which youth follow the news, vote in elections, engage in respectful and productive debates, serve their communities, and judge the accuracy of political claims (Biesta et al., 2014; Kahne & Sporte, 2008; Levine & Kawashima-Ginsberg, 2017). However, students do not have equal access to these opportunities—students of color, low income students, and students with disabilities, are differentially exposed to evidence-based practices such as discussion of current events and controversial issues, learning to tell whether online information is reliable, service learning, and democratic simulations (Bueso, 2022; Kahne & Middaugh, 2009; Kawashima-Ginsberg, 2013; Wolff & Rogers, 2019). Such unequal access is likely exacerbated by three decades of federal education reform that have deprioritized civic education in K–12 schools (Educating for American Democracy, 2021). In fact, an analysis from the Center for American Progress confirmed that only nine states and DC require a full year of civics instruction in high school, 31 states require half a year, and 10 states have no requirement at all (Shapiro & Brown, 2018).

Regardless of your state's commitment to civic education, educators across grade levels and subject areas can incorporate high-quality civic learning opportunities that empower students with disabilities into their practice. For the purposes of this chapter, we focus on one specific learning opportunity—civic action projects—as a way to meaningfully and authentically engage students with disabilities in civic life. We also explain how strategies that promote self-determination, social emotional learning, equity, and inclusion will further support the knowledge, skills, and dispositions necessary for full participation in democratic society (Fullmer et al., 2022; Minarik et al., 2021). Finally, we present practical curricular and pedagogical strategies to help educators design and implement inclusive civic action projects.

WHAT SHOULD CIVIC ENGAGEMENT LOOK LIKE FOR STUDENTS WITH DISABILITIES?

In the *Civic Mission of Schools*, Gibson and Levine (2003) assert that schools are uniquely positioned to prepare generations of students to be informed and thoughtful citizens who participate in their communities, engage politically, and possess moral and civic virtues. They recommend six proven practices to further this goal: (a) classroom instruction, (b) discussion of current events and controversial issues, (c) service learning, (d) extracurricular activities, (e) school governance, and (f) simulations of democratic processes. While research shows that these practices enhance the civic knowledge, skills, and dispositions of the broader student population (Kahne & Sporte, 2008; Levine & Kawashima-Ginsberg, 2017), the extent to which students with disabilities have access to or benefit from them remains understudied (Garwood, 2021; Mann et al., 2015).

Data provided by the National Center for Education Statistics (NCES) suggests schools do not prioritize civic education for students with disabilities. In 2018, only 6% of eighth-grade students with disabilities performed at or above proficient on the National Assessment of Educational Progress (NAEP) civics assessment and these results were not significantly different from previous administrations in 2014, 2010, or 2006 (NCES, 2020). A handful of small-scale studies corroborate the NCES's findings that students with disabilities score significantly lower than their peers on assessments of civic competencies and confirm that school is the primary source of civic knowledge for both students with and without disabilities (e.g., Garwood, 2021; Hamot et al., 2005). Looking beyond assessments, Schur et al. (2003) found that civic skills predicted political participation for a group of 700 individuals with disabilities in adulthood. Ditchman et al. (2017) similarly determined that participation in extracurricular activities and access to civics curriculum was strongly associated with post-school civic engagement among a group of 206 young adults with developmental disabilities. That being said, a recent large-scale study concluded that the civic education experiences provided to students with disabilities in school are significantly different from those provided to students without disabilities, even when controlling for socioeconomic status, race/ethnicity, and gender (Bueso, 2022). In particular, Bueso found that students with disabilities are more likely to be excluded from discussion-based civic learning opportunities, but more likely to be included in service-based civic learning opportunities. These findings may be explained by the fact that students with disabilities frequently miss social studies instruction when they are pulled out of class for related services required by their individualized education programs (IEPs; Garwood, 2021; Teacher-Wagner et al., 2020). They also suggest that educators implicitly (or explicitly) make assumptions about the kinds of learning opportunities that students with disabilities are capable of participating in or contributing to. In other words, educators may believe that students with disabilities can lend a helping hand during a volunteer project but lack the cognitive or communicative competence to engage in class discussions (Bueso, 2022). Any meaningful commitment to preparing students with disabilities for civic engagement, however, requires providing equitable access to a range of civic learning opportunities and ensuring that the opportunities are both high quality and inclusive.

Despite the overall dearth of literature examining the six proven practices for students with disabilities, service learning is more widely researched. A systematic review of 13 studies by Garwood et al. (2022) confirmed that participation in service learning is associated with a wide range of benefits for students with disabilities including, but not limited to, increases in school attendance, peer relationships, cooperation skills, empathy for others, and pride in serving one's community. Unfortunately, much of the research conducted on service learning for students with disabilities described segregated programming, passive participation, or misconstrued notions of "inclusion" as recipients of service, not providers of service (Dymond et al., 2011). Mann et al. (2015) decried the tendency for educators to believe that students with disabilities are best served in segregated learning environments and instead advocated for service learning that encourages and supports the meaningful participation of all students together. Bueso (2022) likewise argued that the inclusion of students with disabilities in service learning must allow for authentic participation that occurs in collaboration with their peers and extends beyond menial task assignments. To do otherwise is to communicate to students with and without disabilities that only certain members of the school community are valued as competent and contributing civic actors.

Self-Determination

One way to support the development of meaningful and authentic civic engagement for students with disabilities is to integrate self-determination strategies into civic education curriculum and pedagogy. As Minarik and Lintner (2016) explain, the component elements of self-determination—choice-making, decision-making, problem-solving, goal setting, self-regulation, self-advocacy, self-efficacy, self-awareness, and self-knowledge—align with the goals of democratic practice. By providing learning opportunities that enhance these skills, educators can empower students with disabilities to act autonomously, improve the quality of their lives, and realize their potential as civic actors (Wehmeyer, 2006). Indeed, research consistently links self-determination with positive in-school and post-school outcomes for students with disabilities including academic productivity and goal attainment (Konrad et al., 2007), access to the general education curriculum (Shogren et al., 2012), student involvement in transition planning (Test et al., 2009), employment and independent living (Wehmeyer & Palmer, 2003), and community participation (Shogren et al., 2015).

Wehmeyer and Field (2007) recommend promoting self-determination through purposeful instruction that begins early in life and takes place across educational settings and experiences. For students with disabilities, the most opportune time to initiate such practices is through the development of the IEP (Vakil et al., 2010). The IEP process requires schools and families to work collaboratively to create a plan for special education and related services that address the unique needs of each student and include a set of annual goals (20 U.S.C. § 1414). As a result, students with disabilities (and their families) have a legal right to actively participate in the IEP process and person-centered approaches can facilitate meaningful and culturally responsive planning for a student's role in the school and community (Sorrells et al., 2004). This could include teaching students to understand their strengths and challenges, share their preferences, and advocate for their educational and postsecondary goals (Salend, 2015). In some cases, students could also lead parts of their IEP meeting, provide input on their IEP goals and services, and write their own transition plans (Williams-Diehm et al., 2008).

While student-directed involvement in the IEP process shows promise for increasing the self-determination of students with disabilities (Lee et al., 2011), these interventions focus on the ability to be autonomous over one's own life. High-quality civic learning opportunities, on the other hand, support the development of skills that may affect change for the individual and collective society (Wehmeyer & Field, 2007). For example, inclusive class discussions about current events can provide students with disabilities with "critical opportunities to engage with issues, share their thoughts and ideas, and have their opinions matter" (Bueso, 2022, p. 78). Along the same lines, instruction about fundamental laws and governmental structures can empower students with disabilities to hold elected officials accountable and advocate for themselves and others as full participants in democracy (Vakil et al., 2010). And when done well, service-learning projects can offer meaningful and authentic experiences that allow students with disabilities to impact their communities while also being treated as competent, contributing citizens (Garwood et al., 2022). Each of these learning opportunities develop critical skills, including active listening, decision-making, cooperation, compromise, and leadership, that will simultaneously support self-determination and preparation for civic life.

Social Emotional Learning

Participation in civic life requires more than self-determination. In a polarized political climate, the strength of our democracy increasingly depends on the social and emotional intelligence of its citizens. As Fullmer et al. (2022) explain, not everyone will get their way in a democracy and therefore students need to know how to regulate their emotions to manage disappointment, take on the perspectives of others to engage in respectful and productive discourse, and develop compassion and empathy to work collaboratively to solve problems. Moreover, social and emotional learning (SEL) frameworks that provide opportunities for students to engage in critical examination and collaborative action around root causes of inequities can be used to address societal issues such as power, privilege, and discrimination (Jagers et al., 2019).

Developmental research confirms that social and emotional competencies support youth civic development (Eisenberg et al., 2010; Sherrod et al., 2010). This makes sense given that many forms of civic engagement require prosocial behaviors in order to prioritize helping others (Metzger et al., 2018). For example, empathy is associated with volunteering and informal helping (Bekkers, 2005), while emotional regulation facilitates goal attainment and problem solving through collective action (Eisenberg & Spinrad, 2004). As another example, advanced prosocial moral reasoning predicted helping behaviors (Carlo et al., 2010) and the ability to contemplate possible outcomes in the future is attributed to increased civic and political engagement among youth (Metzger et al., 2016). Notably, Metzger et al. (2018) found that the predictive value of empathy and emotional regulation on civic engagement was stronger among younger youth (Grades 4–8), whereas the predictive value of prosocial moral reasoning and future-orientation on civic engagement was stronger among older youth (Grades 9–12).

Unfortunately, the large majority of studies examining universal SEL curricula in middle and high schools do not report whether students with disabilities were included in the study samples, which means little is known about whether or how they are benefitting from participation (Daley & McCarthy, 2021). Among the five studies specifically investigating outcomes for students with disabilities, the findings were inconsistent—one showed a decrease in victimization, but another did not; one showed a decrease in bullying, but another did not; and decreases in aggression or fighting occurred for students without disabilities, but not for students with disabilities (see, Espelage et al., 2015; Sullivan et al., 2015). A complementary systematic review of universal SEL curricula in elementary schools found only 20 studies providing outcome data for students with disabilities that vary widely across academic, social, and emotional indicators and offer no disability subgroup analysis (Cipriano et al., 2023). To better understand the impact of universal SEL curricula on students with disabilities, research that considers different disability classifications and provides outcome data on civic engagement would greatly benefit the field.

All things considered, the strong link between SEL competencies and civic engagement suggest high-quality curricula supports the civic development of students with disabilities. In particular, when learning environments lend themselves to collaborative inquiry, deliberation, and problem solving, educators help cultivate skills such as social awareness, self-management, and compromise (Darling-Hammond et al., 2018). The literature indicates that "transformative" versions of such tasks are often action-driven (e.g., project-based learning, youth participatory action research) and encourage responsive, respectful, and inclusive interactions between students, teachers, and the community (Jagers et al., 2019). Examples of key approaches have included: student-centered, culturally responsive activities with balanced group composition and co-constructed group norms (Surr et al., 2018); opportunities for reflection, expression, and agency (Baines et al., 2017); respecting youth as experts about their lived experiences and the required processes for bringing about desired changes (Ozer, 2016); careful attention to adults' sharing of power with students (Ozer et al., 2010); and sustained inquiry that is active, in-depth, and iterative with real-world relevance for students (Jagers et al., 2019). In one of the few experimental studies on a youth participatory action research class, participating students reported higher levels of motivation, persuasiveness, self-efficacy, decision-making, and problem-solving (Ozer & Douglas, 2013). Thus, SEL-infused civic education shows promise as a way to enhance students' capacities as civic actors.

Equity and Inclusion

Equitable access to and meaningful inclusion in high-quality civic learning opportunities is a social justice issue for students with disabilities. Indeed, social studies and special education teachers agree that civics was the content area that received the least amount of attention for students with disabilities (Garwood, 2021). This is particularly disappointing given that social studies teachers have higher caseloads of students with disabilities compared to their colleagues teaching math and English (Mullins et al., 2020). When teachers exclude students with disabilities from vital opportunities to develop civic knowledge, skills, and dispositions, they reinforce able-bodied and able-minded notions of citizenship that prescribe "a particular level and display of intellectual ability, communicative competence, social independence, and behaviour" (Taylor, 2020, p. 53). Instead, a democratic classroom should foster the full acceptance and active participation of all learners through a curriculum that is flexible and accessible (Martin et al., 2021). Put simply, students with disabilities deserve to be treated as competent members of the school community and provided with high-quality civic learning opportunities that will prepare them for civic life.

However, a number of school and classroom level factors related to equity and inclusion have been shown to impact youth civic engagement. When students perceived a more equitable school climate and received opportunities for voice and choice, they were more likely to report positive civic attitudes. Importantly, this association disappeared when schools were seen as inequitable (Jagers et al., 2017). Kupchik and Catlaw (2015) similarly found that punitive school disciplinary policies negatively impacted students' political and civic participation years later. A review of 20 studies across five countries concluded that negative attitudes from supervisors and inaccessible opportunities limited volunteering efforts among youth with disabilities (Lindsay, 2016). Likewise, Carter et al. (2011) confirmed that youth with disabilities are afforded infrequent opportunities to take on leadership roles in high school and are often forced to confront low expectations and stereotypes about their abilities held by teachers, counselors, staff, and peers. In sum, inequitable and exclusionary policies, beliefs, and practices in schools undermine opportunities for civic development.

Educators can mitigate or reverse these effects by establishing a school culture that promotes positive perceptions of disability and students with disabilities. To start, all students should learn about disability history, interrogate exclusionary laws, narratives, and power structures, and participate in collaborative learning experiences with their peers (Minarik et al., 2021). Meanwhile, teachers should evaluate whether high-quality civic learning opportunities are inequitably distributed to students with disabilities and consider how their instructional practices limit full, meaningful, or authentic participation (Minarik & Lintner, 2016). In addition, teachers should prioritize democratic pedagogy that cultivates open dialogue, shared decision making, and respect for diverse opinions (Jagers et al., 2017) as well as self-determination and SEL strategies that expand opportunities for students with disabilities to advocate for themselves and others (Darling-Hammond et al., 2018).

HOW MIGHT EDUCATORS INCLUDE STUDENTS WITH DISABILITIES IN CIVIC ACTION PROJECTS?

Students with disabilities deserve to participate in a wide variety of high-quality civic learning opportunities. This chapter focuses on one specific learning opportunity—civic action projects—because collaborative tasks are an effective way to meaningfully and authentically engage students with disabilities in civic life. To be sure, students need to practice the "arts and habits of citizenship" in order to learn how to engage productively in a democracy (Levinson & Levine, 2013) and civic action projects lend themselves nicely to inclusive modeling. This chapter also aims to dispel any notions that civic action projects should only be attempted by ambitious, veteran teachers. Rather, we offer this practical guide for any teacher ready to empower their students to make real-world change.

Alignment With Academic Standards and Inclusive Pedagogies

The College, Career, and Civic Life (C3) Framework for Social Studies State Standards explicitly advocates for the preparation of students for civic action and centers on the skills of inquiry. As the coalition of authors explain, supporting the development of "knowledgeable, thinking, and active citizens" is necessary to sustain our democratic republic (National Council for the Social Studies [NCSS], 2013). Of course, students need to learn about the history of civic life and the structures and functions of civic institutions in America (e.g., separation of powers, how an idea becomes a law), but that knowledge alone is not enough. All students need to learn to generate and investigate significant questions, and they need to learn to make well-reasoned arguments supported by relevant and reliable sources. Indeed, the C3 framework explicitly calls for students to act upon their values in the larger world as they "apply a range of deliberative and democratic strategies and procedures to make decisions, and take action in their classrooms, schools, and out-of-school civic contexts" (NCSS, 2013, p. 62). Such skill development is particularly important for students with disabilities given the many additional barriers to civic participation that they will face throughout their lives. Yet with adequate support, all students can strengthen these vital capabilities.

In 2021, a broad-based national campaign called Educating for American Democracy (EAD) arose to promote high-quality teaching of history and civics. Emerging America and the Learning Disabilities Association of America (LDAA) drafted an extension to the EAD's research report to highlight and support inclusion for students with disabilities. That extension challenged history and civic educators to consider both the means to support students with disabilities and the academic content and skills that will best address the needs of those students (Emerging America & LDAA, 2021). A central theme of EAD speaks to civic participation. In that context, the extension calls on educators to ask students to consider the following questions:

- What does it mean to be an inclusive classroom community? What actions and processes uphold that community?
- How has civic participation changed over time? Who was granted access to civic learning opportunities and civil rights (e.g., voting) and how were they engaged?

In the sections that follow, we address each of these questions and explore examples of strategies and tools to support civic action projects. But first let's define what we mean: Student-led civic action projects involve students in the nitty gritty of making the world a better place. While traditional service learning or community service projects might include direct assistance like tutoring or serving food at a soup kitchen, civic action projects by definition aim to address the root causes of social issues. That is, students can take action by advocating to policy makers to change laws or by seeking to educate and influence attitudes in the community about an issue. Thus, civic action projects can range from meeting with elected officials or writing letters to the editor of a newspaper, to working with a nonprofit to organize around a community issue or even hosting a public forum.

Establishing an Inclusive Community for Civic Engagement

For educators interested in designing inclusive civic action projects for their students, universal design for learning (UDL) is an effective framework that guides educators in the development of curriculum that meets the needs of every student (Hall et al., 2012). UDL is a critical resource because it helps to identify all the different ways a curriculum needs to be customized so that it is truly accessible. In particular, UDL provides flexibility in the ways information is presented, the ways in which students respond or demonstrate knowledge and skills, and the ways in which students are engaged (CAST, 2018). As a result, UDL leverages learning variability as a strength, makes room for difference in advance, and empowers educators to meet the unique needs of all students.

To begin, UDL asks educators to present information to students using multiple means. With civic action projects, students are given the choice of issues for research and action, but they will need guidance to make this decision. Students with disabilities will have some of the same concerns about the larger community as anyone, so they may want to address issues including climate change, street violence, or public safety. And since many people with disabilities face daily challenges to their very survival, including limited access to transportation and support services, discrimination in hiring and housing, and ableist stereotypes, students with disabilities may feel strongly motivated to work on these issues. In fact, involvement in such projects could lead students to advocate for accommodations or services in school, for particular legislative bills or administrative rules, or for the education of peers and the larger community about the capabilities of people with disabilities and issues that most impact their lives. See Figure 4.1 for a list of sample projects and issues adapted from the blog of Scott Lentine, a

Sample Projects & Issues
Scott Lentine - https://scottlentine.wordpress.com/

- Blog & poetry to share thoughts and strategies
- Expand adaptive arts programs in schools
- Build job skills; support employment programs & transit
- Review legislation and administrative policy
- Support legislation e.g. MA 2014 Autism Omnibus Bill
  - Insurance coverage by MassHealth
  - Strengthen teaching of students with autism
- Register to vote and voter education
- Intern or volunteer with access advocacy organizations
- General issues: street violence, opioid addiction, food access, water pollution, climate change, etc.

Figure 4.1 Sample projects and issues. *Source:* "Civic Engagement for People With Disabilities," by S. Lentine (2017). Adapted with permission.

disability rights activist. Regardless of which issue students choose to investigate, educators must take care to present a wide variety of options relevant to students with and without disabilities. At the same time, the exploration of those options should be presented in multiple formats including, but not limited to, primary source documents, current newspaper and magazine articles, nonfiction texts, documentary films, and podcasts.

Next, UDL asks educators to provide students with multiple means for action and expression. While the end result of a civic action project is inherently flexible—there is no telling where students' research and advocacy will take them—the process by which they get there should be guided and semi-structured. For example, educators can create a list of common ways to take action in one's community (e.g., call or write to a congressional representative, host a community forum, create a public service announcement) and let students choose the best way to address their issue. Educators can also allow students to work alone or in groups and give them the flexibility to summarize their findings in writing (e.g., research paper, op-ed), orally (e.g., slide presentation, news report), artistically (e.g., interpretive dance/song, collage), or any combination of the three.

Finally, UDL asks educators to provide multiple means for engagement of students. Central to inclusive civic action projects is the need to ensure that everyone has meaningful roles and opportunities to contribute. Educators could ask students to use a rubric created by Emerging America (2020) that will help lead students to discuss questions such as, "What can you do to involve people in your group so that everyone gets a voice and has work that plays on their strengths and/or lets them try new things?" Students who are uncomfortable speaking up can get encouragement and feedback on how to "step up" to express and advocate for their ideas. Meanwhile, students who tend to dominate discussions are tasked to learn to "step back" as they listen and encourage others. Educators can also provide students with a list of specific roles to help ensure full participation. These might include typical roles such as timekeeper and recordkeeper, as well as research roles that include drafting interview questions for community-based experts, making phone calls to local organizations, and collecting background information for the group to read together. Students should have choices among roles and be encouraged to rotate to broaden their skill set. This process can be further scaffolded by providing students with a project timeline that includes periodic check-ins where smaller chunks of work are "due" and reviewed with the teacher and any group members (if applicable).

Following the lead of Minarik and Lintner (2016), every lesson on the Accessing Inquiry section of the Emerging America website incorporates the three principles of UDL—engagement, representation, and expression-action—in addition to "cultural considerations" (p. 45). The Accessing Inquiry section also provides a rich variety of primary and secondary sources that are vital to history and civics classes and offer multiple modes of information for students to investigate and express themselves (Morgan & Rasinski, 2012; Waring, 2021).

There is also a powerful alignment between the need for students with disabilities to engage in civic action and their need, commonly identified in IEPs, to develop overall skills and confidence with self-determination. The necessary skills for civics are highly transferable to individual growth: self-reflection, assessment of community resources, prioritizing, decision-making, planning, follow-through, reflection on the process itself, and carrying what has been learned forward into future activities. Helping students to prioritize, learn, and apply these skills should be a key point of collaboration between social studies and special education teachers. Civic action projects offer rich opportunities for alignment between self-determination goals and civic engagement goals. When students choose which project to work on, they can address learning goals such as: "Identify options available in making a decision" and "Identify the short- and long-term impacts of different decisions." Moreover, when presented with meaningful and authentic opportunities for choice, a student may opt to better understand their own disability and/or how to communicate their academic and social-emotional needs. For example, in Jen Groskin's 8th grade civics class, a student with autism addressed such learning goals by developing a slide presentation on autism awareness for younger students and included the following explanation: "I am doing this so I can end stereotypes and assumptions that people make about people who have autism (Groskin & Jensen, 2021). I also wanted to help people understand and [know] what to do when they meet someone on the autism spectrum" (Groskin & Jensen, 2021, p. 15).

Exploring the History of Disability Rights in the United States

A common difficulty for many teachers as well as students is a lack of familiarity with disability rights issues and organizations. Meeting with advocates and researching the issues can be empowering for all, and local or state commissions on disability can be an excellent source of contacts (e.g., Emerging America, 2022). Studying the rich history of advocacy for disability rights gives all students perspectives on ways to think about how to take action for social change. Identity formation and choosing which communities they belong to are central tasks for many students with disabilities. It is especially important for them to gain role models and ideas for effective strategies and tactics. Yet key parts of that narrative are often missing. The history of people with disabilities has been almost wholly neglected in schools (Mueller, 2021). When disability history does come up, it is usually limited to listing "inspiring" leaders with disabilities. Such an approach trivializes people with disabilities and their contributions to society (TED, 2014). Equally disempowering is to focus on people with disabilities solely as victims of tragedy, ignoring the long history of self-advocacy by people with disabilities.

A common reaction by disability activists when they first learn parts of the history of advocacy for disability rights is "Why didn't anyone teach me this?" A full telling of the American story should uplift everyone. When students with disabilities recognize themselves in history, they gain confidence that they too can make a difference. The #TeachDisabilityHistory campaign by Easterseals Massachusetts (n.d.) demonstrates the significance of these narratives. Consider, for example, how deaf leader George Veditz understood early on the power of film to teach and advocate for American Sign Language in the face of well-funded efforts to stamp it out. See Figure 4.2 for a screenshot from Veditz's film *Preservation of the Sign Language*. Analysis of this compelling primary source introduces students to a powerful story of self-advocacy as well as innovative ways that people with disabilities used "new" media for civic action in 1913.

Emerging America (n.d.-a) has compiled a substantial list of curricula and collections of primary and secondary sources on disability history available on the Accessing Inquiry section of its website. The Disability History Museum (https://www.disabilitymuseum.org) and the Longmore Institute on Disability at San Francisco State University (https://longmoreinstitute.sfsu.edu) at San Francisco State University have also published high-quality

84 ▪ L. M. BUESO and R. CAIRN

Figure 4.2 Screenshot from preservation of the sign language. *Note:* George Veditz, president of the National Association of the Deaf. *Source:* "Preservation of the Sign Language," by G. W. Veditz (1913).

source material and lessons for the K–12 classroom. A number of other advocacy organizations make available excellent collections of primary sources, videos, articles, and other secondary resources.

Recognizing the lack of complete, coherent curriculum materials, Emerging America (n.d.-b) developed *Reform to Equal Rights: Disability History Curriculum* with hundreds of primary sources, lessons, slides, and online exhibits. The curriculum emphasizes the agency of people with disabilities in advocating for equal rights, featuring often lesser-known examples such as the work of George Veditz noted above, the direct action tactics of the League of the Physically Handicapped in the 1930s, and the legal activism of Lois Curtis in helping to win the right to self-determination for people in asylums and other institutions. See Figure 4.3 for a photo of Lois Curtis, plaintiff in *Olmstead v. L.C.* (1999), which affirmed the rights of Americans with disabilities to live independently.

When students begin to examine disability history, they will encounter difficult terms, ideas, images, and stories of discrimination and abuse. It is essential to establish ground rules as a class for the respectful use of language, including offensive terms that inevitably appear in the sources. Emerging America's (n.d.-b) *Reform to Equal Rights: Disability History Curriculum* offers strategies and slides to aid this preparation. And while some

Figure 4.3 Lois Curtis meets President Barack Obama for the anniversary of *Olmstead v. L.C.* (1999). *Source:* "Olmstead Champion Meets the President," by S. Jamieson (2011).

students with disabilities will embrace the opportunity to address these issues or talk about their own experiences, others will not want to identify as having disabilities or may need support to address topics that could be personally traumatic. No student should ever be asked to speak for all people with disabilities in general. When possible, talk to students in advance about how they want to address their disabilities, if at all, during the coming period of study. Furthermore, teachers need to stay informed about how the language changes. The National Center on Disability and Journalism (2021) provides a useful resource with a frequently updated *Disability Language Style Guide*.

At the same time, students will encounter leaders on many issues who are increasingly embracing disability as part of their core identity, which may indeed strengthen their capacities. Consider the example of climate change activist Greta Thunberg who proudly proclaimed on Instagram, "I have Asperger's syndrome and that means I'm sometimes a bit different from the norm. And—given the right circumstances—being different is a superpower" (Thunberg, 2019). See Figure 4.4 for a photo of Thunberg at a climate change rally in Denver.

Thunberg also provides a wonderful example of how people with disabilities (including young people) can advocate for change around issues unrelated to their disability or the disability of others. Just as students should never be forced to disclose their disability or speak for all people

Figure 4.4 Greta Thunberg at a climate change rally in Denver. *Source:* Quintano (2019)..

with disabilities, they should never be pigeon-holed into civic action projects that only consider disability-related issues.

Massachusetts: Civic Action in Action

Many states have renewed their focus on civic education in recent years. In 2018, one of the most comprehensive efforts put civics at the heart of Massachusetts state standards for history and social science and newly required an eighth grade civics course. That same year, the Massachusetts legislature required that every student in the state have opportunities to complete nonpartisan civic action projects in eighth grade and again in high school. The state published a flexible, detailed guidebook on planning and carrying out student-directed projects (see Massachusetts Department of Elementary and Secondary Education, n.d.). In response to Emerging America and other disability rights advocates, the state incorporated numerous strategies and tools for inclusion. The guidebook outlines a six-stage process for developing and completing projects that employ all the skills of civic engagement identified above.

Stage 1: Examining Self and Community

Before starting any civic action project, students should be provided with the time and space to explore their identity and relationships to their communities as they generate possible issues to work on. Educators can guide this process by encouraging students to think about "unaddressed or under-addressed" challenges in their lives or the lives of people they care about. Vital questions in the guidebook can help shape teaching practices by asking, for example, "How can I model and support acceptance of student self-determination of identity, recognizing that students' understanding of their identities is often complex and evolving?" Emerging America's rubric for creating an inclusive classroom, described above, supports this stage. The guidebook also offers a variety of worksheets and graphics to aid students to explore such questions as: (a) "What is an asset?"; (b) "What assets does my community offer?"; and (c) "What problems or challenges do people in my community encounter?"

This stage offers an opportunity for all students to reflect on which communities they belong to and how they want to interact with those communities. This can also be a valuable opportunity for students with disabilities to reflect on how they want to position themselves in relation to disability rights advocacy, and there will be a payoff here for those students who studied advocates across history. Moreover, this is a good time to consider intersections between and among identities, including race/ethnicity, socioeconomic status, gender, age, language, and nationality, as well as with personal interests such as athletics, arts, technology, and career. The narratives and perspectives of real advocates will help to illustrate this complexity.

Stage 2: Identifying an Issue

In this stage, students identify the issues that are meaningful to them. As previously discussed, it's an opportunity for all students to learn about a range of community issues including disability rights. The guidebook also offers concrete strategies and tools for a class (or small group) to work toward consensus. This is a vital time to support students with disabilities to speak up. Many students will need explicit instruction and practice to answer questions such as, "What are persuasive techniques and how do we use them to convince others of the importance of a community issue?" Of course, such instruction and practice can also serve as opportunities for students with disabilities to work on self-determination goals in their IEPs.

Stage 3: Research and Investigation

Typically, the most difficult part of the process is researching an issue and identifying and evaluating possible actions to address it. To guide students with research, it can be helpful to provide a list of reliable databases and resources where students can search for information. In some cases, it may even be worthwhile to provide students with specific references to start the research process. Once students understand the basic concepts related to their issue, they can have the freedom to explore additional sources. Students will also need support brainstorming ways to take action on their issue. To do so, educators could lead students in a root cause analysis and show videos of other activists to inspire problem-solving ideas. Moreover, educators should emotionally prepare students to understand that some issues like ending hunger or poverty require ongoing solutions that are unlikely to move the needle within the project timeline. As a result, students who choose local issues (e.g., advocating for their town to help fund construction of a fully accessible food bank) will likely experience more success and have the added benefit of being able to partner with local community organizations. Indeed, the research stage offers a golden opportunity for students with disabilities to interact with and gain information from advocates in the community. The diverse and creative methods of past and current disability rights advocacy can expand their awareness of actions they could take themselves.

Stage 4: Developing an Action Plan

Developing detailed plans for action is another challenging task for most students. But the guidebook outlines specific steps students can take to achieve their objectives and locates rubrics for an effective and inclusive planning process. For example, students will need to consider questions such as, "Who are the decision makers and influencers in our community?" And some students will need substantial help mapping out the details of their plan or even narrowing down their choices so as not to become overwhelmed. As previously noted, students will best understand the tactics that they have seen in their study of history, including creative and tenacious disability rights activism. It is also useful to provide students with graphic organizers and timelines that break down different steps and due dates for the project. This is where social studies and special education teachers can collaborate to provide students with opportunities to practice planning skills. When in doubt, it is always best to start small and then build on those successes as most students need guidance to scale their ambitions to the available time and resources.

Stage 5: Taking Action

Communication with "influencers and decision makers"—those with power in the community—is central to enacting civic action projects. Students should ask themselves, "How do I bring together people and organizations in my community to support my issue?" It is important for students to realize that they do not have to take action by themselves and, in fact, transformative change occurs most often when many people work together. Moreover, many community organizations are already engaged in work that students can choose to join or build upon, which can be a relief for those students trying to reinvent the wheel. In this way, the guidebook focuses on collaborative skills like active listening, building consensus, and working with others. At the same time, the guidebook outlines practical steps that students must take to contact and convince influencers, draft petitions, distribute letter/email campaigns, and organize phone banks. When educators check in with their students during this stage, it is helpful to remind students to cycle between roles so that everyone gets to engage in meaningful tasks and contribute to the project.

Stage 6: Reflecting and Showcasing

The final stage asks students to complete a summative reflection and showcase their work. In particular, the guidebook encourages students to reflect on what they accomplished as well as what worked and what could have been improved. The emphasis here is on applying what has been learned toward future actions, as students consider why certain tactics may have been more effective than others. Although all students will benefit from directed reflection with their peers and thinking about how to apply new insights going forward, these exercises also serve as opportunities for practice for students with self-determination goals in their IEPs. Moreover, no matter what format an educator chooses to adopt for the showcase (e.g., classroom presentations, schoolwide fair, or community event), students will be provided with an authentic opportunity to share their findings and spread awareness about their issue. These moments are incredibly rare and valuable for students with and without disabilities alike. And when students are given the flexibility to showcase their learning in a variety of ways, educators can use this time to highlight the strengths of each student in their classroom, which will build confidence and promote a positive school and classroom climate.

Other Models of Civic Action

Several organizations across the country engage students in civic life and many are organized locally. Chicago-based Mikva Challenge (www.mikvachallenge.org) has grown to involve youth across the nation in "authentic and transformative democratic experiences" and civic skill-building. Project Citizen (www.civiced.org/project-citizen) has offices in a number of states and offers a civics curriculum to support research on issues and skill-building as well as opportunities to showcase projects. Harvard's Democratic Knowledge Project (www.democraticknowledge.fas.harvard.edu) creates curricular resources with teachers and offers professional development and assessment services and the CivXNow coalition (www.civxnow.org/who-we-are/coalition/) brings together many such organizations.

WHERE DO WE GO FROM HERE?

Students with disabilities are an understudied population in the civic education literature. Among extant studies, the majority are small scale and focus on measuring civic competencies (see, e.g., Ditchman et al., 2017; Garwood, 2021), while fewer focus on access to and the quality of civic learning opportunities (Bueso, 2022). A larger body of research linking civic engagement and SEL is available, but most studies fail to provide or collect disaggregated demographic data based on disability classification and educational placement or exclude students with disabilities from the study population altogether (see, e.g., Cipriano et al., 2023; Daley & McCarthy, 2021). This often occurs because students with disabilities are considered a vulnerable population in the research review process and it is much more difficult to get permission to study their classes, services, and IEPs. But precisely because students with disabilities are a vulnerable population, we need more data to identify the best ways to support them. As a result, there is a general need for additional research in this field, but targeted studies examining whether subgroups of students with disabilities have variable needs would greatly benefit scholars and practitioners.

Within schools and classrooms, all educators—but especially social studies and special education teachers—need robust training on providing high-quality civic learning opportunities (Levine & Kawashima-Ginsberg, 2017) and integrating self-determination and SEL strategies in civic education (Espelage et al., 2015; Vakil et al., 2010). However, the root issue always leads back to equity and inclusion. Teachers need help reflecting on how and why their practices may exclude students with disabilities from critical civic learning opportunities (Mann et al., 2015; Taylor, 2020) as well as what they can do to create democratic classrooms that foster acceptance and full participation (Martin et al., 2021). At the same time, district and school administrators must examine how punitive policies are making places of learning feel inequitable and inaccessible for students with disabilities (Jagers et al., 2017; Kupchik & Catlaw, 2015). As we recommend in this chapter, educators can begin this crucial process by providing all students with opportunities to learn about, from, and alongside students with disabilities, especially through high-quality civic learning opportunities.

REFERENCES

Baines, A., DeBarger, A. H., De Vivo, K., & Warner, N. (2017). *Why social and emotional learning is essential to project-based learning.* Lucas Education Research. https://www.lucasedresearch.org/wp-content/uploads/2021/02/SEL-White-Paper.pdf

Bekkers, R. (2005). Participation in voluntary associations: Relations with resources, personality, and political values. *Political Psychology, 26*(3), 439–454.

Biesta, G., De Bie, M., & Wildemeersch, D. (Eds.). (2014). *Civic learning, democratic citizenship and the public sphere.* Springer.

Bueso, L. (2022). Civic equity for students with disabilities. *Teachers College Record, 124*(1), 62–86.

Carlo, G., Mestre, M. V., Samper, P., Tur, A., & Armenta, B. E. (2010). Feelings or cognitions? Moral cognitions and emotions as longitudinal predictors of prosocial and aggressive behaviors. *Personality and Individual Differences, 48*(8), 872–877.

Carter, E. W., Swedeen, B., Walter, M. J., Moss, C. K., & Hsin, C. T. (2011). Perspectives of young adults with disabilities on leadership. *Career Development for Exceptional Individuals, 34,* 57–67.

CAST. (2018). *The universal design for learning guidelines.* https://udlguidelines.cast.org/

Cipriano, C., Naples, L. H., Eveleigh, A., Cook, A., Funaro, M., Cassidy, C., McCarthy, M. F., & Rappolt-Schlichtmann, G. (2023). A systematic review of student disability and race representation in universal school-based social and emotional learning interventions for elementary school students. *Review of Educational Research, 93*(1). https://doi.org/10.3102/00346543221094079

Daley, S. G., & McCarthy, M. F. (2021). Students with disabilities in social and emotional learning interventions: A systematic review. *Remedial and Special Education, 42*(6), 384–397.

Darling-Hammond, L., Cook-Harvey, C., Flook, L., Gardner, M., & Melnick, H. (2018). *With the whole child in mind: Insights from the Comer School Development Program.* ACSD.

Ditchman, N., Haak, C., & Corrigan, P. (2017). *Civic engagement among young adults with disabilities: Summary of survey findings.* Illinois Institute of Technology.

Dymond, S. K., Renzaglia, A., & Slagor, M. T. (2011). Trends in the use of service learning with SWD. *Remedial and Special Education, 32*(3), 219–229.

Easterseals Massachusetts. (n.d.). *Teach disability history.* Retrieved November 14, 2022 from https://www.easterseals.com/ma/get-involved/advocacy/teach-disability-history/

Educating for American Democracy. (2021). *Educating for American democracy: Excellence in history and civics for all learners.* iCivics. https://www.educatingforamericandemocracy.org/wp-content/uploads/2021/02/Educating-for-American-Democracy-Report-Excellence-in-History-and-Civics-for-All-Learners.pdf

Eisenberg, N., Eggum, N. D., & Di Giunta, L. (2010). Empathy-related responding: Associations with prosocial behavior, aggression, and intergroup relations. *Social Issues and Policy Review, 4*(1), 143–180.

Eisenberg, N., & Spinrad, T. L. (2004). Emotion-related regulation: Sharpening the definition. *Child Development, 75,* 334–339.

Emerging America. (n.d.-a) *Accessing inquiry.* Retrieved September 27, 2022 from http://www.emergingamerica.org/accessing-inquiry

Emerging America. (n.d.-b). *Reform to equal rights–disability history curriculum.* Retrieved September 27, 2022 from http://www.emergingamerica.org/curriculum/reform-equal-rights-disability-history-curriculum

Emerging America. (2020). *Assessment of student inclusion in civic engagement projects: Single-point rubric.* https://docs.google.com/document/d/1NdtVHOVmqSPeflCUt8D1D5jnClrhpihz4eukDKbtPPM/edit?usp=sharing

Emerging America. (2022). *Disability advocacy groups.* https://drive.google.com/file/d/1C_iUWsFYN7W3UsSLCvnPX2syikjpFdbY/view

Emerging America and Learning Disabilities Association of America. (2021). *Educating for American democracy roadmap disability history and civics extension*. https://drive.google.com/file/d/1ug5kNxt7jeSo4tH1hSm1olj9itNAqrbv/view

Espelage D. L., Rose C. A., & Polanin J. R. (2015). Social-emotional learning program to reduce bullying, fighting, and victimization among middle school students with disabilities. *Remedial and Special Education, 36*(5), 299–311.

Fullmer, L. M., Bond, L. F., Molyneaux, C. N., Nayman, S. J., & Elias, M. J. (2022). *Students taking action together: 5 teaching techniques to cultivate SEL, civic engagement, and a healthy democracy*. ACSD.

Garwood, J. D. (2021). The absence of civics interventions for students with disabilities: A Mixed-methods investigation. *Exceptionality, 29*(4), 280–293.

Garwood, J. D., Peltier, C., Ciullo, S., Wissinger, D., McKenna, J. W., Giangreco, M. F., & Kervick, C. (2022). The experiences of students with disabilities actually doing service learning: A systematic review. *Journal of Experiential Education, 46*(1). https://doi.org/10.1177/10538259221109374

Gibson, C., & Levine, P. (2003). *The civic mission of schools*. The Center for Information and Research on Civic Learning and Engagement and the Carnegie Corporation of New York. https://media.carnegie.org/filer_public/9d/0a/9d0af9f4-06af-4cc6-ae7d-71a2ae2b93d7/ccny_report_2003_civicmission.pdf

Groskin, J., & Jensen, J. (2021). *Civics project virtual support forum: Students with disabilities* [Google slides]. Massachusetts Department of Elementary and Secondary Education. https://docs.google.com/presentation/d/1bGAL1aMfndmpUM6gjTVjM2rvzNr6UNsHfcFAblI2Hk8/edit#slide=id.ga6dfbeac14_0_677

Hall, T., Meyer, A., & Rose, D. (2012). *Universal design for learning in the classroom: Practical applications*. Guilford Press.

Hamot, G. E., Shokoohi-Yekta, M., & Sasso, G. M. (2005). Civic competencies and students with disabilities. *Journal of Social Studies Research, 29*(2), 34–45.

Ho, S., Eaton, S., & Mitra, M. (2020). *Civic engagement and people with disabilities: A way forward through cross-movement building*. The Lurie Institute for Disability Policy and the Ford Foundation's Civic Engagement and Government Program. https://heller.brandeis.edu/lurie/pdfs/civic-engagement-report.pdf

Individuals With Disabilities Education Improvement Act of 2004, Pub. L. No. 108-44 (codified as amended at 20 U.S.C. § 1400 et seq. (2015)).

Jagers, R. J., Lozada, F. T., Rivas-Drake, D., & Guillaume, C. (2017). Classroom and school predictors of civic engagement among black and latino middle school youth. *Child Development, 88*, 1125–1138.

Jagers, R. J., Rivas-Drake, D., & Williams, B. (2019). Transformative social and emotional learning (SEL): Toward SEL in service of educational equity and excellence. *Educational Psychologist, 54*(3), 162–184.

Jamieson, S. (2011, April 22). *Olmstead champion meets the president*. The White House President Barack Obama. https://obamawhitehouse.archives.gov/blog/2011/06/22/olmstead-champion-meets-president

Kahne, J., & Middaugh, E. (2009). Democracy for some: The civic opportunity gap in high school. In J. Youniss & P. Levine (Eds.), *Engaging young people in civic life* (pp. 29–58). Vanderbilt University Press.

Kahne, J. E., & Sporte, S. E. (2008). Developing citizens: The impact of civic learning opportunities on students' commitment to civic participation. *American Educational Research Journal, 45*(3), 738–766.

Kawashima-Ginsberg, K. (2013). *Do discussion, debate, and simulations boost NAEP civics performance?* The Center for Information and Research on Civic Learning and Engagement. https://circle.tufts.edu/sites/default/files/2020-01/discussion_debate_naep_2013.pdf

Konrad M., Fowler C. H., Walker A. R., Test D. W., & Wood W. M. (2007). Effects of self-determination interventions on the academic skills of students with learning disabilities. *Learning Disability Quarterly, 30,* 89–113.

Kupchik, A., & Catlaw, T. J. (2015). Discipline and participation: the long-term effects of suspension and school security on the political and civic engagement of youth. *Youth & Society, 47*(1), 95–124.

Lee, Y., Wehmeyer, M. L., Palmer, S. B., Williams-Diehm, K., Davies, D. K., & Stock, S. E. (2011). The effect of student-directed transition planning with a computer-based reading support program on the self-determination of students with disabilities. *The Journal of Special Education, 45*(2), 105–117.

Lentine, S. (2017). *Civic engagement for people with disabilities.* Emerging America. http://www.emergingamerica.org/programs/inclusive-civics-education

Levine, P., & Kawashima-Ginsberg, K. (2017). *The republic is (still) at risk_and civics is part of the solution.* Jonathan M. Tisch College of Civic Life, Tufts University. https://civxnow.org/sites/default/files/resources/SummitWhitePaper.pdf

Levinson, M., & Levine, P. (2013). Taking informed action to engage students in civic life. *Social Education, 77*(6), 339–341.

Lindsay, S. (2016). A scoping review of the experiences, benefits, and challenges involved in volunteer work among youth and young adults with a disability. *Disability and Rehabilitation, 38,* 1533–1546.

Mann, J. A., Dymond, S. K., Bonati, M. L., & Neeper, L. S. (2015). Restrictive citizenship: Civic-oriented service-learning opportunities for all students. *Journal of Experiential Education, 38*(1), 56–72.

Martin, M., Minarik, D., & Lintner, T. (2021). Inclusive practices in social studies classrooms: Including all students in all aspects of learning. In A. Samuels & G. L. Samuels (Eds.), *Fostering diversity and inclusion in the social sciences* (pp. 69–84). Information Age Publishing.

Massachusetts Department of Elementary and Secondary Education. (n.d.) *Civics project guidebook.* Retrieved September 29, 2022 from https://www.doe.mass.edu/instruction/hss/civics-project-guidebook/index.html#/

Metzger, A., Alvis, L. M., Oosterhoff, B., Babskie, E., Syvertsen, A., & Wray-Lake, L. (2018). The intersection of emotional and sociocognitive competencies with civic engagement in middle childhood and adolescence. *Journal of Youth and Adolescence, 47,* 1663–1683.

Metzger, A., Syvertsen, A. K., Oosterhoof, B., Babskie, E., & Wray-Lake, L. (2016). How children understand civic actions: A mixed methods perspective. *Journal of Adolescent Research, 31,* 507–535.

Morgan, D. N., & Rasinski, T. V. (2012). The power and potential of primary sources. *The Reading Teacher, 65*(8), 584–594.

Minarik, D., Grooten, R., & Lintner, T. (2021). A justice-oriented approach to addressing disability in social studies. In R. W. Evans (Ed.), *Handbook on teaching social issues* (2nd ed., pp. 337–346). Information Age Publishing.

Minarik, D., & Lintner, T. (2016). *Social studies and exceptional learners*. National Council for the Social Studies.

Mueller, C. O. (2021). I didn't know people with disabilities could grow up to be adults: Disability history, curriculum, and identity in special education. *Teacher Education and Special Education, 44*(3), 189–205.

Mullins, R. D., Williams, T., Hicks, D., & Mullins, S. B. (2020). Can we meet our mission? Examining the professional development of social studies teachers to support SWD and emergent bilingual learners. *Journal of Social Studies Research, 44*(1), 195–208.

National Center for Education Statistics. (2020). *The nation's report card: Student group scores and score gaps*. Institute of Education Sciences, U.S. Department of Education. https://www.nationsreportcard.gov/civics/results/groups/

National Center on Disability and Journalism. (2021, August). *Disability language style guide*. Arizona State University, Walter Cronkite School of Journalism and Mass Communication. https://ncdj.org/style-guide/

National Council for the Social Studies. (2013). *College, career, and civic life (C3) framework for social studies state standards*. https://www.socialstudies.org/system/files/2022/c3-framework-for-social-studies-rev0617.2.pdf

Olmstead v. L. C., 527 U.S. 581 (1999).

Ozer, E. J. (2016). Youth-led participatory action research: Developmental and equity perspectives. In S. S. Horn, M. D. Ruck, & L. S. Liben (Eds.), *Equity and justice in developmental sciences: Theoretical and methodological issues* (pp. 189–207). Oxford University Press.

Ozer, E. J., & Douglas, L. (2013). The impact of participatory research on urban teens: An experimental evaluation. *American Journal of Community Psychology, 51*, 66–75.

Ozer, E. J., Ritterman, M. L., & Wanis, M. G. (2010). Participatory action research (PAR) in middle school: Opportunities, constraints, and key processes. *American Journal of Community Psychology, 46*(1–2), 152–166.

Quintano, A. (2019). *File: Greta Thunberg climate change rally in Denver Colorado 2019 (49203885236).jpg*. Wikimedia Commons. https://commons.wikimedia.org/wiki/File:Greta_Thunberg_Climate_Change_Rally_In_Denver_Colorado_2019_(49203885236).jpg

Salend, S. J. (2015). *Creating inclusive classrooms: Effective, differentiated, and reflective practices* (8th ed.). Pearson Education.

Schur, L., & Kruse, D. (2019). *Fact sheet: Elected officials with disabilities*. Rutgers School of Management and Labor Relations. https://smlr.rutgers.edu/sites/default/files/Documents/Centers/Program_Disability_Research/Fact%20Sheet%20Elected%20Officials%20Disabilities.pdf

Schur, L., & Kruse, D. (2021). *Disability and voting accessibility in the 2020 elections: Final report on survey results*. U.S. Election Assistance Commission. https://www.eac.gov/sites/default/files/voters/Disability_and_voting_accessibility_in_the_2020_elections_final_report_on_survey_results.pdf

Schur, L., Shields, T., & Schriner, K. (2003). Can I make a difference? Efficacy, employment, and disability. *Political Psychology, 24*(1), 119–149.

Shapiro, S., & Brown, C. (2018). *The state of civics education*. Center for American Progress. https://www.americanprogress.org/wp-content/uploads/2019/12/020618_CivicsEducation-UPDATED.pdf

Sherrod, L. R., Torney-Purta, J., & Flanagan, C. (Eds.). (2010). *Handbook of research on civic engagement in youth*. John Wiley & Sons.

Shogren K. A., Wehmeyer M. L., Palmer S. B., Rifenbark G. G., & Little T. D. (2015). Relationships between self-determination and postschool outcomes for youth with disabilities. *Journal of Special Education, 53*, 30–41.

Shogren, K. A., Wehmeyer, M. L., Williams-Diehm, K., & Little, T. (2012). Effect of intervention with the self-determined learning model of instruction on access and goal attainment. *Remedial and Special Education, 33*(5), 320–330.

Sorrells, A. M., Rieth, H. J., & Sindelar, P. T. (2004). *Critical issues in special education access, diversity, and accountability*. Pearson Education.

Sullivan, T. N., Sutherland K. S., Farrell A. D., & Taylor K. A. (2015). An evaluation of second step: What are the benefits for youth with and without disabilities? *Remedial and Special Education, 36*(5), 286–298.

Surr, W., Zeiser, K., Briggs, O., & Kendziora, K. (2018). *Learning with others: A study exploring the relationship between collaboration, personalization, and equity*. American Institutes for Research.

Taylor, A. (2020). The metaphor of civic threat: Intellectual disability and education for citizenship. In L. Ware (Ed.), *Critical readings in interdisciplinary disability studies: (Dis)Assemblages* (pp. 53–67). Springer.

Teacher-Wagner, A., Kawashima-Ginsberg, K., & Hayat, N. (2020). *The state of civic education in Massachusetts*. The Center for Information and Research on Civic Learning and Engagement. https://circle.tufts.edu/sites/default/files/2021-01/MA_DESE_civics_full_report.pdf

TED. (2014, June 9). *I'm not your inspiration, thank you very much: Stella Young* [Video]. YouTube. https://www.youtube.com/watch?v=8K9Gg164Bsw

Test, D. W., Fowler, C. H., Richter, S. M., White, J., Mazzotti, V., Walker, A. R., Kohler, P., & Kortering, L. (2009). Evidence-based practices in secondary transition. *Career Development for Exceptional Individuals, 32*, 115–128.

Thunberg, G. [@gretathunberg]. (2019, August 31). When haters go after your looks and differences, it means they have nowhere left to go. And then you know you're winning! I have Asperger's syndrome and that means I'm sometimes a bit different from the norm. And—given the [Instagram photo]. Retrieved from https://www.instagram.com/p/B12ChnkioB9/?igshid=YmMyMTA2M2Y=

Vakil, S., Welton, E. N., & Ford, B. A. (2010). Citizenship and self-determination for individuals with cognitive disabilities: The interdependence of social studies and special education. *Action in Teacher Education, 32*(2), 4–11.

Veditz, G. W. (1913). *Preservation of the sign language*. [video] Library of Congress. https://www.loc.gov/item/mbrs01815816/

Waring, S. M. (2021). *Integrating primary and secondary sources into teaching: The SOURCES framework for authentic investigation*. Teachers College Press.

Wehmeyer, M. L. (2006). Self-determination and individuals with severe disabilities: Re- examining meanings and misinterpretations. *Research and Practice for Persons With Severe Disabilities, 30*(3), 113–120.

Wehmeyer, M. L., & Field, S. L. (2007). *Self-determination: Instructional and assessment strategies.* Corwin Press.

Wehmeyer, M. L., & Palmer, S. B. (2003). Adult outcomes for students with cognitive disabilities three-years after high school: The impact of self-determination. *Education and Training in Developmental Disabilities, 38*(2), 131–144.

Williams-Diehm, K., Wehmeyer, M. L., Palmer, S. B., Soukup, J. H., & Garner, N. W. (2008). Self-determination and student involvement in transition planning: A multivariate analysis. *Journal on Developmental Disabilities, 14*(1), 27–39.

Wolff, J., & Rogers, J. (2019). *Resources and readiness: Exploring civic education access and equity in six New York high schools.* The Center for Educational Equity. https://cee.tc.columbia.edu/media/centers-amp-labs/cee/publication-pdfs/Resources-and-Readiness-Full-Report-.pdf

CHAPTER 5

EMBRACING UNIVERSAL DESIGN FOR LEARNING

Planning for Inclusive Social Studies Classrooms

Kari A. Muente
Martin Luther College

Designing a social studies environment where a diverse group of learners share their learning experiences is essential for promoting an equitable and inclusive education. As social studies teachers, we play a central role in designing and implementing instructional practices that adequately meet the needs of all learners, both with and without disabilities. This task has proven more complicated in recent years.

As social studies classrooms become more academically, culturally, and linguistically diverse, educators face a rapidly increasing challenge of teaching content and integrating a body of instructional knowledge all while relating to diverse groups of learners. The research reinforces how classroom teachers feel ill-prepared to instructionally meet the needs of diverse learners, especially students with disabilities ([SWD]; Florian & Linklater, 2010; Forlin,

Creating an Inclusive Social Studies Classroom for Exceptional Learners, pages 97–119
Copyright © 2024 by Information Age Publishing
www.infoagepub.com
All rights of reproduction in any form reserved.

2010; Ko & Boswell, 2013; Kratz, 2014), as well as understand the challenges that face them in accessing complex social studies content (Garrick-Duhaney, 2014; Scruggs et al., 2010). These challenges amplify our struggles as teachers wrestle with understanding and defining what inclusive education looks like and how it applies to a diverse learning environment.

Defining inclusion in social studies education reflects an understanding of diversity and inclusion through a multi-dimensional and intersectional lens that focuses on "being more inclusive." In this model, educators adapt a curricular and instructional approach that celebrates and appreciates differences. However, for many social studies scholars, making room to celebrate differences "fails to explain why particular identities, cultures, languages, and traditions are centered and considered normal while others get pushed to the margins or attacked" (Rodriguez & Swalwell, 2021, p. 28). Notions of diversity and inclusion become distinguished by the questions that we ask. The National Council for the Social Studies (NCSS) C3 Framework encourages these perceptions through the inquiry design model ([IDM]; Grant et al., 2017) for instructing social studies teachers on how to engage our students in the critical elements of the Inquiry Arc—questions, tasks, and sources. Inclusion education becomes a multi-perspective, civic-driven inquiry-based learning approach that advocates for changing student outcomes to celebrate and appreciate what makes us uniquely different.

When defining inclusive education through the lens of educating the exceptional learner, the Individuals With Disabilities Education Act's (IDEA, 2004) least restricted environment (LRE) principle requires SWDs to be educated, to the maximum extent appropriate, in general education settings. In this sense, inclusion restructures education to create a learning environment that is accessible, considers the use of specially designed instruction (SDI), is equitable, and recognizes cultural considerations (diversity, equity, inclusion [DEI]) for students with or without disabilities. This is a complex task with high demands on instructing all students toward meaningful learning outcomes (Ladson-Billings, 2011). Our learning environment must acknowledge our students' learning variability, including their readiness to learn, interest and cultural background, and learning preferences not just across one environment but across all environments (Ladson-Billings, 2021; Nelson, 2021). We must be mindful of how our learners' previous experiences shape meaning and connect to their daily lives (Kieran & Anderson, 2019; Tomlinson, 2014). Recognizing students' unique learning preferences and backgrounds generates a learning community with a sense of belonging, creating a growth mindset that living and learning together benefits everyone, not just students receiving special education services.

Inclusion is also a belief system, or mindset, that needs to replace the traditional instructional belief of a "one-size-fits-all" approach with an accessible model that meets the needs and promotes an equitable education for students with or without disabilities (Azam et al., 2021; Griful-Freixenet et al., 2021). This begins with an awareness of how biases and stereotyping of students can impact the learning environment (DeCuir-Gunby et al., 2010; Fritzgerald, 2020). As teachers plan lessons, this mind shift requires a curriculum decision-making process that focuses on going beyond "being more inclusive" to examining how content choices may impact student engagement and learning. Also, educators need to see special education not as a physical space where an individual enters and exits through a multitiered system, but rather a learning environment where all learners' needs, both with and without disabilities, are met through flexibility and equitable access. Overall, educators need to embrace the belief system that focuses on creating a universally designed equitable learning environment that recognizes that the average learner does not exist and "one-size-fits-all" is a poor instructional design model. Inclusive education requires maintaining a learning environment designed around firm goals through flexible means so all students can become expert learners.

Designing social studies curriculum and instruction that meets the needs of every student is difficult. First, we must let go of the one-size-fits-all approach and embrace learner variability to build expert learners. It also requires us to self-reflect on how our instructional decisions create barriers for our students (Chardin & Novak, 2020; Meyer et al., 2014), creating levels of vulnerability and inefficacy. Embracing an inclusive decision-making process that reinforces and values the power of learning for students with and without disabilities is not something that happens overnight. Advocating for better equitable learner outcomes takes a team. Social studies teachers, special educators, and school administrators must work together to provide the necessary support, collaboration, and resource for meeting learner variability. One essential support and resource is the Universal Design for Learning (UDL) framework. This framework offers principles and guidance in designing instruction that creates an inclusive social studies classroom environment that addresses learner variability and equitable access.

UNIVERSAL DESIGN FOR LEARNING: THEORETICAL FRAMEWORK

Inspired by the architectural concepts of universal design (UD), the UDL framework is a collection of research findings culled from educational psychology and neuroscience on how and why people learn differently through an interrelationship of recognition, strategic, and affective networks in the brain (Meyer et al., 2014). UDL builds on the premise that *all* students learn differently and, at the same time, integrates the UD architecture challenge to plan and create a product, or a curriculum and instructional design, with everyone in mind rather than adapting to individual needs after the fact (Connell et al., 1997). Through their early assistive technology work, the Center of Applied Special Technology (CAST) applied the UD principles to their research and development of the UDL framework, creating a research-based instructional practice through principles, guidelines, and checkpoints. As noted in Figure 5.1, CAST's UDL Guidelines support classroom instruction that develops expert learners who are purposeful, motivated, resourceful, and strategic (CAST, 2018). Applying UDL guidelines and checkpoints teaches students how to learn, set goals, and share what they know in meaningful ways. An inclusive social studies classroom begins with empowering students to become more self-determined, and the UDL principles and guidelines have educators recognize learner variability and transfer power to the students, giving students a voice in deciding what to learn and to demonstrate new knowledge.

UDL's three foundational principles provide a blueprint for creating instructional goals, materials, and assessments. Integrating these principles prompts us to recognize learner variability and anticipate any predictable

Figure 5.1 UDL Guidelines version 2.2 Note: UDL Guidelines version 3.0 are expected to be released in 2024 with a focus on updating the guidelines through an equity lens. Source: CAST (2018). Universal design for learning guidelines version 2.2 [graphic organizer]. https://udlguidelines.cast.org

barriers while designing an environment with options to personalize learning (CAST, 2018; Hall et al., 2012). The three UDL principles are:

- Multiple means of engagement ("why" of learning—affective network),
- Multiple means of representation ("what" of learning—recognition network), and
- Multiple means of action and expression ("how" of learning—strategic network).

The UDL framework serves as a foundational lens, or growth mindset, for understanding how our instructional design and learning environment may hinder a learner's development or impede their ability to gain skills beyond the lesson. The UDL principles embrace curriculum development that works for all students—with or without disabilities. It is not a single, one-size-fits-all solution, but a proactive, intentional, flexible approach that supports inclusion.

In practice, applying the UDL framework to our curricular and instructional decision-making process leads us to become proactive, purposeful planners, similar to engineers. Basham and Marino (2013) reinforce how engineering design is an essential concept in implementing UDL. The UDL framework adopts an engineering mindset that includes systems thinking, creativity, optimism, and attention to ethical considerations (Bashman & Marino, 2013; Fritzgerald, 2020). The UDL mindset drives intentional curriculum and instructional decisions around establishing firm goals through flexible means that support learner variability.

UDL encourages educators to proactively engineer inclusive education accessible around learner variability by recognizing and reducing predictable learning barriers before a student enters the learning environment. Therefore, we focus on the classroom environment rather than any particular student (Rose & Meyer, 2002). Our designing mind shifts away from instructionally planning for and instructing a singular to intentionally planning for and teaching all learners.

To be sure, differentiated instruction (DI) is essential in our social studies classrooms. Responding to a learner's individual needs through SDI, accommodations, and at times modifications, is critical for serving our students, with and without disabilities. Rooted in the belief that variability exists, DI, similar to UDL, leads teachers to expect student diversity and adjust whole class instruction accordingly through the examination of content, process, and product (Tomlinson, 2014). However, DI varies from UDL's responses to those who need support. DI draws on responding, or adapting, to SWDs or learner variability, by adding supports or accommodations to the existing classroom as a student enters and exits the learning environment. In contrast, UDL intentionally designs a learning environment that eliminates and overcomes the learning barriers before the student enters.

Representation Options for presenting content	Emgagement Options for emgaging student interest	Expression Options for demonstrating student learning	Diversity, Equity, and Inclusion Considerations
• Artifacts • Pictures • Graphic organizers • Video Clips • Audio Recordings • Lab • Lecture • Other _____	• Cooperative Group Work • Partner Work • Manipulatives • Movement • Debates • Role plays or simulations • Other _____	• Written response • Illustrated response • Oral response • Model creation or construction • Project-based • Other _____	• Nature of content includes learners' perspectives, values, and needs (culturally responsive) • Lesson supports components of SEL: Empathy, Resilience, and Relationship building • SDI _____ • Accommodations and/or modifications • Other _____
CONTENT	PROCESS	PRODUCT	

Figure 5.2 Lesson plan UDL chart. *Source:* Adapted from Minarik & Lintner (2016).

The UDL framework provides the means for us to create a learning environment whereby the needs of SWDs have already met.

Differentiation and UDL are not in competition with each other. One need not be chosen over the other—they need to work in tandem. As Figure 5.2 shows, a lesson plan can include both elements of UDL and differentiation. DI provides the necessary scaffolding for a student with or without disabilities to reach an identified learning goal.

That goal often does not look the same for every student. Evidence collected from formative assessments may lead to small-group interventions or more targeted instruction. Expectation levels are adapted so the individual learner can be successful. The limitation of DI is that not all students have access to the same opportunities to learn, nor do they have the opportunity to reflect on their learning (Novak, 2022). On the other hand, UDL's intentional design of firm goals through flexible means provides a student with choice and reflective feedback. As evidence is collected and shared, the UDL framework provides the means to target specific learners through DI, thus, creating more pathways for students to reach their learning goals in meaningful ways.

The same holds when applying a student's SDI. The tandem work of DI and UDL is a vital consideration when planning for instruction. SDI is defined as "adapting, as appropriate to the needs" of a student's individual goals, providing modifications or accommodations to content, and providing access to the general education curriculum (IDEA, 2004). The UDL framework emphasis is eliminating and overcoming learning barriers. A student's individualized education program (IEP) already outlines various student strengths and challenges, complete with clear goals and a path for overcoming such challenges. As a UDL engineer, SDI, through an IEP, provides another means for recognizing barriers and planning options for all learners. As such, a student's SDI barrier becomes a predictable barrier for all. As students share their learning through flexible assessment, the teacher can use the evidence to target groups of learners through DI. The learning environment has now become more accessible, allowing every student to participate and engage with the content in their own unique way while acquiring the skills to become an expert learner.

As previously mentioned, we must recognize that "one-size-fits-all" is an inadequate instructional design decision. A social studies curriculum that defines meaningful goals while generating access to content that celebrates and appreciates diversity, must also recognize, and address the barriers that go beyond a learner's ability or language. This includes race, class, gender, religion, and ethnic backgrounds (Chardin & Novak, 2020; Fritzgerald, 2020). Through UDL, every student is provided with opportunities that challenge and support their academic journey (Fritzgerald, 2021). As a result, students feel safe and welcome and achieve academic success. A UDL classroom provides more students with opportunities to recognize problems, create strategies to solve those problems, and, ultimately to contribute to making a better world. Our classrooms must reflect powerful and purposeful instruction where content is relevant to a learner's life. UDL empowers our students, with and without disabilities, to personalize their pathways, building classroom equity and celebrating unique identities.

Adapting UDL begins with self-reflection and self-assessment. We must first examine our educational practices, instructional tools, and selected resources to check for biases, not only in the content and its delivery, but also how our students engage within the learning environment. UDL leads us to design a learning environment where students learn how to learn, set goals, and share what they know in authentic and meaningful ways (Meyer et al., 2014). It is a process that calls us to relinquish power to our students, so they have—and create—purposeful, relevant options and choices. Building a teacher-student relationship, where all students are respected and honored, can be difficult. Fortunately, we have a framework that provides the means to shape the social studies classroom to be more inclusive. Applying the UDL framework opens the learning environment to recognize and celebrate diversity while embracing equity for all learners.

SOCIAL STUDIES EDUCATION: IDM AND UDL

A social studies classroom generates lessons, activities, and resources around the inquiry process. Inquiry is the fundamental element of learning. The act of inquiry goes beyond developing fact-based knowledge by undertaking a journey to enhance meaningful learning. In our social studies classrooms, inquiry is its heart, propelling students towards the understanding ideas, people, actions, or events. In 2013, NCSS published the C3 Framework and the Inquiry Arc, a curricular tool used to enhance inquiry-based learning in the social studies classroom. The Inquiry Arc identifies four steps or dimensions to inquiry: (a) developing questions and planning inquiries for students to answer throughout a unit of study; (b) applying discipline focus concepts and tools to assist students in answering their questions; (c) learning how to evaluate sources and use evidence to support students in answering their questions; (d) communicating evidence-based claims towards taking informed action (Swan et al., 2018). The IDM gave us a distinctive blueprint to create instructional material representing the Inquiry Arc's key elements—questions, tasks, and sources. The C3 Framework and IDM became the cornerstone for preparing social studies students for the 21st century.

As curriculum gatekeepers, we learn to balance curricular decision-making between social studies content and our support of inclusion (Grossman et al., 2009; Thornton, 2005). For several of us, engaging a diverse group of learners, especially SWDs, with inquiry-based practices challenges the traditional teacher-to-student relationship. Inquiry-based instruction empowers our students to actively engage in their learning and development. It requires teachers to relinquish some level of content-skill acquisition and shift to a more student-center active learning approach. Although IDM promotes the effective use of scaffolding to build a student-center learning environment, it makes little mention of how best to proactively engage SWDs in the inquiry-design process. In the same manner, NCSS (2013) published a bulletin outlining the purpose, practices, and implications of the C3 Framework, specifically expressing how the framework is largely silent on the different abilities children bring into the classroom.

As subject matter experts, we tend to focus on making the content more inclusive rather than recognizing learner variability. Signaling a reflective pause requires reevaluating how educational decisions influence how students, both with and without disabilities, personalize their learning, share their voices, and actively become expert learners. The UDL framework provides the tools and resources to reflect on learner variability and engineer curriculum and instruction around building a more vital teacher-student educational trust through inquiry-based instruction. It also requires an educational paradigm shift in how educators think about what we teach, who we teach, and why we teach. Building trusting student-teacher relations begins with acknowledging that the average learner no longer exists, that learner vulnerability is the rule, not the exception, and that all students can learn when barriers are eliminated (Meyer et al., 2014). Applying UDL to the IDM empowers students in active inquiry learning, opening pathways for honoring our students while creating a learning environment that empowers our students' voices and choices.

IDM QUESTIONS: UDL MULTIPLE MEANS OF ENGAGEMENT (*WHY* OF LEARNING)

The IDM frames grade-level curriculum topics around inquiry, which begins with a compelling question. A compelling question addresses critical issues and subjects found within the academic disciple while reflecting on the ideas and experiences that students bring into the classroom (Grant et al., 2017). A challenge for many of us is not with the content knowledge per se, but in student engagement and acquisition. Applying the UDL framework to the IDM begins with recognizing that all students, both with and without disabilities, can engage in the content and inquiry process.

As acknowledged earlier, a diverse group of students enter the learning environment with various levels of prior knowledge, interest, and goals. Consequently, IDM aims to create a compelling question that all students find interesting while respecting and honoring individual efforts to engage in complex content. This moves the social studies classroom from a fact-based instruction and acquisition structure to a structure grounded in honest and genuine questions associated with a content angle that is interesting and relevant to the students (Swan et al., 2018; Wineburg, 2018). Identifying a content angle requires strong content knowledge and draws upon a teacher's pedagogical expertise to craft student inquiry. A good content angle provides the means for students to connect critically and emotionally to their own lives. However, no two individuals are alike. How one person responds to a situation or setting varies, with often different responses to the same situation or setting. How a person responds to a situation affects their ability to learn, remember and reply (Meyer et al., 2014). As the content angle begins to take shape to form compelling questions, so do the predictable barriers facing students.

When applying UDL to the IDM, a social studies lesson and learning environment are designed around flexible options to awaken the appropriate brain networks of the learner. The UDL principle of engagement awakens the affective network of the brain and addresses the "why" of learning. Knowing the why sparks excitement and curiosity as learning strengthens activities that are personalized and contextualized to a student's life (Meyer et al., 2014; Nelson, 2021). Constructing a compelling question through the UDL mindset of utilizing relevance through authentic, meaningful activities opens pathways for students to overcome the predictable barriers, allowing all students to engage in and with the content in meaningful ways.

Connecting UDL with IDM also prompts educators to keep learner variability at the forefront of their curriculum decisions. As we engineer our content angle to formulate compelling questions, we maintain content rigor through firm goals while involving all learners in the inquiry process. Involving students at these levels includes setting goals to break down the why of learning, empowering students to take charge of their learning, and fostering a safe environment in which student can take risks. The UDL principle of engagement helps address how students emotionally connects to the topic, the setting, the mode of delivery, the teacher delivering the information, and how other students can support learning and content acquisition (Daley et al., 2014; Rose & Meyer, 2002). Engaging our students in inquiry instruction enables us to evaluate patterns and connect an emotional significance between the content and the student.

Structured around three guidelines, the principle of engagement engineers curriculum and instruction around providing options for (a) recruiting interest by knowing who our learners are and identifying their interests; (b) sustaining student effort and persistence by providing opportunities to work with peers in small groups, maintaining focus on the task at hand, while receiving direct and supported feedback from teachers; and (c) practicing self-regulation where students learn skills to gauge behavior and take charge of their learning (Meyer et al., 2014). As designing content angles and compelling questions generate predictable barriers, the UDL principle of engagement opens pathways to overcome or eliminate such barriers by optimizing individual choice and autonomy.

Giving students choice is not about lowering expectations or providing the means to follow the path of least resistance. Choice must be structured to lead students to understand how they learn and what motivates them to do so. Remember, UDL is about developing expert learners. In the principle of engagement, expert learners are purposeful and motivated. For a student to successfully engage in a compelling question, they must interact with the content by finding common ground between the big content ideas and what they know and value (Swan et al., 2018). This interaction requires us to recognize the scope of the social studies curriculum yet manage it in ways that honor the students we teach (Fritzgerald, 2020; Swan et al., 2018).

An essential function of a compelling question is using disciplinary content and skills to comprehend and articulate understandings. However, with the breadth and depth of the social studies curriculum, this is a daunting task for many students. Successful student engagement varies fand is both definitional and contextual. For many students, often simple tasks (skill acquisitions) can become significant barriers in sparking student interest when approaching compelling questions. Students enter our classrooms with varying levels of both academic readiness and inherent motivation to learn. This is especially true when the demands of the social studies content reveal clear academic gaps.

In many classrooms, academic gaps are addressed through differentiating instruction, SDI, or by scaffolding disciplinary skills to connect old knowledge to new knowledge. As we apply a UDL lens to our compelling questions, Table 5.1 provides reflective considerations for intentionally designing inquiry-based instruction and disciplinary content skills to overcome barriers *before* a student with disabilities enters the classroom. Reflecting on these considerations allows students to access information via appropriate, flexible, and scaffolded resources. Digital resources and assistive technology have provided a plethora of scaffolding options, allowing students with and without disabilities increased freedom to choose a resource that is challenging yet appropriately scaffolded for success.

An inquiry-based compelling question needs to excite students and engage their curiosity. IDM outlines several staging activities to access prior knowledge and experiences to build early student interest and engagement (Swan et al., 2018). Applying the the principle of engagement asks educators to first define learning goals, consider learner variability in the instructional planning process, which, in turn, helps to mitigate—if not eliminate—barriers to content acquisition prior to students entering our classroom. Students with and without disabilities will often not find the same activities or information equally relevant or valuable. In supporting SWDs in our social studies classrooms, crafting relevant, valuable, and meaning compelling questions is imperative.

IDM TASK: UDL MULTIPLE MEANS OF ACTION AND EXPRESS (*HOW* OF LEARNING)

In the first stage of UDL, instruction is crafted through a content angle that presents a rigorous and relevant compelling question. Here, students wrestle with ideas and synthesize information. The second concept in the IDM, the Task, focuses on argumentation. IDM emphasizes the relationship between the compelling question and constructing an evidence-based summative argument task (Swan et al., 2018). Assessment or performance tasks provide a simple means for checking student understanding through various formative and summative formats. Despite seeming rather simplistic, assessing student historical thinking and argumentative skills are complicated by the demand for teacher accountability, the ubiquity of high-stakes testing, and the implementation of IEP accommodations.

Assessment tasks are designed to get students thinking about what they are learning, what they thought about the learning process, and to monitor and record (and demonstrate) what they are learning. How students

TABLE 5.1 IDM Content Angle and Compelling Questions Predictable Barriers and UDL Engagement Reflection Questions and Considerations

Providing multiple means of Engagement Affective Network The "WHY" of Learning	IDM Compelling Questions Predictable Barriers	UDL Reflection questions and considerations
Provide options for *Recruiting Interest* • Optimize individual choice and autonomy • Optimize relevance, value, and authenticity • Minimize threats and distractions.	Lack of background knowledge Varying interests, passions, and curiosity Lack of understanding of subject-matter content, vocabulary, or concepts. Lack of understanding of the purpose or goals for why students need to engage in the content and the compelling questions. Lack of personal goals for why the need to ask or answer questions.	What content angle questions are we asking students to lead them to share their interests, ideas, and knowledge? How do we design our classroom environment to ensure students, both with and without disabilities, feel safe enough to take risks and share what they know and their interests? How do we design our content angles and compelling questions to be culturally responsive while building on prior knowledge and bridging the gaps around content understanding, terms, and concepts?
Provide options for *Sustaining Effort & Persistence* • Heighten salience of goals and objectives • Vary demands and resources to optimize challenges • Foster collaboration and community • Increase master-oriented feedback	Fear of working with other students, speaking in class, or sharing one's thoughts due to English being a second language, attention or memory issues, or speech impairments. Lacks the ability to self-regulate or be self-motivated Respond with high anxiety levels when engaging in stressful, frustrating, or challenging situations.	How do we design our compelling questions so all students know the purpose and why it is essential? How do our supporting questions provide options so students can choose pathways that appropriately challenge and support them? What strategies do we put into place, so students with and without disabilities have meaningful collaboration with each other? How do we offer ongoing feedback or additional supporting questions through the inquiry process to provide opportunities for students to self-reflect, engage in peer review and provide instructional feedback?
Provide options for *Self-Regulation* • Promote expectations and beliefs that optimize motivation • Facilitate personal coping skills and strategies • Develop self-assessment and reflection	Recognizing components of SEL and culturally responsive teaching; Empathy, Resilience, and Relationship building Acknowledge the student's SDI, Accommodations and/or modifications.	How do our content angle and compelling questions build excitement and motivate students to engage in the content? How do we create an environment and scaffold content angles and compelling questions to prevent students from getting upset, frustrated, or quitting when challenged?

choose to strategize and what tools they use to demonstrate their thinking/learning affect how they communicate to others what they know and understand (Rose & Meyer, 2002). In a traditional classroom, students typically demonstrate understanding in limited ways. All students benefit from demonstrating their understanding in multi-modal ways (Rose et al., 2018). By providing students with options for learning and demonstrating what they have learned, we value and support the unique gifts, backgrounds, and experiences they bring into our social studies classrooms (Chardin & Novak, 2020; Fritzgerald, 2020). The UDL principle of action and expression addresses the "how" of learning.

Measuring what diverse learners know presents an array of predictable barriers in balancing *assessments for learning* (progress; Wiggins, 1998) with *assessments as learning* (growth; Earl, 2012). Assessments for learning and assessments as learning recognize the power of ongoing diagnostics to drive student autonomy, reflection, and learning in authentic ways (Novak & Tucker, 2021; Rose et al., 2018). Assessment for learning help determines where students presently are in their learning, where they need to go next, and the actionable steps to get them there. This type of formative assessment then provides the information to modify or differentiate instruction to target misconceptions or underdeveloped skills. In comparison, assessment as learning encourages students to actively assess themselves, rather than be passive recipients of predefined learning outcomes. This ongoing process allows students to focus on developing and supporting metacognition. Students learn to reflect on what is going well—and why—and what they need to improve on—and how. Such formative assessments lead students to self-assess, self-reflect, and self-report, allowing them to purposefully direct and own their learning.

In many social studies classrooms, these two types of formative assessments—for learning (progress) and as learning (growth)—provide important data points to inform instructional decisions in meeting the needs of all students. They facilitate the redirection of understandings, mitigate misconceptions, and ensure proper scaffolding (Swan et al., 2018). The IDM provides a blueprint for designing compelling questions that are rigorous and relevant, connecting content acquisition, and crafting a particular outcome—an evidence-based argument.

The relationship between the compelling question, the formative performance task, and the summative argument task is the central focus of IDM (Swan et al., 2018). For SWDs, connecting content, skills, inquiry, and performance generates several predictable barriers hindering their ability to successfully complete requisite tasks. Engaging in a formative performance task or summative argument task tends to reflect a more traditional assessment approach. Since students differ in how they engage and express what they know, traditional pen-to-paper assessments generate numerous formative roadblocks for diverse learners. Many SWDs struggle with poor recall or memory, possess low-level reading and writing ability, and lack of strong test-taking skills. If instructional decisions focus on assessing the average student, those who struggle now have limited opportunities to demonstrate what they know. Applying the principle of action and expression to developing a summative argumentative task allows students to piece together the information and demonstrate their understanding of that information in ways that are relevant and meaningful (Meyer et al., 2014; Rose et al., 2018).

The principle of action and expression provide various options for students to access materials, tools, and technologies to articulate what they know while enhancing their abilities to set goals, plan, and manage information (CAST, 2018). Table 5.2 outlines how to apply the action and expression guidelines that reduce learning barriers and support differentiated learning constructs. For example, instead of students writing a response, allow them to create a video, record an audio response, or making a visual (or oral) presentation. No assessment tool is equally suited for all learners. Yet providing assessment alternatives for students with and without disabilities allows them to more accurately—and personally—demonstrate what they know.

Providing more options around assessment for learning and assessment as learning allows us to consider the unique strengths and challenges facing our SWDs while also using evidence-based, universally designed, and culturally responsive practices supported through assistive and instructional technologies (Meyer et al., 2014; Spencer, 2015). Connecting UDL to IDM performance tasks allows students to actively identify their struggles, articulate how they learn best, and advocate for demonstrating their social studies learning in ways that are relevant and meaningful to them.

IDM SOURCES: UDL MULTIPLE MEANS OF REPRESENTATION (*WHAT* OF LEARNING)

In the IDM, sources and questions work together to deepen student knowledge while honing argumentation skills. Sources supply the background knowledge and spark inquiry-based thinking essential in constructing—and making—evidence-based arguments (Swan et al., 2018). Engaging students in source evaluation challenges them to think beyond what they already know. This takes intention, structure, and time. In the case of social studies instruction, active learning, or "doing history," focuses on historical interaction and deliberation with historical events, people, or topics (Levstik & Barton, 2015; Wineburg, 2010). In the IDM task, measuring a student's active learning is evident through the summative argumentative task. Here, students access and evaluate a collection of primary and secondary sources and synthesize claims as they relate to the initial compelling question.

Embracing Universal Design for Learning • 111

TABLE 5.2 IDM Performance Task Predictable Barriers and UDL Action & Expression Reflection Questions and Considerations

Providing multiple means of Action & Expression Strategic Networks The "HOW" of Learning	IDM—Performance Task Argumentative Writing Predictable Barriers	UDL Reflection questions and considerations
Provide options for *Physical Action* • Vary the methods for response and navigation • Optimize access to tools and assistive technology	Lack of proper keyboard or handwriting skills. Lack of proper inquiry and research skills. Struggle with completing tasks in a timely manner.	What type of assistive technology or other technology tools are available to students to assist them in formulating their performance tasks, and how do we instruct and encourage them to use them? How much time do we allow students to complete performance tasks, and how do we assist them in navigating the time given for completing tasks?
Provide options for *Expression & Communication* • Use multiple media for communication • Use multiple tools for construction and composition • Build fluencies with graduated levels of support for practice and performance	Struggle with categorizing and organizing information. Struggle with basic literacy skills and has below grade level reading ability. Struggle to recall language and content knowledge necessary for responding. Struggle with spelling and other language conventions due to English being a second language, attention or memory issues, or speech impairments.	How often do we provide flexible performance tasks so students with and without disabilities have options to share what they know? What tools and scaffolds do we provide to students with and without disabilities to successfully complete performance tasks and can share their appropriate level of learning more independently?
Provide options for *Executive Function* • Guide appropriate goal-setting • Support planning and strategy development • Facilitate managing information and resources • Enhance capacity for monitoring progress	Recognizing components of SEL and culturally responsive teaching; Empathy, Resilience, and Relationship building Acknowledge the student's SDI, Accommodations and/or modifications.	How do we encourage students to set goals and monitor their learning process through self-assessments? What process do we have in place to assist students in reflecting on their performance tasks, receiving feedback, and having opportunities to revise work?

Sources impact all aspects of IDM. Finding substantive, reliable sources that spark curiosity, build content knowledge, and develop and hone argumentative skills comes with challenges. When initially locating sources, IDM asks teachers to consider these specific source characteristics: type, complexity, and perspective (Swan et al., 2018). IDM encourages introducing a variety of source types, positioned from multiple perspectives to both deepen student content knowledge and improve requisite analytic skills. The intentional selection of source variety provides students with a rich array of information to evaluate evidence and ultimately draw claims. Despite the well-intentioned use of source variety, barriers nonetheless exist when a student struggles with source acquisition, evaluation, and synthesis.

The UDL principle of representation allows students to identify and interpret what comes to them through their senses. Our senses help us to find concrete, abstract, simple, and complex meaning (Meyer et al., 2014; Nelson, 2021). Through multiple means of representation, we consider how students' previous experiences influence the skills they need to acquire and ultimately organize sources used to support (or refute) an argument or claim.

When making the UDL paradigm shift, the principle of representation is a good starting point. For many teachers, finding resources, tools, and strategies to access information, ideas, concepts, and themes, while generating support for decoding and comprehending information is at the heart of teaching. In social studies education, we have—and should use—multiple resources for presenting material and instructional practices for integrating history and literacy (Monte-Sano et al., 2014; Wineburg et al., 2012). These curriculum guides model instructional strategies and outline evidence-based practices to support historical thinking, reading, and argumentative writing, thus supporting the "what" of learning (Nelson, 2021). The guidelines of representation strengthen a teacher's decision-making process for addressing learner variability and, concomitantly, eliminating barriers. Knowing there is no singular means of representing social studies content, the principle of representation does provide more robust options for displaying and customizing visual and auditory information, supporting students in understanding text, numbers, symbols, and language, and deepening comprehension skills (CAST, 2018). When recognizing barriers through reflection questions, as outlined in Table 5.3, the "what" of learning opens the door to how students perceive information and our role in supporting knowledge and skill acquisition.

In connecting the principle of representation to IDM sources, we must recognize how a student's academic levels, cultural background, and second language acquisition influence how they approach and unpack sources in making an argumentative claim. Engineering our lessons around the principle of representation demonstrates to our students that we honor their academic levels, background knowledge and experience, and community

Embracing Universal Design for Learning • 113

TABLE 5.3 IDM Performance Sources Predictable Barriers and UDL Representation Reflection Questions and Considerations

Providing multiple means of Representation Recognition Network The "WHAT" of Learning	IDM—Sources Predictable Barriers	UDL Reflection questions and considerations
Provide options for *Perception* • Offer ways of customizing the display of information • Offer alternative for auditory information • Offer alternatives for visual information	Lacks background knowledge and experience. Struggles with basic literacy skills, like decoding text and reads below grade level. Struggle to recall basic vocabulary or comprehend content-level concepts.	When providing direct instruction, how do you utilize multimedia tools, both audio and visual components, to ensure that all students build understanding and can learn at high levels? How do we provide culturally responsive content and multi-perspective evidence that will inform students' perspectives, values, and needs? How do we reflect on our perspectives, biases, and interpretations of content, classroom material, and classroom environment to ensure our pedagogy and methodology are not barriers to student learning?
Provide options for *Language & Symbols* • Clarify vocabulary and symbols • Clarify syntax and structure • Support decoding of text, mathematical notions, and symbols • Promote understanding across languages • Illustrate through multiple media	Struggle with visual and written language conventions due to English being a second language, attention or memory issues, or a hearing or visual impairment. Recognizing components of SEI and culturally responsive teaching; Empathy, Resilience, and Relationship building	When assigning text, how do you supplement or provide alternatives to standard text by providing audio, visuals, and translations for students to build comprehension? What tools and scaffolds do we provide students with and without disabilities to successfully learn and engage in the sources and build vocabulary and comprehension at their appropriate level of learning? If English is a Second Language for students, what techniques do you use to honor a student's first language and support their English language development?
Provide options for *Comprehension* • Activate or supply background knowledge • Highlight patterns, critical features, big ideas, and relationships • Guide information processing and visualization • Maximize transfer and generalization	Acknowledge the student's SDI, Accommodations and/or modifications.	As students learn the content, what scaffolds are put into place to guide students' engagement with key content concepts, themes, and terms? How do you guide students to see how they can use the new information in other classes, units, or settings? How do you activate student background knowledge during each lesson?

and cultural references (Fritzgerald, 2020; Ladson-Billings, 2021). Teachers must always consider how individual differences affect learning and align instructional decisions to address those differences effectively.

At the same time, we must recognize what influences our purpose for teaching social studies and reflect on the instructional decisions we make. Doing so validates and supports learner variability and reduces potential barriers to learning. When selecting and presenting multiple sources to support and enhance inquiry building, it is essential to create firm, measurable learning goals while providing flexible options centered on student learning preferences. Swan et al. (2018) acknowledge the value of providing students a variety of complex sources, including more accessible sources for students with learning difficulties. Overall, the type of sources used in the social studies classroom provides an opportunity to modify learning to meet the needs of diverse learners. Applying UDL to source selection shifts the emphasis from the number of sources used to the way(s) in which students demonstrate their understanding of the source.

SHIFTING TO UDL

As our social studies classroom becomes more diverse, teachers are challenged with teaching the content and integrating a body of instructional knowledge on how the content relates to students from various academic, cultural, and linguistic levels. Designing a social studies environment where diverse learners thrive is essential in promoting equitable and inclusive education. The shift to implementing UDL into the IDM design process must begin slowly and intentionally, with meaningful, continual self-reflection.

In engineering inquiry-driven curriculum, teachers play a central role in designing and implementing instructional practices that adequately meet the needs of all learners. Once inquiry-based practices and the core values of UDL are aligned, strategies continue to evolve and are flexible and iterative based on students' voices and needs (Novak & Woodlock, 2021). The UDL framework replaces the one-size-fits-all mindset that recognizes learner variability as a rule, not the exception. UDL provides the means to create an inquiry-based social studies classroom that allows students with and without disabilities to become expert learners.

However, understanding and adapting the UDL framework can be overwhelming. Implementation is a process. First, we must understand the big picture of why we teach, to whom we teach, and how that translates to student success. Next, we design learning with all learners in mind, both with and without disabilities. Learner variability must be embraced. Accomplishing this requires that we both know and articulate lesson goals and objectives and differentiate instruction appropriately (Meyer et al., 2014; Nelson,

2021; Novak, 2022). For many social studies teachers, these guidelines are already being implemented. Yet, we need to be mindful that using one or two guidelines within lesson planning does not make full UDL implementation. UDL is not a checklist but a belief system that learner variability exists while proactively and intentionally planning curriculum and instruction to eliminate barriers.

Shifting to UDL needs to begin slowly, following a design cycle that allows for small implementations focused on student engagement, reflection, and repetition. The first step in applying the UDL principles to an inquiry-designed curriculum and instruction is revisiting and revising current standard-aligned goals. To meet the needs of all learners, goals need to be inherently flexible (CAST, 2018). Keeping learner variability in mind, creating flexible goal statements acknowledges learner differences and serves to reduce potential barriers students may face.

To understand the barriers facing students with or without disabilities, educators must question each step of the planning process through each UDL principle. The UDL principles remind us to ask the following questions (CAST, 2018; Novak, 2022):

- How are we designing our class to ensure that every student sees themselves in the curriculum, in the classroom, and within the learning expectations?
- How do our inquiry-based lessons provide a variety of challenges so students can choose pathways that appropriately engage and support them?
- How do we help our students stay motivated and provide appropriate resources to prevent frustrations?
- How do we supplement our sources by providing audio, visual, and translation materials for students to facilitate comprehension?
- How do we teach complex vocabulary to ensure students build and comprehend grade-level terms and concepts to successfully construct an argumentative task?
- How do we activate students' unique background knowledge, build interest, and find personal relevance to successfully engage in the content angle to answer the compelling question?
- What scaffolds do we use to bring students' attention to the most critical content and build confidence in contextualizing sources to produce evidence-based arguments?
- How do we encourage students to set individual learning goals and monitor those goals through self-assessment?
- How often do we provide flexible assessment, so all students have the option/choice to share what they know?

As we reflect on the questions above, we commit to inclusive practices through the UDL belief systems of learner variability, firm goals, and expert learning. We recognize that applying the UDL principles to the IDM blueprint serves to mitigate the common barriers that prevent students from becoming motivated, purposeful, knowledgeable, and goal-directed learners. Through the UDL principles, inquiry-based learning creates more pathways for ensuring an equitable, inclusive classroom.

Another critical aspect of applying UDL to the IDM is providing students with mastery-oriented feedback. Within the UDL principles, feedback takes on both a new definition and new direction. Master-oriented feedback is not providing constructive comments to/on student work. Here, feedback facilitates student recognition and reflection. Mastery-oriented feedback shifts the student mindset from what perceive they cannot do to realizing, in fact, what they can do. Students understand that learning is often a struggle but, through structured feedback, they begin to look for, identify, and utilize strategies and supports to guide appropriate goal-setting skills and monitor their own learning progress (Meyer et al., 2014; Nelson, 2021). When we help our students focus on the process, learning becomes continuous, and they grow closer to becoming expert learners.

CONCLUSION

Inquiry-based instruction requires intelligent, thoughtful, and dedicated teachers. The same is true for educating a diverse group of learners. IDM is a design process for engaging students in the inquiry process, while UDL is a design framework for ensuring all students become expert learners. Both require teachers to be iterative, creative, and personal. Developing IDM social studies lessons is processional and continual and should not be assigned to a single assignment or unit of study. IDM aims to get students engaged and connected to and with the content. Teachers must customize the IDM blueprint around the unique needs of our students and this may, in fact, require the purposeful construction and contextualization of assignments and materials (Swan et al., 2018). Unfortunately, modifying the inquiry process may not be enough to overcome the barriers SWDs face when accessing social studies content.

At the same time, teachers may link UDL to the various content decisions, resources, cultural considerations, and differentiation instructional practices they use. Admittedly, these are great starts and certainly a sign of responsible, reflective teaching. Yet we must remember that UDL is not a simple list of actions that, if adopted, lead to a more equitable and inclusive learning environment. UDL is a set of values that recognizes and respects the skills and attitudes students bring into our social studies classrooms

(Meyer et al., 2014). Integrating the UDL framework with IDM offers multiple means for successfully overcoming academic, cultural, linguistic, and environmental barriers while actively engaging diverse learners, both with and without disabilities, in the inquiry process. However, UDL cannot transform inquiry-based teaching and learning unless teachers value variability, equity, and inclusion.

As our social studies classroom become increasingly more diverse, teachers are challenged with covering the required curriculum while making instructional decisions that value student difference. Designing a learning environment whereby all students engage in—and share—their own learning, is essential for promoting equitable and inclusive social studies education.

Social studies teachers play a key role in designing and implementing instructional practices that adequately meet the needs of all learners. Once inquiry-based practices are aligned to the core values of UDL, reflective, engaging strategies emerge and are flexible and iterative and rooted in student needs (Novak & Woodlock, 2021). The UDL framework recognizes learner variability as a rule, not the exception. It affirms that, when adequately supported, and barriers are removed, all students, both with and without disabilities, can access and understand social studies content in various, relevant ways. UDL can help support an inquiry-based social studies classroom where all learners become active, engaged, participatory expert learners.

REFERENCES

Azam, S., Goodnough, K. C., Moghaddam, A., Arnold, C., Penney, S., Young, G. D., & Maich, K. (2021). Becoming inclusive teacher educators: Self-study as a professional learning tool. *International Journal for the Scholarship of Teaching and Learning, 15*(2), Article 4.

Basham, J. D., & Marino, M. T. (2013). Understanding STEM education and supporting students through universal design for learning. *Teaching Exceptional Children, 45*(4), 8–15.

CAST. (2018). *Universal design for learning guidelines, version 2.2* [graphic organizer]. http://udlguidelines.cast.org

Chardin, M., & Novak, K. (2020). *Equity by design: Delivering on the power and promise of UDL.* Corwin Press.

Connell, B., Jones, M., Mace, R., Mueller, J., Mullick, A., Ostroff, E., Sanford, J., Steinfeld, E., Story, M., & Vanderheiden, G. (1997). *The principles of universal design: Version 2.0.* The Center for Universal Design.

Daley, S. G., Willett, J. B., & Fischer, K. W. (2014). Emotional responses during reading: Physiological responses predict real-time reading comprehension. *Journal of Educational Psychology, 106*(1), 132–142.

DeCuir-Gunby, J. T., DeVance Taliaferro, J., & Greenfield, D. (2010). Educators' perspectives on culturally relevant programs for academic success: The American excellence association. *Education and Urban Society, 42*(2), 182–204.

Earl, L. M. (2012). *Assessment as learning: Using classroom assessment to maximize student learning.* Corwin Press.

Florian, L., & Linklater, H. (2010). Preparing teachers for inclusive education: Using inclusive pedagogy to enhance teaching and learning for all. *Cambridge Journal of Education, 40*(4), 369–386.

Forlin, C. (2010). Teacher education reform for enhancing teachers' preparedness for inclusion. *International Journal of Inclusive Education, 14*(7), 649–653.

Fritzgerald, A. (2020). *Antiracism and Universal Design for Learning: Building expressways to success.* CAST Professional Publishing.

Garrick Duhaney, L. M. (2014). Disproportionate representation in special education: A persistent stain in the field. In F. E. Obiakor & A. F. Rotatori (Eds.), *Multicultural education for learners with special needs in the twenty-first century* (pp. 101–124). Information Age Publishing.

Grant, S. G., Swan, K., & Lee, J. (2017). *Inquiry-based practice in social studies education: Understanding the inquiry design model.* Routledge.

Griful-Freixenet, J., Struyven, K., & Vantieghem, W. (2021). Toward more inclusive education: an empirical test of the universal design for learning conceptual model among preservice teachers. *Journal of Teacher Education, 72*(3), 381–395.

Grossman, P., Hammerness, K., & McDonald, M. (2009). Redefining teacher: Reimagining teacher education. *Teachers and Teaching: Theory and Practice, 15*(2), 273–290.

Hall, T. E., Meyer, A., & Rose, D. H. (2012). *Universal Design for Learning in the classroom.* Guilford Press.

Individuals With Disabilities Education Act, 20 U.S.C. § 1400 (2004).

Kieran, L., & Anderson, C., (2019). Connecting Universal Design for Learning with culturally responsive teaching. *Education and Urban Society, 5*(9), 1202–1216.

Ko, B., & Boswell, B. (2013). Teachers' perceptions, teaching practices, and learning opportunities for inclusion. *Physical Educator, 70*(3), 223.

Kratz, J., (2014). Implementing the three-block model of Universal Design for Learning: Effects on teachers' self-efficacy, stress, and job satisfaction in inclusive classrooms K–12. *International Journal of Inclusive Education, 19*(1), 1–20.

Ladson-Billings, G. (2011). Is meeting the diverse needs of all students possible? *Kappa Delta Pi Record, 47*(1), 13–15.

Ladson-Billings, G. (2021). *Culturally relevant pedagogy: Asking a different question.* Teachers College Press.

Levstik, L. S., & Barton, K. C. (2015). *Doing history: Investigating with children in elementary and middle schools.* Routledge.

Meyer, A., Rose, D. H., & Gordon, D. T. (2014). *Universal design for learning: Theory and practice.* CAST Professional Publishing.

Minarik, D., & Lintner, T. (2016). *Social studies and exceptional learners.* National Council for the Social Studies.

Monte-Sano, C., De La Paz, S., & Felton, M. (2014). *Reading, thinking, and writing about history: Teaching argument writing to diverse learners in the Common Core classroom, Grades 6–12.* Teachers College Press.

National Council for the Social Studies. (2013). *Social studies for the next generation: Purposes, practices, and implications of the college, career, and civic life (C3) framework for social studies state standards*. NCSS Publishing.

Nelson, L. L. (2021). *Design and deliver: Planning and teaching using Universal Design for Learning*. Brooks Publishing.

Novak, K. (2022). *UDL now! A teacher's guide to applying Universal Design for Learning*. CAST Professional Publishing.

Novak, K., & Tucker, C. R. (2021). *UDL and blended learning: Thriving in flexible learning landscapes*. Impress.

Novak, K., & Woodlock, M. (2021). *UDL playbook for schools and district leaders*. CAST Professional Publishing.

Scruggs, T. E., Mastropieri, M. A., Berkeley, S., & Graetz, J. E. (2010). Do special education interventions improve learning of secondary content? A meta-analysis. *Remedial and Special Education, 31*(6), 437–449.

Spencer, S. A. (2015). *Making the Common Core writing standards accessible through universal design for learning*. Corwin Press.

Swan, K., Grant, S. G., & Lee, J. (2018). *The inquiry design model: Building inquiries in social studies. C3 inquiry series*. NCSS Publishing.

Thornton, S. J. (2005). *Teaching social studies that matters: Curriculum for active learning*. Teachers College Press.

Tomlinson, C. A. (2014). *The differentiated classroom: Responding to the needs of all learners*. ASCD.

Rodriguez, N. N., & Swalwell, K. (2021). *Social studies for a better world: An anti-oppressive approach for elementary educators (Equity and social justice in education)*. W. W. Norton & Company.

Rose, D. H., & Meyer, A. (2002). *Teaching every student in the digital age: Universal Design for Learning*. ASCD.

Rose, D. H., Robinson, K. H., Hall, T. E., Coyne, P., Jackson, R. M., Stahl, W. M., & Wilcauskas, S. L. (2018). Accurate and informative for all: Universal Design for Learning (UDL) and the future of assessment. In S. N. Elliott, R. J. Kettler, P. A. Beddow, & A. Kurz (Eds.), *Handbook of accessible instruction and testing practices* (pp. 167–180). Springer.

Wiggins, G. (1998). *Educative assessment: Designing assessments to inform and improve student performance*. Jossey-Bass Publishers.

Wineburg, S. (2010). Thinking like a historian. *Teaching With Primary Sources Quarterly, 3*(1), 2–4.

Wineburg, S. (2018). *Why learn history (when it's already on your phone)*. Chicago Press.

Wineburg, S. S., Martin, D., & Monte-Sano, C. (2012). *Reading like a historian: Teaching literacy in middle and high school history classrooms*. Teachers College Press.

PART III

INCLUSIVE INSTRUCTION

CHAPTER 6

ADDRESSING THE LEARNING NEEDS OF STUDENTS WITH DISABILITIES THROUGH EFFECTIVE QUESTIONING

Darren Minarik
Radford University

Janis A. Bulgren
University of Kansas

How do teachers effectively lead all students through higher levels of understanding using questions? Questioning is a critical skill necessary to promote meaningful learning experiences for students in the social studies classroom. Good questioning in social studies education fosters student engagement and retention of information while enhancing the critical thinking and problem-solving skills necessary for effective inquiry. It also encourages student self-reflection and metacognition skills that help students take ownership of the learning experience. Although teachers learn about effective questioning techniques to assess student learning and encourage

Creating an Inclusive Social Studies Classroom for Exceptional Learners, pages 123–134
Copyright © 2024 by Information Age Publishing
www.infoagepub.com
All rights of reproduction in any form reserved.

critical thinking during their teacher preparation programs, many still struggle with implementing these effective practices in the classroom (Walsh & Sattes, 2017). Furthermore, when teaching students with disabilities (SWDs), "smart, thoughtful, and imaginative" social studies teachers are left to their own discretion and expertise when considering how to scaffold effective questioning techniques (National Council for the Social Studies, 2013, p. 15). Although we agree there are many talented teachers in the field who successfully use questioning to promote inquiry-based learning for diverse groups of students, it is still important to provide guidance for those teachers looking to better meet the needs of their students, especially those with individualized education programs (IEPs).

To address the need for SWDs to be included more in classroom questioning activities that encourage higher level thinking and reasoning, we begin this chapter by examining the importance of effective questioning in the social studies classroom, especially for SWDs who may not be included in questioning exercises because of perceived abilities. We define effective questioning and explore its importance in creating a learning environment that supports both content acquisition and higher order thinking and reasoning. We then discuss how to plan for effective questioning and provide some specific strategies and scaffolds to support questioning that engages all learners in an inclusive classroom. These strategies offer explicit steps to follow that help include students with a variety of support needs. Finally, we explore potential challenges and barriers to effective questioning in inclusive classrooms and provide guidance for future research on this topic, encouraging social studies educators to not shy away from challenging all students, regardless of disability labels.

WHAT IS EFFECTIVE QUESTIONING?

Effective, well-crafted questions are those that align with student learning objectives, capture students' attention, stimulate curiosity, and invite students to become active participants in their own learning (Bain, 2004; Walsh & Sattes, 2017). This active participation leads to more motivated learners who take ownership of their learning, and eventually develop a deeper understanding of the content (Kramer Ertel, 2021). Good questions have a clear purpose and align to the objectives of the lesson (Walsh & Sattes, 2017). When teachers question effectively, they provide opportunities for response and reflection throughout the lesson. Typically, teachers will ask questions at the beginning of a lesson when they are reviewing previous material and establishing interest or gauging prior knowledge in anticipation of the lesson topic. During the lesson, teachers interweave questions to check for understanding and encourage critical thinking when the opportunity arises. Throughout this process, teachers provide continuous feedback to students, engaging them in the learning process and even encouraging students to ask their own questions (Rosenshine, 2012). Quality questions should elicit correct or at least substantive answers, promote discussion, and guide students toward higher order thinking and reasoning when possible.

Effective questions are aligned and sequenced across taxonomies and hierarchies of responding and thinking ranging from a focus on a demonstration of basic knowledge or comprehension of information to more complex skills such as application, analysis, evaluation, and judgment to critical thinking, and creativity (Anderson & Krathwohl, 2001; Bloom, 1956). Questions come in different forms that serve a variety of purposes. The most common form is factual or close-ended questions where teachers are attempting to assess student comprehension of the content. Answers to these questions are often considered either right or wrong. For example, a teacher might ask, "What was the form of writing used in ancient Mesopotamia by the Sumerians?" Like factual questions, convergent questions also lead to specific answers or conclusions, but these questions require a higher level of cognition, encouraging students to show deeper comprehension through an application and analysis of content knowledge. A convergent question would go beyond factual recall and ask, "Why did civilizations form in river valleys?" or "What is needed to characterize a society as a civilization?" These questions require students to group content knowledge and then make comparisons and connections. Divergent questions are another type of questioning utilized in the social studies classroom. These questions are more open-ended in nature, requiring students to analyze, synthesize, or evaluate information. Divergent questions promote creativity and exploration, examination from multiple perspectives, and at times produce intellectual risk-taking that pushes students out of their comfort zones (Gallavan & Kottler, 2012). Students in a U.S. History class might be asked, "Is American exceptionalism really exceptional?" as part of a project-based inquiry. This question requires students to determine both those aspects of history that people would identify as exceptional and reveal historical events that do not represent an exceptional society. All these different question types can be combined in a variety of ways to support learning in the classroom. Within these question types, teachers utilize probing or follow-up questions to dig deeper into student responses. This process encourages metacognitve skills as students consider their own responses and how or why they came to certain conclusions.

APPROACHES IN PLANNING AND IMPLEMENTING EFFECTIVE QUESTIONING STRATEGIES

Planning is an essential first step in ensuring quality questions in lessons. Although there are many frameworks available to teachers, two that really support inclusive classrooms are Wiggins and McTighe's Understanding by Design (UbD) and SMARTER planning developed by the University of Kansas Center for Research on Learning (Lenz, 2016; Lenz et al., 2004; Minarik & Lintner, 2016; Wiggins & McTighe, 2012). The UbD model begins by having teachers consider desired student outcomes and how teachers will collect evidence of student learning. Teachers develop essential questions to determine what will be assessed in the unit. The unit is organized into lessons where strategies, activities, and well-prepared questions are introduced to help students meet essential unit outcomes. The more comprehensive essential questions are broken down into supporting questions that provide a scaffold for individual learning needs.

SMARTER planning also has teachers develop essential questions and consider central themes of a unit before organizing the content and planning for instruction. Often, SMARTER planning is aligned with the Unit Organizer Content Enhancement Routine (Bulgren et al., 2007). Unit Organizers (see Figure 6.1) are devices that visually represent the parts of a unit for students and help guide the planning and implementation of the unit for teachers. The Unit Organizer identifies the previous unit, current unit, and next unit of study, and determines the overall big idea of the unit.

A section called the unit map provides an organized visual graphic of each part of the unit. The unit map is aligned to several essential unit self-test questions students would answer in the unit lessons. These unit questions are aligned to skills students use to answer those questions. As an example, teachers might ask students, "What events caused the American Revolution?" The knowledge structure used to respond to this question would be "cause and effect." The SMARTER planning acronym can be applied to the Unit Organizer or any unit planning tool that teachers might consider. The acronym has teachers *shape* essential questions, *map* critical content, *analyze* the learning difficulties, *reach* enhancement decisions, *teach* strategically, *evaluate* mastery, and *revisit* outcomes. Using SMARTER planning, teachers are directed to develop lessons that consider potential learning difficulties and encourage the selection of activities and methods that strategically address learning needs. Both UbD and SMARTER planning provide these opportunities for differentiated instruction, which support the diverse learning needs of students.

Part of planning effective questions is alignment with lesson objectives. When writing objectives for an inclusive lesson, teachers should use a tiered approach (King-Sears et al., 2015; Murawski & Spencer, 2011). To do this, it is important for teachers to ask, "What essential content do I expect all

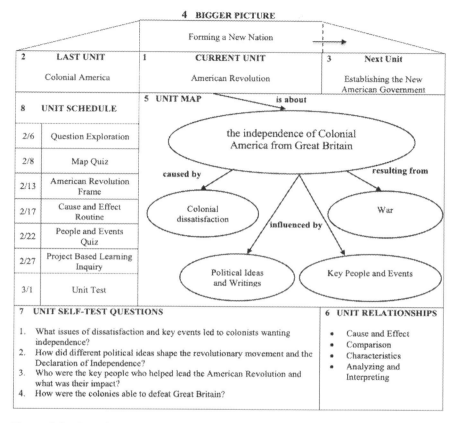

Figure 6.1 Sample unit organizer from a sixth grade social studies classroom.
Source: Adapted from Lenz et al. (1994).

students to learn? What content can some students learn? What content will be reached by a few students during the lesson?" These tiers are not intended to assume certain abilities in the classroom. Teachers should presume that all students have the potential to reach the objectives identified as those reached "by a few." If a teacher uses this approach to planning lessons, it will help determine what content is essential and make it easier to scaffold questions to assist students in learning the more challenging content (Minarik et al., 2021).

PLANNING WITH THE C3 FRAMEWORK AND INQUIRY DESIGN MODEL

The C3 Framework and Inquiry Design Model (IDM) are two additional tools specific to social studies that provide guidance when planning instruction, especially for students who need additional support (Dague, 2020; Grant et al., 2015). Utilizing the C3 Framework and inquiry design model is a way for teachers to encourage inquiry-based learning in the classroom while moving away from a more traditional emphasis on content coverage, memorization, and recall. Although most research in social studies as it relates to SWDs focuses on content recall, there is some limited evidence that SWDs are successful when an emphasis is placed on higher order thinking (Curtis & Green, 2021; Mullins et al., 2020; Nokes & De La Paz, 2018). IDM provides a structure and opens opportunities for social studies teachers in collaboration with special education, to create scaffolded inquiry-based learning for SWDs. Let us examine how the C3 Framework incorporates compelling questions.

Similar in design to the essential questions in UbD or the essential questions noted in SMARTER planning, compelling questions in the C3 Framework address broad themes and concepts. These questions are addressed within Dimension 1: Developing Questions and Planning Inquiries. For questions to be compelling rather than essential, they should spark interest, curiosity, discussion, and debate, but they do not always provide a definitive final answer (Grant et al., 2015). They always inspire higher order thinking and reasoning and often produce additional questions about the topic. Also, compelling questions are frequently interdisciplinary in nature, crossing content areas within social studies disciplines and other fields of study. A compelling question requires that the student examines the historical, governmental, geographical, and economic connections. Students collect essential information, analyze the information, and then make decisions rather than simply focusing on memorization.

The supporting questions within Dimension 1 serve as scaffolds, breaking down the larger compelling question and filling in pieces needed to develop an informed and thorough response. When accommodating the needs of SWDs, the teacher might allow students to develop their own supporting questions or develop supporting questions in peer groups. However, students with more complex special education needs might require support from explicit prompts, the definition of key terms, and the use targeted strategies or graphic organizers to scaffold the development of supporting questions. Students may need the supporting questions developed in advance along with strategies to help find answers to the provided supporting questions. It is important that teachers challenge all learners with compelling questions and not assume that some students are incapable of responding to such questions.

In Dimension 2, teachers are provided a way for organizing content using conceptual themes rather than providing specific topics. This broad approach was intentional to encourage use of the C3 Framework within existing state standards and to support development of new standards when needed. The content is divided into the four core social studies disciplines, civics, economics, geography, and history. Dimension 3 begins with the understanding that complex skills are needed for evaluating sources and using evidence. The ability to communicate views and take informed action is the skill emphasized in Dimension 4, where students are asked to develop sound arguments using evidence from a variety of sources, draw conclusions from those arguments, and then take action to inform others. Students advocate for their beliefs in a variety of formats from print and social media to oral debate.

Grant, Swan, and Lee (2022), authors of the inquiry design model (IDM) provide guidelines and templates for developing an inquiry using the C3 Framework Inquiry Arc at https://c3teachers.org/inquiry-design-model/. The Design Path document addresses ten steps built within three phases: (a) framing the inquiry, (b) filling the inquiry, and (c) finishing the inquiry. The working blueprint templates address each part of the IDM. Figure 6.2 provides a sample completed template with accommodations built in to support an inclusive classroom. The main template begins by having the teacher identify the compelling question and the standard aligned to the question. It also asks the teacher to identify the disciplinary practice and provide an activity to stage the question for the students. Then, the template provides a section for supporting questions. Each supporting question developed aligns to a formative performance task and lists sources used to help respond to the question. The next part of the template has the teacher develop a summative performance task that asks students to construct an argument and provides an extension exercise. This feature allows students to work at their own pace and it provides enrichment for those who completed the inquiry sooner. The taking informed action step has three parts, understand, assess, and act. Grant, Lee, and Swan note that these tasks can be woven throughout the inquiry or completed after the summative tasks (Grant et al., 2015; Grant et al. 2022).

STRATEGIES FOR EFFECTIVE QUESTIONING

When considering strategies for questioning in an inclusive classroom, it is important to consider the individual needs of students. SWDs all have specific challenges and teachers should not assume certain needs based on a disability label. It is important to consult and collaborate with the special education teacher and other support personnel when developing questioning strategies to fully include SWDs in the classroom. There are some general considerations that social studies teachers can begin with when selecting questioning strategies to reach the diverse learning needs of their students. For example, students with visual impairments often benefit from

Is American exceptionalism really exceptional?		
Standard: Virginia Standards of Learning (2015)	GOVT.4b The student will apply social science skills to understand the Constitution of the United States by (b) evaluating the purposes for government stated in the Preamble VUS.1 The student will demonstrate skills for historical thinking by a) synthesizing evidence from artifacts and primary and secondary sources to obtain information about events in United States history; d) constructing arguments, using evidence from multiple sources; e) comparing and contrasting historical, cultural, economic, and political perspectives in United States history; f) explaining how indirect cause-and-effect relationships impact people, places, and events United States history; g) analyzing multiple connections across time and place; h) using a decision-making model to analyze and explain the incentives for and consequences of a specific choice made; and j) investigating and researching to develop products orally and in writing.	
Staging the Compelling Question	Share the poem. "Let America Be America Again" by Langston Hughes. Have students read the poem while listening to it: https://youtu.be/b6Im4b3kdfc Ask students to do the following during the poem (pause at least 3 times): (1) Mark any phrases or words you found interesting (2) Identify any words we should consider defining as a class (3) place question marks next to any words or phrases where you want clarification. (4) What groups does the speaker include in this poem? What is the relationship between these disenfranchised groups? (5) Hughes writes, "O, let America be America again—The land that never has been yet." What do you think he means by this?	
Supporting Question 1	Supporting Question 2	Supporting Question 3
What were the origins of the concept of American exceptionalism?	What events in U.S. History support American greatness/exceptionalism?	What events in U.S. History challenge American greatness/exceptionalism?
Formative Performance Task	Formative Performance Task	Formative Performance Task
Identify and explain historical documents and events that helped create the idea of American Exceptionalism.	Compare and evaluate events in U.S. History and determine how various events contribute to the nation in positive and negative ways.	Compare and evaluate events in U.S. History and determine how various events contribute to the nation in positive and negative ways.
Featured Sources	Featured Sources	
Source A: Constitution, Preamble Source: B: Common Sense, Thomas Paine Source C: Democracy in America, Alexis de Tocqueville Source D: American Exceptionalism: A Short History https://foreignpolicy.com/2012/06/18/american-exceptionalism-a-short-history/	Source E: PBS Learning Media U.S. History Collection https://www.pbslearningmedia.org/collection/us-history-collection/era/america-into-the-21st-century-2001present/ Source F: Smithsonian's History Explorer https://historyexplorer.si.edu/ Source G: Library of Congress U.S. History Primary Source Timeline https://www.loc.gov/classroom-materials/united-states-history-primary-source-timeline/	
Summative Performance Task	**Argument** Should we characterize the United States as exceptional? Construct an argument using the Cross-Curricular Argumentation Routine that responds to the compelling question using specific claims and relevant evidence from sources while acknowledging competing views (Bulgren, 2020).	
	Extension Analyze and evaluate the "more perfect Union" statement in the Preamble of the Constitution. How can we make our union "more perfect" for everyone?	
Taking Informed Action	**Understand** Research recent events taking place in our nation's schools regarding state standards and how teachers are expected to teach U.S. History.	
	Assess How do you think U.S. history should be taught in our schools?	
	Act Choose a direct action you can take related to this issue in your own community.	

Figure 6.2 Sample IDM for twelvth grade U.S. government. *Source:* Adapted from the IDM Working Blueprint Templates. Retrieved from https://c3teachers.org/inquiry-design-model/ (CC BY-SA 4.0).

auditory cues and tactile materials built into questions. Auditory cues might include clear and concise verbal explanations of questions that break down vocabulary and difficult concepts along with repetition to reinforce understanding. Our tone and inflection when asking questions can indicate the emotion within the question or important points to keep in mind. Tactile materials might include 3-D models and embossed or raised maps and images that students can touch and feel. Tactile materials are also helpful for some students with hearing impairments when asking questions. In addition, if a sign language interpreter is present, the interpreter needs your questions prepared in advance to make sure nothing is lost in the interpretation process.

Students with intellectual disabilities and those with autism or other developmental disabilities benefit from structured and predictable question formats in plain language that are used on a routine basis in the classroom. The Autistic Self Advocacy Network (ASAN) has an excellent guide that describes plain language and other ways to make language accessible (https://autisticadvocacy.org/wp-content/uploads/2021/07/One-Idea-Per-Line.pdf). Scaffolding questions with definitions of key terms or breaking down more complex questions into smaller parts is also helpful. Students with attention-deficit hyperactivity disorder and learning disabilities also benefit from these same scaffolds and structures when developing and asking questions. All students benefit from wait time, a brief pause after posing a question that allows students to process the question and generate responses. Additionally, educators can use various peer-to-peer questioning and collaboration questioning techniques like think–pair–share, Socratic questioning, questioning circles, and peer-led questioning to foster collaboration, active engagement, and deeper understanding among students.

Graphic Organizers and acronyms spelling out explicit steps can be powerful tools for supporting effective questioning for SWDs. One useful acronym is the RESPOND! inquiry inspired by IDM and developed by the American Civics Center (Minarik, 2020). This acronym identifies seven explicit steps to lead students through an inquiry. Students *reveal* the compelling question, *explore* supporting questions, *search* for supporting answers (using sources), *prepare* a response, *offer* alternative responses, *note* similarities and differences (compare/contrast), and *develop* connections to bigger ideas. The exclamation point represents the "take action and get excited" step. Chapter 7 goes into detail about higher order thinking and reasoning routines developed by the University of Kansas Center for Research on Learning. One of those routines, the question exploration routine (Bulgren et al., 2011; Bulgren et al., 2007), guides students through the higher order thinking and reasoning required to answer a critical question. The Question Exploration graphic organizer follows steps using the acronym ANSWER: *ask* a critical question, *note* and explain key terms, *search* for supporting questions and answers, *work* out the main idea answer, *explore* the main idea within a related area, and *relate* the idea to today's world. The steps of the question exploration routine move students toward higher-order learning by exploring a critical question, breaking apart that complex question into smaller questions to answer, arriving at a clear, concise main idea answer, and engaging in generalization of the main ideas to other complex issues in the same content area, and to issues in the real world. The key terms section required in the routine provide an important scaffold for students who need additional understanding of vocabulary to complete the routine. An example of a question exploration guide along with a more detailed description of its use in a social studies classroom is provided in Chapter 7.

CONCLUSION

Well-planned, thoughtful, and targeted questioning in lessons is important for all learners and is critical if teachers want to meet the learning needs of SWDs in social studies classrooms. It is imperative that social studies educators implement effective questioning strategies as a tool to create inclusive and engaging learning environments for students. This chapter provides guidance for educators as they consider how to make questioning in the classroom more inclusive for SWDs. Teacher educators need to emphasize the importance of good questioning to their pre-service teachers and consider ways to have the students gain practice opportunities to model good questioning.

There will be challenges and barriers to effective questioning in inclusive classrooms. Planning ways to address questions for a variety of learning needs is not an easy task and teachers may initially not recognize the learning benefits of using the strategies in this chapter, or they may feel some SWDs are not capable of participating in questioning activities that encourage inquiry-based higher order thinking and reasoning. One way to address these doubts is for researchers to consider more studies that look specifically at questioning strategies and their impact on SWDs. We know what good questioning looks like in social studies but have little research on how these strategies support diverse learning needs in the social studies classroom. We know that teachers incorrectly think they ask fewer low-level questions and more questions that challenge their students to higher order thinking and reasoning (Barikmo, 2021). It is time for teachers and teacher educators to address this issue and answer the question, "How can we use effective questioning techniques and strategies to help students connect more deeply with content and cognitive processes in an inclusive social studies classroom?"

REFERENCES

Anderson, L. W., & Krathwohl, D. R. (2001). *A taxonomy for learning, teaching, and assessing: A revision of Bloom's taxonomy of educational objectives.* Longman.

Bain, K. (2004). *What the best college teachers do.* Harvard University Press.

Barikmo, K. R. (2021). Deep learning requires effective questions during instruction. *Kappa Delta Pi Record, 57*(3), 126–131.

Bloom, B. S. (1956). *Taxonomy of educational objectives.* Longman.

Bulgren, J. A. (2020). *Teaching cross-curricular argumentation.* The University of Kansas Center for Research on Learning.

Bulgren, J., Deshler, D. D., & Lenz, B. K. (2007). Engaging adolescents with LD in higher order thinking about history concepts using integrated content enhancement routines. *Journal of Learning Disabilities, 40*(2), 121–133.

Bulgren, J. A., Marquis, J. G., Lenz, B. K., Deshler, D. D., & Schumaker, J. B. (2011). The effectiveness of a question exploration routine for enhancing the content learning of students. *Journal of Educational Psychology, 103*(3), 578–593.

Curtis, M. D., & Green, A. L. (2021). A systematic review of evidence-based practices for students with learning disabilities in social studies classrooms. *The Social Studies, 112*(3), 105–119.

Dague, C. T. (2020). In support of students' needs: Exploring the benefits of the inquiry design model. *Social Education, 84*(1), 66–71.

Gallavan, N. P., & Kottler, E. (2012). Advancing social studies learning for the 21st century with divergent thinking. *The Social Studies, 103*(4), 165–170.

Grant, S. G., Lee, J., & Swan, K. (2015). *The inquiry design model.* C3 Teachers.

Grant, S. G., Swan, K., & Lee, J. (2022). *Inquiry-based practice in social studies education: Understanding the inquiry design model.* Taylor & Francis.

King-Sears, M. E., Janney, R., & Snell, M. E. (2015). *Collaborative teaming* (3rd ed.). Paul H. Brooks Publishing Co.

Kramer Ertel, P. A. (2021). Key principles and strategies for enhancing student engagement and learning. *Kappa Delta Pi Record, 57*(3), 120–125.

Lenz, B. K. (2016). *The SMARTER instructional cycle.* https://simvilledev.ku.edu/sites/default/files/PD%20Resources/SMARTER%20InstCycle%20Lenz%202016.pdf

Lenz, B. K., Bulgren, J. A., Kissam, B. R., & Taymans, J. (2004). SMARTER planning for academic diversity. *Teaching content to all: Evidence-based practices in middle and secondary schools* (pp. 47–77). Pearson.

Lenz, K., Bulgren, J. A., Schumaker, J. B., Deshler, D. D., & Boudah, D. A. (1994). *The unit organizer routine.* Edge Enterprises.

Minarik, D. (2020). *RESPOND!* American Civics Center.

Minarik, D., & Lintner, T. (2016). *Social studies and exceptional learners.* National Council for the Social Studies Publications.

Mullins, R. D., Jr., Williams, T., Hicks, D., & Mullins, S. B. (2020). Can we meet our mission? Examining the professional development of social studies teachers to support students with disabilities and emergent bilingual learners. *The Journal of Social Studies Research, 44*(1), 195–208.

Murawski, W. W., & Spencer, S. (2011). *Collaborate, communicate, and differentiate! How to increase student learning in today's diverse schools.* Corwin.

National Council for the Social Studies. (2013). *The college, career, and civic life (C3) framework for social studies state standards: Guidance for enhancing the rigor of K–12 civics, economics, geography, and history*. http://www.socialstudies.org/c3

Nokes, J., & De La Paz, S. (2018). Writing and argumentation in history education. In S. A. Metzger & L. McArthur Harris (Eds.), *The Wiley international handbook of history teaching and learning* (pp. 551–578). Wiley.

Rosenshine, B. (2012). Principles of instruction: Research-based strategies that all teachers should know. *American Educator, 39*, 12–19.

Walsh, J. A., & Sattes, B. D. (2017). *Quality questioning: Research-based practice to engage every learner*. Corwin Press.

Wiggins, G. P., & McTighe, J. (2012). *The understanding by design guide to advanced concepts in creating and reviewing units*. Association for Supervision and Curriculum Development.

CHAPTER 7

SUPPORTING INCLUSION WITH HIGHER ORDER THINKING AND REASONING

Janis A. Bulgren
University of Kansas

Darren Minarik
Radford University

Among challenges facing teachers in social studies classes are the dual needs to teach students to apply complex reasoning skills across history, civics, geography, and economics, and to assure that all students, including those with a variety of disabilities fully benefit from that instruction. A response to this dual challenge may be illustrated by how social studies teachers implement research and evidence-based strategies to support inclusion for students with a range of learning needs and supports. In this chapter, we propose that social studies educators implement instructional procedures called *higher order thinking and reasoning* (HOTR) routines developed and researched with attention to both the needs of a wide range of student needs and the increasingly rigorous thinking and reasoning standards required in our social studies classrooms (National Council for the Social Studies [NCSS], 2013). It is our belief that teachers do not need to reduce rigorous thinking and reasoning to provide access to the content for diverse populations, and HOTR routines provide a pathway to create more inclusive social studies classrooms.

Social studies standards emphasize using HOTR to understand and compare concepts, analyze central ideas and themes, explain the causes and effects of important events, and analyze claims and arguments. These types of reasoning skills are addressed across state and national standards relevant to social studies (e.g., Common Core State Standards Initiative, 2010; Adler & NCSS, 2010). Specifically for social studies, the Dimensions of Learning in the Inquiry Arc of the 3C Framework (NCSS, 2013) present four critical instructional components that require reasoning: (a) developing questions and planning inquiry; (b) applying disciplinary concepts and tools; (c) evaluating sources and using evidence; and (d) communicating conclusions. Combined with these social studies learning standards are the requirements addressed through federal legislation such as the Individuals with Disabilities Education Act (IDEA, 2004) and the Elementary and Secondary Education Act (U. S. Department of Education, 2004), recommending all students with disabilities are provided with rigorous and effective instruction and that this instruction takes place in the general education content classrooms to the maximum extent possible (Baglieri & Shapiro, 2017).

In this chapter, we introduce HOTR routines as a structured and engaging way to support teacher instruction and impact learning for all students in an inclusive social studies classroom. We begin with a brief examination of HOTR routines and how they fit within a larger series of instructional devices called *content enhancement routines*. We then address each of the HOTR routines, sharing how to develop and implement each routine in the classroom while also providing the research supporting their effectiveness. Finally, we suggest additional ways the routines could benefit inclusive social studies classrooms and provide suggestions for future research and support for both pre-service and in-service teachers.

HIGHER ORDER THINKING AND REASONING ROUTINES

Higher order thinking and reasoning (HOTR) routines provide an evidence- and research-based set of instructional procedures and supports designed to address challenges related to HOTR (Bulgren, 2014; Bulgren, 2018; Bulgren, 2020; Bulgren et al., 2001; Bulgren et al., 1995). HOTR routines are part of strategic instruction model (SIM™) developed at the University of Kansas Center for Research on Learning (KUCRL) called *content enhancement routines* (CERs). CERs are sets of instructional tools that use powerful teaching devices, strategies, and procedures to plan for and teach rigorous content (for additional information on the SIM and the variety of CERs located in Table 7.1, please visit https://sim.ku.edu/). These routines support teachers as plan ways to help students learn including the HOTR routines (Bulgren et al., 2007; Bulgren et al., 2013).

HOTR routines are designed to respond to increasingly rigorous reasoning challenges. For example, HOTR routines helps students make comparisons with the concept comparison routine (Bulgren et al., 1995) answer critical questions with the question exploration routine (Bulgren et al., 2001), trace cause-and-effect relationships with the teaching cause and effect routine (Bulgren, 2014), make decisions with the teaching decision-making routine (Bulgren, 2018), and engage in argumentation across different content areas with the cross curricular argumentation routine (Bulgren, 2020).

Common components used across all HOTR routines include (a) a graphic organizer tailored to each reasoning challenge, (b) a cognitive reasoning strategy with a guiding acronym embedded within the steps of the graphic organizer, and (c) common instructional procedures. Built into the instructional procedures are other recommendations such as advance and post organizers, interactive exploration of topics, collaborative learning opportunities, and continuous review. Research on HOTR routines demonstrated both the effectiveness in helping a diverse range of students

TABLE 7.1 Content Enhancement Routines in the Strategic Instruction Model

Content Enhancement Routines				
Planning and Leading Learning	Increasing Performance	Explaining Text, Topics, and Details	Teaching Concepts	Higher Order Thinking and Reasoning
Course Organizer	Quality Assignment	Framing	Concept Mastery	Question Exploration
Unit Organizer	Recall Enhancement	Clarifying	Concept Anchoring	Teaching Cause and Effect
Lesson Organizer	Vocabulary LINCing	Survey	Concept Comparison	Concept Comparison
				Cross-Curricular Argumentation
				Teaching Decision-Making
				Scientific Argumentation

Note: Concept comparison falls under both the teaching concepts and HOTR categories. More detailed information about each of these routines can be found at https://sim.ku.edu/sim-content-enhancement-routines

including those with disabilities learn complex content and the practicality of teacher implementation in general education inclusive classes taught by expert content area teachers (Bulgren, 2004; Bulgren, 2014; Bulgren, 2018; Bulgren, 2020; Bulgren et al., 2001; Bulgren et al., 2013; Bulgren et al., 2011; Bulgren et al., 2009; Bulgren et al., 1995). HOTR routines feature other research-based components that support student learning such as explicit instruction (Hughes et al., 2017), graphic organizers (Pashler et al., 2007), Universal Design for Learning (Gargiulo & Metcalf, 2022), the use of explanatory questioning (Beck & McKeown, 2002), and built in continuous review (Rosenshine, 2012).

EXAMPLES OF HOTR ROUTINES IN SOCIAL STUDIES

As part of the HOTR planning process, teachers create a draft of the graphic organizer in preparation for the lesson. Then in the introductory process, teachers introduce the content topic and the HOTR routine chosen for the lesson. Teachers share with their students how the device will support their learning. During the instructional process, teachers use the draft as a guide and co-construct the routine with students. Students will not necessarily construct a graphic organizer that looks exactly like the teacher example because it is important that students collaborate in the interactive development to create a graphic organizer. However, it is critical that the teacher has a guide for assuring critical coverage of the topic. After completion of the routine, students summarize the CER and apply it to other lessons and assignments. This review process is an important step and those who implement CERs are encouraged to provide multiple opportunities to review and revisit content to support long-term understanding of the content taught (Rosenshine, 2012).

Concept Comparison Routine

The concept comparison routine (CCR) provides an approach to help compare, contrast, and distinguish a range of social studies facts and issues. For example, in Dimension 2: Civics and Political Institutions for students in grades three through five in the C3 Framework (D2.Civ.1.3-5), the CCR is an effective tool for comparing the responsibilities and power of government officials at various levels and branches of government and in different times and places (NCSS, 2013). Furthermore, the CCR responds to Dimension 2 challenges in Grades 6 through 8 to compare deliberative processes used by a wide variety of groups in different settings (D3.Civ.9.6-8).

The CCR helps teachers to guide students as they analyze and explain the similarities and differences between or among two or more concepts

Supporting Inclusion With Higher Order Thinking and Reasoning ▪ **139**

or examples of concepts. After identifying critical characteristics of each, students and teacher collaborate to identify which characteristics are alike, which are different, the categories into which each alike and different characteristic fit, and then to summarize understanding and use the ability to compare and contrast in a new challenge. Research on the routine demonstrated that teachers using the routine in inclusive general education social studies and science classes saw a significant increase in correct test responses for all students, including those with disabilities, compared to teachers that did not use the routine (Bulgren et al., 2002).

The CCR includes the cognitive reasoning strategy shown in Table 7.2 and cued by the acronym COMPARING. These steps provide guidance for both the teacher and students as they compare two or more concepts within the lesson. To implement the CCR, teachers may use a graphic organizer like the one modeled in Figure 7.1 to support the instructional process.

The CCR graphic organizer is a one-page teaching tool used to visually display information. The organizer contains forms and spaces to write information, and each of these spaces contains a set of steps that guide the thinking and reasoning required. In instruction, teachers introduce concepts or examples of concepts, and collaborate with students to explore the similarities and differences of each. To use the routine, the teacher would cue the lesson by introducing the concept comparison guide, the procedure that the students follow to complete the guide, and how using this routine will help them learn more about the topic. In the "do" phase of instruction, the teacher and students co-construct the CCR using the COMPARING steps. As outlined in Figure 7.1, the teacher would begin by *communicating* the targeted concepts of Judaism and Islam. Next, the teacher works with students to *obtain* or identify the overall concept of monotheistic religions to

TABLE 7.2   Concept Comparison COMPARING Linking Steps
Linking Steps
Communicate Targeted Concepts
Obtain the overall concept
Make a list of known characteristics
Pin down like characteristics
Assemble like categories
Record unlike characteristics
Identify unlike categories
Nail down a summary
Go beyond the basics

Note: Reprinted from *Concept Comparison Routine*, by J. Bulgren et al., 1995, Edge Enterprises, Inc. Copyright 1995 by Janis Bulgren. Reprinted with permission.

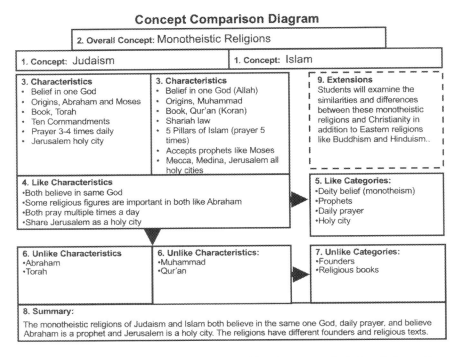

Figure 7.1 Concept comparison diagram addressing monotheistic religions. *Note:* Visual device reprinted from *Concept Comparison Routine*, by J. Bulgren et al., 1995, Edge Enterprises, Inc. Copyright 1995 by Janis Bulgren. Text in visual device written by Darren Minarik. Reprinted with permission.

which the targeted concepts belong. This assures understanding of the big picture of the content lesson. Once the concepts are identified, the teacher and students then collaborate to *make* lists of characteristics of each of the targeted concepts. The next steps are important for guiding students to see the big picture of how concepts relate to each other in an efficient way. Then, the students and teacher *pin* down or pick the most critical characteristics for each concept that are alike and collaborate to *assemble* or identify the like categories. The process is repeated for unlike characteristics and unlike categories in steps in which they *record* unlike characteristics and *identify* unlike categories. Students then *nail* down a summary, using the like and unlike categories along with the target concepts and overall concept to create a summary statement that demonstrates their understanding. After the students develop a summary of the similarities and differences in the concepts or examples being compared, they can review the information on the graphic to confirm understanding. After understanding is assured, the teacher can guide students to review the steps of the routine to prompt generalization of learning. The last step is to *go* beyond basics by taking the knowledge learned and applying it to other content. For example, after learning about the similarities and differences between Judaism and Islam, students may add Christianity to the comparison. They also might compare monotheistic religions to polytheistic religions.

Question Exploration Routine

The question exploration routine (QER) is a tool for teachers to guide students through the higher-order reasoning required to answer compelling questions and engage in inquiry aligned to challenges in the 3C Framework (Bulgren et al., 2001). For one example, prompted by thinking and reasoning demands in Dimension 1 of the C3 Framework (NCSS, 2013), the QER helps teachers and students respond to challenges in grades three through five (D1.4.3-5) to explain how supporting questions help answer compelling questions. Furthermore, in grades six through eight (D1.3.6-8), the QER responds to the challenge of explaining key questions in a field followed by constructing supporting questions (Bulgren et al., 2011).

The QER routine includes the question exploration guide, a graphic organizer with spaces to write information, along with steps to guide the thinking and reasoning required using the acronym ANSWER. As noted in Table 7.3, the QER progressively moves a student toward higher-order learning by exploring a critical question and key terms, breaking apart that complex question into smaller questions to answer, arriving at a clear, concise main idea answer, and engaging in generalization of the main ideas to other complex issues in the same content area, and to issues in the real world.

Studies were conducted in middle school social studies and science classes to examine the effectiveness of the QER (Bulgren et al., 2011). Results of the research indicated that diverse groups of students including those with learning disabilities who received the QER instruction answered

TABLE 7.3 Question Exploration ANSWER Linking Steps

Linking Steps
Ask a critical question
Note and explain key terms
Search for supporting questions and answers
Work out the main idea answer
Explore the main idea within related area
Relate the idea to today's world

Note: Reprinted from *Question Exploration Routine*, by J. Bulgren et al., 2001, Edge Enterprises, Inc. Copyright 2001 by Janis Bulgren. Reprinted with permission.

Question Exploration Guide

① What is the Critical Question?
Is American Exceptionalism really exceptional?

② What are the Key Terms and explanations?
- Preamble
- Exceptionalism
- Perfect
- Civil rights

- The introduction to the U.S. Constitution that begins with "We the people"
- Unique, distinctive, and exemplary compared to others
- A good as something can possibly be
- Personal rights guaranteed and protected by the U.S. Constitution and federal laws

③ What are the Supporting Questions and answers?

1. What does "a more perfect union" mean in the Preamble to the U.S. Constitution?
2. What were the origins of the concept of American Exceptionalism?
3. What events in our history support American greatness/exceptionalism?
4. What events in our history challenge American greatness/exceptionalism?

1. We are always striving to be better as a nation
2. American exceptionalism was first suggested in Alexis de Tocqueville's *Democracy in America*
3. Events include but are not limited to scientific and technical achievements, our role in WWII, a shared belief system established in Preamble, and so on.
4. Events include but are not limited to slavery, treatment of Indigenous American tribes, Japanese American internment, and so on.

④ What is the main idea answer?
Although the United States has had some dark times in history, the idea that we are always trying to become "a more perfect union" and that we demonstrate this through the achievements and diversity of our citizens makes the U.S a distinctive and unique experiment in democracy.

⑤ How can we use the main idea?
American literature frequently reflects periods in our history that support and challenge the idea of exceptionalism. Have students read "Let America be America Again" by Langston Hughes or parts of Alexis de Tocqueville's *Democracy in America* to discuss the concept of American Exceptionalism further.

⑥ Is there an Overall Idea? Is there a real-world use?
Today, there are differing views about how we should teach U.S. history. Some believe that it's okay to highlight our flaws and challenges, while others feel that the focus should be on our strengths as a nation and those aspects that might be considered exceptional. How do you think U.S. history should be taught in our schools?

Figure 7.2 Question exploration guide examining American exceptionalism.
Note: Visual device reprinted from *Question Exploration Routine*, by J. Bulgren et al., 2001, Edge Enterprises, Inc. Copyright 2001 by Janis Bulgren. Text in visual device written by Darren Minarik. Reprinted with permission.

a significantly higher percentage of total questions than those receiving traditional lecture-discussion instruction. In another study, the QER was shown to support students' ability to write essays (Bulgren et al., 2009).

To implement the QER, teachers may use a guide such as that shown in Figure 7.2 to teach a lesson on a complex topic like American exceptionalism. The instruction and co-construction of the QER is guided by the cue–do–review instructional sequence. To use the QER, the teacher would cue the lesson by introducing the guide and procedures the class will follow to complete the guide and explain how using this routine will help them learn. During the do phase of the lesson, the teacher and students co-construct the question exploration guide using the ANSWER linking steps located in Table 7.3.

In the example QER provided in Figure 7.2, the teacher *asks* the critical question, "Is American Exceptionalism really exceptional?" Typically, the use of interrogatives like "how" and "why" often elicit the type of thinking and reasoning found in the standards. In this instance, the teacher is using an ironic yes/no compelling question structure to create interest in the topic (Swan et al., 2018). Next, students *note* the words that they find confusing or are unsure about the definition or meaning. The vocabulary lists might be based on the learning needs of individual students, providing a scaffold to support the learning process. These first two steps respond to reasoning challenges associated with knowledge of necessary facts and comprehension of the context of the question.

Once critical vocabulary is identified and defined, the teacher and students then *search* for possible supporting questions and answers to answer the critical question posed in the first step. Students could work individually, in small groups as with the whole class. The C3 Framework (NCSS, 2013) points out the critical importance not only of compelling questions but also supporting questions and this third step of the QER responds to this challenge with the spaces for supporting smaller questions and with guidance on answering those questions. This step responds to reasoning challenges associated with analysis and synthesis.

Students use the answers to the smaller, supporting questions to help *work* out the answer to the larger critical question. Again, this can be done individually or in small groups depending on the environment of the classroom and needs of the students. The last two steps of the QER encourage students to expand their reasoning beyond the initial question and main idea answer. As noted in Figure 7.2, students are asked to *explore* the main idea answer in other ways in the content or related area by connecting the answer to literature like the Langston Hughes poem, "Let America Be America Again" and Alexis de Tocqueville's "Democracy in America." Finally in the last step, students *relate* the topic addressed to real-world examples. For example, the teacher can ask students to examine recent debates in state legislatures regarding what histories should be taught in our classrooms and how those histories should be taught. These final two steps respond to reasoning challenges associated with application, evaluation, and generalization.

During the "review" phase of the lesson, teachers and students may use the explicit cognitive reasoning steps to prompt a review of both the content learning and the procedural steps. This type of review may serve to prompt independent future use of the cognitive strategic thinking and reasoning. Teachers would revisit the completed QER, making connections to future content and reviewing essential information.

Cause-and-Effect Routine

The cause-and-effect routine helps teachers and students to explain causes and effects of an event. An event may be an action such as a conflict, an assertion, procedures such as legislative actions or a decision made by companies or the government. As an example within Dimension 2 of the C3 Framework (NCSS, 2013), the cause-and-effect routine can address how economic decisions affect the well-being of individuals, businesses and society (D2.His.14.3-5) and analyze the multiple and complex causes and effects of past events (D2.His.14.6-8; D2.His.14.9-12).

The cause-and-effect routine helps students in the identification, analysis, evaluation, and explanation of cause-and-effect relationships by focusing on clear understanding a critical event with its preceding causes and subsequent effects (Bulgren, 2014). The routine provides for clarifying the question and exploring background knowledge as well as making critical connections from causes to the event and from the event to the effects. Students who received instruction using the routine performed better than those who did not on their ability to apply cause and effect reasoning to a new task (Bulgren, 2014; Hock et al., 2017). In addition, correlations between performance on the task and knowledge of the steps of the cognitive strategy and between performance on the task and quality of notetaking were found.

The graphic organizer for this routine, the cause-and-effect guide (CEG), is like those used in other routines, a one-page teaching tool used to visually display information. Again, the graphic organizer contains forms and spaces to write information, and each of these spaces contains a set of steps that guide the thinking and reasoning required. The CEG follows the acronym REASON as noted in Table 7.4. Teachers still follow the cue–do–review sequence as they guide students through the introduction to the routine, each of the linking steps, and a continuous review of the content after completion of the CEG.

The CEG in Figure 7.3 provides an example of its use in social studies by examining the causes and effects of the Great Depression. To use the routine, the teacher would cue the lesson by introducing the CEG, the procedure that the students follow to complete the guide, and how using this routine will help them learn more about the events leading up to the Great Depression and the results created from those events. During the do sequence of the lesson, the students and teacher co-construct sections of the guide while following the REASON linking steps. The teacher begins by *restating* the question:

TABLE 7.4 Cause-and-Effect REASON Linking Steps

Linking Steps
Restate the question
Examine key terms
Analyze critical event and background information
Specify causes and connections
Organize effects and connections
Nail down the answer

Note: Reprinted from *Teaching Cause and Effect*, by J. Bulgren, 2014, University of Kansas Center for Research on Learning. Copyright 2014 by Janis Bulgren. Reprinted with permission.

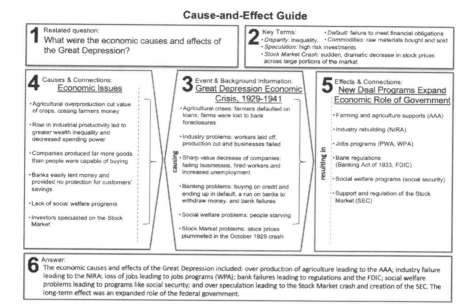

Figure 7.3 Examining the causes and effects of the Great Depression. *Note:* Visual device reprinted from *Teaching Cause and Effect* by J. Bulgren, 2014, University of Kansas Center for Research on Learning. Copyright 2014 by Janis Bulgren. Text in visual device written by Janis Bulgren. Reprinted with permission.

"What were the economic causes and effects of the Great Depression?" After defining critical vocabulary during the *examine* key terms step, the students and teacher proceed to *analyze* the event and other information needed to complete their understanding. Then, students *specify* causes and connections to the event, proceeding to *organize* connections from the event to the effects. As noted in Figure 7.3, students list economic events and then make connections with New Deal programs created because of those events. The final step is to *nail* down an answer where students use the guide they filled out to construct the answer to the initial question.

As part of the review phase, after the students develop an answer to the question posed in the first step of the routine, they can review what was learned as well as the steps of the strategy they used. Students can then make cause and effect comparisons in later units when economic downturns are discussed.

Teaching Decision-Making Routine

Teaching decision-making is an instructional routine that helps students identify an issue or problem, explore options for addressing or solving the situation, ways to analyze components of each option, consider potential compromises, and come to conclusions (Bulgren, 2018). The routine aligns well with many thinking and reasoning skills noted in social studies standards and the C3 Framework. For example, in Dimension 2 of the C3 Framework (NCSS, 2013) students are asked to examine positive and negative influences that influence decisions as well as explore how economic decisions affect the well-being of individuals, businesses and society (D2.Eco.2.3-5; D2.Eco.1.6-8). The decision-making routine provides a way to help explain how people can work together to make decisions (D2.Civ.9.3-5) and allows the teacher and students to learn and use procedures for making decisions (D2.Civ.11.3- 5).

The graphic organizer for this routine, the decision-making guide (DMG), is like those used in other routines. The DMG is a one-page teaching tool used to visually display information and help students make decisions related to different options. The graphic organizer contains spaces to write information, and each space is a linking step that guides the thinking and reasoning required. As identified in Table 7.5 the guiding steps spell out the acronym DECISION.

Research conducted on decision-making indicated that students who received instruction using this routine performed better than those who did not. Students demonstrated knowledge of the steps of the cognitive strategy, an ability to apply the strategy to a new decision-making task, and the ability to generalize the use of the strategy to a decision-making task in a different content area in which they had not been taught the routine in that class (Bulgren, 2018).

The DMG in Figure 7.4 provides an example of its use in a social studies geography or civics classroom. To use the routine, the teacher would cue the lesson by introducing the DMG, the procedure that the students follow

TABLE 7.5 Decision-Making DECISION Linking Steps

Linking Steps
Decide the issue
Enter options
Create a list of important information
Identify reasons to support each option
Set rank for each reason
Identify compromises or alternatives
Offer a decision
Name reasons for the decision

Note: Reprinted from *Teaching Decision-Making*, by J. Bulgren, 2018, University of Kansas Center for Research on Learning. Copyright 2018 by Janis Bulgren. Reprinted with permission.

Decision-Making Guide

1. Decide the issue				
Hybrid Vehicles versus Electric Vehicles to Address Climate Change				
3. Create important information	**2. Enter Option A**		**2. Enter Option B**	
- Combustion engine: runs on fuel (gas, ethanol/gas) - Hybrid vehicle: combines electric motor with gasoline engine that is the primary engine - Electric vehicle: runs on battery power - Plug-in hybrid vehicle: combines electric motor that is the primary engine with a gasoline engine - Hydrogen fuel-cell vehicle: runs on pure hydrogen fuel - Emissions: exhaust released into the air - Climate Change: long-term shift in temperatures and weather - Carbon footprint: amount of carbon compounds emitted	Hybrid Vehicle (HVs)		Electric Vehicles (HVs)	
	4. Identify reasons for option A	**5. Set Rank**	**4. Identify reasons for option B**	**5. Set Rank**
	- Great fuel economy and quick to fuel up	1	- No emissions leading to better air quality	2
	- Significantly cheaper than EVs to produce and to buy	3	- Cheaper to charge compared to gas powered	3
	- Not as big of a change for the consumer used to combustion engines	5	- Less maintenance than cars containing combustion engines	1
	- Do not require a charger	6	- Quicker acceleration	5
	- Less carbon-intensive to make compared to EVs	2	- Less of a carbon footprint in the long-term life of the vehicle	2
	- Can travel longer distances (300+ miles)	4	- Battery charge is starting to surpass 300 miles	4
6. Identify compromises/alternatives				
Plug-in hybrids and hydrogen fuel-cell vehicles are providing additional options. People can also use public transportation when available as an alternative to reduce emissions.				
7. Offer a Decision				
Overall, there are more appealing reasons to move toward EVs instead of producing and driving more HVs.				
8. Name reasons for the decision				
Less maintenance than cars containing combustion engines, no emissions leading to better air quality, and less of a carbon footprint in the long-term life of the vehicle were the primary reasons for this decision.				

Figure 7.4 Deciding between hybrid and electric vehicles to address climate change. *Note:* Visual device reprinted from *Teaching Decision-Making*. by J. Bulgren, 2018, University of Kansas Center for Research on Learning. Copyright 2018 by Janis Bulgren. Text in visual device written by Darren Minarik. Reprinted with permission.

to complete the guide, and how using this routine will help them learn more about how hybrid and electric vehicles address climate change.

During the do sequence of the lesson, the students and teacher co-construct sections of the guide while following the DECISION linking steps. The teacher begins by helping students in *deciding* the issue, "hybrid vehicles versus electric vehicles to address climate change." This is followed by brainstorming and *entering* options in response to the issue. Next, after *creating* a list of important information about the vehicle types, students can discuss and *identify* reasons for supporting each option and *select* numbers to rank the importance of difference reasons. This is followed by the *identify* compromises and alternatives step where additional ideas for addressing the issue are presented. The final two steps are to *offer* a decision and *name* the reasons for the decision. As part of the review phase, students develop a response to the issue posed in the first step of the routine and then share their responses, comparing the information and insights. At this point, both the teacher and students review critical points of learning in addition to the learning process they followed to come to a decision.

Cross-Curricular Argumentation Routine

The cross-curricular argumentation routine (Bulgren, 2020) is a teaching procedure to help teachers guide students to understand and use argumentation. Components of the routine focus on ways to understand and evaluate claims, evidence, reasoning, counterarguments, rebuttals, corroboration, and explanation of conclusions across content areas. These components align with many skills listed in Dimension 3 and 4 of the C3 Framework Inquiry Arc (NCSS, 2013). For example, within Dimension 3: Evaluating Sources and Using Evidence, the cross-curricular argumentation routine (CCAR) helps students and teachers to analyze claims (D3.3.6-8), identify limitations of evidence and develop claims and counterclaims with the strengths and weaknesses of each (D3.3.6-8). For Dimension 4: Communicating Conclusions and Taking Informed Action, the CCAR supports constructing arguments using precise and evidence weaknesses (D4.1.9-12) and constructing explanations using sound reasoning (D4.2.9-12).

The CCAR shares components with the Scientific Argumentation Routine (Bulgren et al., 2014). The similarity in component parts of the scientific argumentation and the CCAR provide evidence and confidence for the extension to different content areas with ongoing research. Overall, a significant difference and large effect size were found in favor of students in the experimental condition on an assessment of a claim based on a scientific research study.

The CCAR represents one of the most challenging types of reasoning. In argumentation the reasoning is used to show how the evidence supports the claim. The reasoning component has been referred to as developing a "chain of reasoning" (Bulgren et al., 2014). A chain of reasoning is a paraphrase of what evidence the author of the claim included *and* how the evidence is shown to be strong enough and well-connected to the claim to lead to acceptance.

The routine includes the cross-curricular argumentation guide graphic organizer with spaces to write information, and steps that guide the thinking and reasoning required using the acronym CLAIMS noted in Table 7.6.

The lesson begins with the cue phase when the teacher introduces a blank copy of the guide and shares the cognitive strategic linking steps. The teacher explains how the device will help the students better analyze and evaluate a claim.

Figure 7.5 provides a sample claim looking at voting as a civic duty. During the do phase, the teacher facilitates co-construction of the device using the linking steps. The *clarify* step in the routine is designed to help students understand and analyze the claim, "Voting is a civic duty and a powerful way for citizens to influence public policy and shape the future of their country." During the *list* the evidence step, students find and paraphrase the evidence presented by the author of the claim. Students can determine if the evidence consists of facts and data, opinions, or theories used to support the claim.

TABLE 7.6 Cross-Curricular CLAIMS Linking Steps

Linking Steps

Clarify the claim with any clarifier and define key terms

List the evidence

Analyze the reasoning

Identify other arguments for or against the claim

Make a judgment about the quality of evidence, the reasoning, and other arguments

State why you accept or reject the claim

Note: Reprinted from *Teaching Cross-Curricular Argumentation*, by J. Bulgren, 2020, University of Kansas Center for Research on Learning. Copyright 2020 by Janis Bulgren. Reprinted with permission.

Cross-Curricular Argumentation Guide

1. Clarify the claim with any qualifier and define key terms (including author, date, source, era).

Voting is a civic duty and a powerful way for citizens to influence public policy and shape the future of their country.
- *Voting* is a democratic process by which eligible individuals express their preferences on various issues or the selection of representatives
- *Civic duty* refers to the responsibilities and obligations that individuals have as members of a community or society
- *Public policy* refers to the plans and actions undertaken by government to address societal problems and meet public needs

2. List the evidence (facts, data, authority, theory precedent)

1. Written into the U.S. Constitution, 15th, 19th, 24th, and 26th amendments
2. The history of the U.S. and many countries wanting democracy includes significant struggles to achieve the right to vote.
3. Candidates often base platforms on the issues that resonate with voters and voters choose candidates who align with interests of the voters and will enact public policy that meets public needs.

3. Analyze the reasoning (cause-effect, correlation, corroboration)

1. The Constitution protects the rights of citizens from various backgrounds, cultures, and perspectives to have a say in shaping policies that affect their lives.
2. If people struggle to gain the right to vote, then this demonstrates how voting is a fundamental aspect of democracy, as it promotes the principles of political equality and majority rule.
3. Without voting, a government could become disconnected from the will of the people and potentially lead to authoritarianism or an unrepresentative government.

4. Identify other arguments for or against the claim (rebuttal, counterargument, corroboration)

In addition to it being a constitutional right, some argue that registered voters should be required to vote. Others argue that registration and voting should be made easier. There are also arguments that people are not informed enough and not everyone should vote as a result. Some question if election fraud is widespread, but there is no evidence of widespread fraud in the U.S.

5. Make a judgment about quality of evidence (accurate, adequate, objective, relevant), **reasoning** (type of reasoning), **and other arguments.**

The evidence, arguments, and reasoning are based on hundreds of years of debate and discussion as well as constitutional amendments and actual election outcomes that support the reasoning.

6. State why you accept or reject the claim

We accept the claim that voting is a civic duty because it helps people have influence over the future of our society. We believe that without voting, government is at greater risk for more authoritarian rule.

Figure 7.5 Voting as a civic duty. *Note:* Visual device reprinted from *Teaching Cross-Curricular Argumentation*, by J. Bulgren, 2020, University of Kansas Center for Research on Learning. Copyright 2020 by Janis Bulgren. Text in visual device written by Darren Minarik. Reprinted with permission.

Next, the teacher and students *analyze* the reasoning of the author, identifying how the author linked or connected the evidence to the claim.

In the fourth step, students *identify* other arguments for or against the claim, and this typically involves examination of additional sources. Once students complete these steps, then they need to *make* judgments about the quality of evidence, reasoning, and other arguments. As noted in Figure 7.5, the students determined that the evidence was strong because it had gone through hundreds of years of debate as well as constitutional amendments and court cases. These judgments help students *state* why they accept or reject the claim. Depending on the nature of the claim, students might be divided on accepting or rejecting a claim, creating an opportunity for using the routines to support dialogue. After the review phase of the both the content learning and the process of learning with the reasoning steps, students may then use the guide as a tool to either write an argumentative essay or present information on the topic.

HOTR Responses to Speaking and Writing Expectations in the C3 Framework

Targeted research on the use of HOTR routines also provides data responding to Dimension 4 of the C3 Framework, Taking Informed Action (NCSS, 2013). Specifically, students in this dimension of learning are expected to communicate and critique conclusions through writing, visual representations, and speech (NCSS, 2013). As a group, HOTR routines provide a structure for developing written responses and in preparation for sharing conclusions visually or through speech in a variety of formats (e.g., Bulgren et al., 2009). Following instruction with a HOTR routine, the graphic organizer and embedded strategy steps provide guidance as students use the information collected to develop essays (Bulgren et al., 2009). For example, within Dimension 4 the visual device and linking steps in cross-curricular argumentation (2020) provides a structure for students to construct arguments based on claims (D4.1.6-8), recognize the strengths and weaknesses within the arguments (D4.2.6-8) and present arguments and explanation in a written, visual, or oral format (D4.3-6-8). Studies of HOTR routines also supported the development of student note-taking skills, acquisition of knowledge through strategy steps (Bulgren, 2017) and the generalization of use of the reasoning steps from one content area to another (Bulgren, 2018; Bulgren, 2020; Bulgren et al., 2011).

HOTR ROUTINES IN PRESERVICE AND INSERVICE PROGRAMS

Professors and researchers in higher education face the same issues as teachers in K–12 education. Teacher educators must address increasingly complex demands across state and national standards as they prepare their students or teachers to respond to those standards and teach students representing a range of learning needs. In addition, educators and researchers have additional challenge: to go beyond methods coursework and think broadly about the introduction of instructional routines such as the HOTR routines through research, publications, professional presentations, and professional development in K–12 schools. There is a network of SIM professional developers and teacher educators can obtain the micro-credentials or professional developer certification needed to provide high quality professional development at both the pre-service and in-service level (see https://sim.ku.edu/sim-micro-credentials). HOTR routines used as a group provide a menu of procedures that respond to the different types of reasoning required within the social studies discipline.

Teacher educators in social studies could provide a long-term benefit to the field by exploring with student teachers how content in the various disciplines within social studies afford opportunities for the development of HOTR skills. Furthermore, there is an opportunity for teacher preparation programs to incorporate HOTR routines across multiple education courses, creating the potential for increased student learning based on intensity of instruction resulting from use of HOTR across courses. These education courses may focus on components of Universal Design of Learning (UDL), differentiation, and explicit instruction that align well with the teaching elements embedded within HOTR routines and other routines in the content enhancement series (Minarik & Lintner, 2011, 2016). Repeated use of HOTR routines may support students as they become more flexible and skilled in making connections and using those skills in multiple ways across different content and in response to real world issues. In addition, use of HOTR routines has the potential to be even more powerful when educators across different departments or content areas also use HOTR routines.

Instructors at various educational levels can be leaders in advocating for instructional tools such as HOTR routines that respond to the needs of a wide range of student learning needs while not watering down rigorous content. Instruction using HOTRs routines have been shown to be beneficial learning of a wide range of students. For example, various research on HOTR routines have shown to benefit learning and performance for students with learning disabilities, students as a group with disabilities who have IEPs, those identified as gifted, as males or females, and those whose grades indicate performance levels as low, average, or high (Bulgren et al., 2014). Such awareness can set the stage for teachers in inclusive content area classes, special education intervention classes, and co-taught classes to collaborate more effectively to meet the needs of students with IEPs.

FINAL THOUGHTS AND RECOMMENDATIONS FOR FUTURE RESEARCH

Preservice and in-service educators have an opportunity to use their expertise and communication outlets to share with the educational world the advantages and importance of research-and evidence-based strategies that promote HOTR, such as HOTR routines. Teachers and administrators should think of the instructional procedures in HOTR routines as gateways to planning and teaching so that all students can succeed in social studies classrooms. HOTR routines provide teachers and students with ways to teach and learn that are aligned with individual needs and these routines incorporate proven methods that support learning in an inclusive classroom setting. HOTR routines help expand awareness of and the ability to engage in reasoning across broad areas of subject matter, educational settings, life experiences, and careers. The skills addressed in these routines are essential to support the development of an educated and engaged citizenry.

This chapter provides a pathway for educators as they consider how HOTR routines support inclusive practice in the social studies classroom. We recognize there are challenges and barriers to supporting HOTR in inclusive classrooms. Developing these HOTR routines takes time and teachers may initially not recognize the learning benefits of using HOTR routines in the classroom, especially for students perceived as being cognitively unable of inquiry-based HOTR. To address these potential doubts, academics need to expand the number of studies and research-to-practice articles examining the impact of these routines on students with disabilities, especially those students with developmental disabilities. As more students with autism, intellectual disabilities, and multiple disabilities are fully included in general education classrooms, teachers need the tools and evidence of what works. As noted in this chapter, we have numerous studies examining the impact of HOTR routines on students with learning disabilities in inclusive classrooms, but there is a clear need to expand research into other disability categories. The field of social studies continues to demand rigorous thinking and reasoning within our state and national standards, and it is time to recognize the value of HOTR routines as a way to fully include students in this higher level of instruction.

REFERENCES

Adler, S. A., & National Council for the Social Studies. (2010). *National curriculum standards for social studies: A framework for teaching, learning and assessment.* National Council for the Social Studies.

Baglieri, S., & Shapiro, A. (2017). *Disability studies and the inclusive classroom: Critical practices for creating least restrictive attitudes.* Routledge.

Beck, I. L., & McKeown, M. G. (2002). Questioning the author: Making sense of social studies. *Educational Leadership, 60*(3), 44–47.

Bulgren, J. A. (2004). Effective content-area instruction for all students. In T. E. Scruggs & M. A. Mastropieri (Eds.), *Advances in learning and behavioral disabilities: Research in secondary schools, Volume 17* (pp. 147–174). Emerald Group Publishing.

Bulgren, J. A. (2014). *Teaching cause and effect.* University of Kansas Center for Research on Learning.

Bulgren, J. A. (2017). *The use and effectiveness of the cause-and-effect routine to help students learn and apply a cause-and-effect reasoning strategy* [Unpublished manuscript]. University of Kansas Center for Research on Learning.

Bulgren, J. A. (2018). *Teaching decision-making.* University of Kansas Center for Research on Learning.

Bulgren, J. A. (2020). *Teaching cross-curricular argumentation.* The University of Kansas Center for Research on Learning.

Bulgren, J. A., Deshler, D. D., & Lenz, B. K. (2007). Engaging adolescents with LD in higher order thinking about history concepts using integrated content enhancement routines. *Journal of Learning Disabilities, 40*(2), 121–133. https://doi.org/10.1177/00222194070400020301

Bulgren, J. A., Ellis, J. D., & Marquis, J. (2014). The use and effectiveness of an argumentation and evaluation intervention in science classes. *Journal of Science Education and Technology, 23*(1), 82–97. https://doi.org/10.1007/s10956-013-9452-x

Bulgren, J. A., Lenz, B. K., Deshler, D. D., & Schumaker, J. B. (2001). *The question exploration routine.* Edge Enterprises.

Bulgren, J. A., Lenz, B. K., Schumaker, J. B., Deshler, D. D., & Marquis, J. G. (2002). The use and effectiveness of a comparison routine in diverse secondary content classrooms. *Journal of Educational Psychology, 94*(2), 356.

Bulgren, J. A., Marquis, J. G., Deshler, D. D., Lenz, B. K., & Schumaker, J. B. (2013). The use and effectiveness of a question exploration routine in secondary-level English language arts classrooms. *Learning Disabilities: Research and Practice, 28*(4), 156–169. https://doi.org/10.1111/ldrp.12018

Bulgren, J. A., Marquis, J. G., Lenz, B. K., Deshler, D. D., & Schumaker, J. B. (2011). The effectiveness of a question exploration routine for enhancing the content learning of students. *Journal of Educational Psychology, 103*(3), 578–593. https://doi.org/10.1037/a0023930

Bulgren, J. A., Marquis, J. G., Lenz, B. K., Schumaker, J. B., & Deshler, D. D. (2009). Effectiveness of question exploration to enhance students' written expression of content knowledge and comprehension. *Reading and Writing Quarterly, 25*(4), 271–289. https://doi.org/10.1080/10573560903120813

Bulgren, J. A., Schumaker, J. B., & Deshler, D. D. (1995). *The concept comparison routine.* Edge Enterprises.

Common Core State Standards Initiative. (2010). *Common core state standards for English language arts & literacy in history/social studies, science, and technical subjects* (Appendix A). National Governors Association Center for Best Practices and the Council of Chief State School Officers.

Gargiulo, R. M., & Metcalf, D. (2022). *Teaching in today's inclusive classrooms: A universal design for learning approach.* Cengage Learning.

Hock, M. F., Bulgren, J. A., & Brasseur-Hock, I. F. (2017). The strategic instruction model: The less addressed aspects of effective instruction for high school students with learning disabilities. *Learning Disabilities Research & Practice, 32*(3), 166–179.

Hughes, C. A., Morris, J. R., Therrien, W. J., & Benson, S. K. (2017). Explicit instruction: Historical and contemporary contexts. *Learning Disabilities Research & Practice, 32*(3), 140–148. https://doi.org/10.1111/ldrp.12142

Minarik, D. W., & Lintner, T. (2011). The push for inclusive classrooms and the impact on social studies design and delivery. *Social Studies Review, 50*(1), 52–55.

Minarik, D., & Lintner, T. (2016). *Social studies and exceptional learners.* National Council for the Social Studies Publications.

National Council for the Social Studies. (2013). *The college, career, and civic life (C3) framework for social studies state standards: Guidance for enhancing the rigor of K–12 civics, economics, geography, and history.* National Council for the Social Studies Publications.

Pashler, H., Bain, P. M., Bottge, B. A., Graesser, A., Koedinger, K., McDaniel, M., & Metcalfe, J. (2007). *Organizing instruction and study to improve student learning. IES practice guide* (NCER 2007-2004). National Center for Education Research.

Rao, K. (2017). UDL and intellectual disability: What do we know and where do we go? *Journal of Intellectual and Developmental Disability, 55*(1) 37–47.

Rosenshine, B. (2012). Principles of instruction: Research-based strategies that all teachers should know. *American Educator, 39,* 12–19. https://eric.ed.gov/?id=EJ971753

Swan, K., Lee, J. K., & Grant, S. G. (2018). *Inquiry design model: Building inquiries in social studies.* National Council for the Social Studies.

U.S. Department of Education. (2004). *Individuals With Disabilities Education Act.* U.S. Department of Education, Office of Planning, Evaluation and Policy Development.

U.S. Department of Education. (2010). *ESEA blueprint for reform.* U.S. Department of Education, Office of Planning, Evaluation and Policy Development.

CHAPTER 8

ACTIVE AND ENGAGING SOCIAL STUDIES INSTRUCTION FOR HIGHER LEVEL LEARNING

Melissa Martin
University of South Carolina Aiken

Alison Puliatte
State University of New York Plattsburgh

In 2010, the National Council for the Social Studies (NCSS) published revised standards for K–12 classrooms. These standards provide a framework for educators promoting civic competence and focusing on themes related to culture, time and place, individuals, power and governance, goods and services, and science and technology (NCSS, 2022). That is, these standards are meant to teach and instill a sense of civic responsibility among K–12 learners by outlining the needed competencies to positively impact society. Moreover, the authors of these standards indicated the goal was for

Creating an Inclusive Social Studies Classroom for Exceptional Learners, pages 155–173
Copyright © 2024 by Information Age Publishing
www.infoagepub.com
All rights of reproduction in any form reserved.

students to be knowledgeable about the world and to use and apply this knowledge in their own lives (NCSS, 2022).

In order to think critically to make informed decisions and problem solve, K–12 students must practice these skills in the classroom. They simply cannot memorize content and take tests and quizzes. Instead, students must be actively engaged in intentionally designed instruction that promotes civic engagement and an understanding about the world around them during both the school years and across the lifespan. Thus, it is critical that K–12 social studies educators provide strategies that promote the transfer of learning, so students with and without disabilities can acquire knowledge, and generalize and maintain requisite skills across both time and setting.

This chapter will outline higher level strategies that can be implemented in social studies classrooms to help students transfer learning to the real world. Specifically, teachers can implement project-based learning, simulations, kinesthetic learning, experiential learning, role play, and cognitive strategy instruction in classrooms. Providing strategies that promote critical thinking and problem solving are important for students as they engage in their classrooms, communities, and across with the world.

PROJECT-BASED LEARNING

Minarik and Lintner (2016) defined project-based learning (PBL) as a learning experience in which students "apply information they learn about a topic to a real-life or simulated situation" (p. 52). Using PBL, students can *make sense* of societal challenges by thinking critically to analyze the potential impact of these challenges on communities (Duke et al., 2021). Duke and colleagues (2021) noted this "sensemaking" includes "opportunities for students to inquire, interpret, elaborate, and link new learning to their prior knowledge and experiences" (p. 163). This helps students to not view assignments or classroom-based tasks or discussions as occurring in isolation. Instead, it helps them generalize and adapt their knowledge and skills to other disciplines and make connections to the real world.

Because the use of the PBL strategy requires students to analyze, evaluate, and solve authentic real-world problems, it has been shown to increase student learning, especially when used during social studies instruction (Brooks & Rock, 2018; Kingston, 2018). Kingston (2018) examined nine studies utilizing PBL in Grades 2–12. Overall, PBL improved learning as compared to traditional social studies instruction.

Additionally, Brooks and Rock (2018) noted the use of PBL in PreK to 12th grade classrooms increases engagement among learners. PBL is by nature collaborative. That is, it enlists a team to solve authentic tasks and problems. Although students may need lectures and notes to learn the foundational knowledge prior to an activity, PBL is hands-on and requires group collaboration. Thus, it promotes student engagement. For students with disabilities, the teacher may need to model how to work collaboratively and give explicit instruction about the PBL activity before asking groups to begin thinking critically and start problem solving.

Furthermore, the skills associated with PBL require students to connect new learning to existing knowledge. For students with disabilities, this may be challenging as they may not know the needed content knowledge, or they may not be fluent in this knowledge to make meaning or connect it to new skills.

Practical and Engaging Strategies

The content included in social studies curriculum and standards lends itself to the implementation of PBL. Some practical strategies are described below:

1. Geography: Students are asked to evaluate the impact of rezoning schools. Districts and counties assign students and families to specific schools based on where they live. Teachers could ask students to evaluate a potential rezoning of schools. Students can analyze the impact of these changes on the community (e.g., population size, transportation/buses).
2. Economics: The movement of goods is a fundamental logistic. Students can analyze the potential lack of fuel supply for diesel trucks and its impact on transporting goods to various communities (e.g., urban, suburban, and rural).
3. Government: Local, state, and federal elections are consequential in our lives. Students can analyze the impact of elections by hosting a mock campaign and election.

Implementation and Suggestions for the Future

It is well-documented that PBL improves student learning (Kingston, 2018) and engagement (Brooks & Rock, 2018). To provide access to students with disabilities, it may be imperative to implement accommodations. These may include activating background knowledge, defining key terms, explicitly teaching new skills related to the PBL task/activity, or intentionally grouping students to provide peer supports or more intensive teacher support.

To implement PBL, teachers should consider utilizing direct instruction pedagogy to first teach the students the foundational knowledge prior to participating in PBL. This may include a preassessment to determine students' prior knowledge and differentiated instruction to address the varied levels of student knowledge. In addition to direct instruction, teachers should consider if the PBL opportunities consist of potentially sensitive information or scenarios that may trigger an emotional response from students. This will allow teachers to be proactive by providing students with support prior to the PBL to assist them with applying effective coping skills.

SIMULATIONS

Simulations are real world tasks students actively engage in to determine an outcome. This is different than a game or reenactment in which students are recreating events that have already happened or that have a predetermined ending. The foundational principle of a simulation is that students are active participants who are making decisions that will directly or indirectly impact the outcome of the activity (Wright-Maley, 2015a). Research indicates the use of simulations in social studies classrooms increases both critical thinking and democratic skills among students (Wright-Maley, 2015a). Furthermore, researchers have outlined four criteria to define simulations: (a) reflect the real world; (b) portray significance; (c) engage learners actively; and (d) facilitate learning through intentional collaborations with the teacher (Wright-Maley, 2015b; Wright-Maley, 2015c).

The use of simulations in classrooms has resulted in increased achievement, engagement, retention, and use of critical thinking and problem-solving skills (Wright-Maley, 2015a). Wright-Maley (2015b) examined 16 studies published between 1981 and 2015. Although some (six) of these studies outlined specific challenges of implementing simulations (e.g., time consuming, teacher as facilitator, lack of background knowledge to complete activity), most of the studies outlined at least one benefit of this strategy including (a) understanding real-world problems, (b) fostering empathy and democratic skills in students, and (c) recognizing problems are complex and intricate.

Simulations may be a part of the implementation of PBL (Lo, 2017). Lo (2017) contends the use of simulations can help students garner the needed skills and knowledge associated with real-world tasks (the goal of PBL). Therefore, it may be impactful to integrate both strategies in social studies curriculum and instruction.

Practical and Engaging Strategies

Teachers need to ensure students are active participants in simulations. Some examples of how to implement this strategy are briefly described below.

1. Pandemic: Students can simulate the outbreak of a pandemic and analyze how the perspectives of health officials, world leaders, communities, and families may differ. They could then analyze how specific decisions can have tremendous impact on various stakeholders.
2. Immigration at the Southern Border: Students can be asked to simulate the part of various stakeholders impacted by immigration. This may include local government, farmers/ranchers, community citizens, immigrants, as well as local, state, and national policymakers. Students can simulate the impact of decisions on the other stakeholders to truly understand this complex real-world problem.
3. Poverty: Students can simulate a family living in poverty. They can be provided with an array of situations and are asked to problem-solve mitigants or solutions (e.g., losing a job; lack of money to use public transportation).

All of these examples provide students with scenarios in which their decisions impact the outcome of the simulation.

Implementation and Suggestions for the Future

Because the use of simulations in the classroom is complex, it is important teachers are mindful when implementing this strategy. First, teachers need to ensure students are active and that their decisions truly impact the result or outcome of the simulation. This is different than role-playing, games, and reenactments. This strategy is much more purposeful and requires extensive consideration and planning. It is important not to trivialize the topic of the simulation by attempting to have students put themselves in the experience (Dack et al., 2016). Rather, students in a simulation need to understand the hard history and should be asking, what did people do in these situations and what options did they have?

For students with disabilities, simulations may be an effective way to practice and apply their skills in authentic, meaningful ways. As noted previously, it is vital that students have the required background content knowledge to have access to this strategy. If you ask students to evaluate immigration, they must first know about this topic and its impact on people's lives. If they lack the foundational knowledge, their ability to apply and transfer knowledge will be limited. Thus, teachers need to ensure they have still taught students the social studies content related to the activities being implemented. Simply introducing content through an activity may be ineffective and lack the potential impact on students with disabilities.

KINESTHETIC LEARNING TO SUPPORT CRITICAL THINKING

Kinesthetic learning activities allow students to physically engage in the learning process by using "movements and other kinesthetic senses that provide an authentic learning experience to actively engage students in a lesson, create connections with real-world situations, and make learning more enjoyable and fun" (Jabonetea & Mejarito, 2021, p. 2). Kinesthetic learning is supported by the embodied cognition theory which purports the human body impacts the function of the brain and cognitive processes (Foglia & Wilson, 2013). This theory supports the idea that the body, through physical movements, is capable of changing the function of the brain. Pedagogy that supports the embodied cognition theory includes physical activities that aim to improve cognition.

Martin et al. (2021) describe three benefits of kinesthetic learning: (a) makes learning relevant to students by connecting to their interests and experiences, (b) fosters creativity, innovation, and curiosity, and (c) supports activities focused on exploration, evaluation, and action. Additionally, kinesthetic activities help to increase students' academic performance (Richards, 2012) and their emotional and psychological development (Sibley & Etnier, 2003). The benefits of kinesthetic activities as an instructional practice include improvement in language and reading comprehension skills (Cassar & Jang, 2010) and improved learning and understanding of both mathematics and science concepts and content (Abrahamson, 2013; Ayala et al., 2013; Kellman & Massey, 2013; Hall & Nemirovsky, 2012). Additionally, movement integrated into lessons results in positive attitudes in students as seen through their increased participation, interest, and concentration (Strean, 2011).

In the context of students with disabilities, kinesthetic activities have shown promising outcomes. Kosmas et al. (2018) explored the effects of the motion-based technology Kinect-based educational games with elementary students with disabilities. The game uses a Microsoft Kinect camera to detect body movements. The game had a positive impact on students' short-term memory skills as measured through a word recall test as well as their emotional state as related to their learning experience. Additionally, Martin et al. (2021) purport kinesthetic learning "mitigates the lecture-read-show-write instructional model that may hinder content comprehension for many students, including students with exceptionalities" (p. 27).

Practical and Engaging Strategies

Martin et al. (2021) described kinesthetic learning activities for social studies content in inclusive classrooms aimed to teach social studies concepts and have students physically engaged in learning. Two examples of the activities described are human maps and anchoring devices.

1. Human maps involve having students use their bodies to physically map events. Students stand on a large floor map of Washington, DC to physically represent important landmarks including the Capitol, Supreme Court Building, Library of Congress, House and Senate Office Buildings, and White House. Additional students represent a piece of proposed legislation and they physically walk through the map to model the steps that are taken for a bill to become law.
2. Anchoring devices support student learning by connecting new learning to previous learning that involves physical movement—this is the anchor. For example, an anchor may be the game of tug-of-war (Martin et al., 2021). The teacher makes connections between the game tug-of-war and the characteristics of the Cold War. The students then engage in a game of tug-of-war. After the game, the students revisit the characteristics of the Cold War. The use of the kinesthetic anchoring device, in this case, the game of tug-of-war, helps students remember the characteristics of the historical event.

Implementation and Suggestions for the Future

While kinesthetic activities are an engaging and motivating way for students to learn social studies content, it is important for educators to be cognizant of the physical demands of such activities to prevent the unintended exclusion of students with physical disabilities from class activities (Gravett, 2018). Educators should be aware of ableism that may be present during kinesthetic activities that exclude less able-bodied students. This concern can be avoided by planning inclusive activities through a Universal Design of Learning (UDL) lens. For example, activities that require students to move around the classroom should be organized in a manner that allows for ease of movement for all students by taking into consideration the space needs of students with mobility devices.

In an age where remote learning is common, the extent to which remote learning activities incorporate kinesthetic learning needs to be considered. Kinesthetic learning activities are important components to include in remote instruction to increase student motivation, attention, and connection making between concepts and prior knowledge. However, asynchronous learning modules seldom integrate kinesthetic activities (Jabonetea & Mejarito, 2021). There is a need for educators to create activities for remote instruction that incorporate kinesthetic learning into their lessons such as hands-on learning, songs, music, role play, drama, games, and creative movements such as dance (Jabonetea & Mejarito, 2021).

EXPERIENTIAL LEARNING

Experiential learning theory (ELT) is based on a model of learning whereby students actively reflect on their experiences, apply their learning to new situations, and act based on their new learning (Kolb, 1984; McCarthy, 2016). Thinking is transformed when students reflect on concrete experiences and makes connections and comparisons between these new experiences. Students then apply their learning by modifying future actions based on the experiential learning acquired.

According to ELT, learning takes place when students move through a four-stage model: (a) concrete experience, (b) transformation of experience, (c) abstract conceptual, and (d) active experimentation (Kolb & Kolb, 2017). During the concrete experience stage, students acquire new information without bias through real-world hands-on new experiences. The transformation of experience stage allows students to reflect, from different perspectives, on the experience presented in the first stage. In the abstract conceptual stage, students translate their observations from the first stage into theories or practices. During the active experimentation stage, students apply their learning to new and more complex scenarios. The stages are cyclical therefore access can begin at any of the four stages. However, for meaningful learning to take place, students must experience all four stages.

Experiential education includes four pedagogical principles: authenticity, active learning, drawing on student experience, and providing mechanisms for connecting experience to future opportunity (Carver, 1996). The principle of authenticity refers to meaningful activities, rewards, and consequences that are relevant to the students' lives. The principle of active learning requires students to be physically and cognitively engaged in their learning. Drawing on student experiences involves guiding students in making connections between new learning and their prior knowledge and experiences. And providing mechanisms for connecting experience to future opportunity requires the teacher to assist students with reflecting on their learning with the goal of applying their learning to future contexts.

The benefits of incorporating experiential learning activities into social studies instruction include an increase in students' understanding of social issues and expanded learning experiences outside of the classroom (Burch et al., 2019). Experiential learning activities also provide students with opportunities to analyze primary documents, develop evidence-based arguments, self-examine their own beliefs, and examine the point of view of others (Provenzo et al., 2008).

Experiential learning is particularly beneficial when students are learning about social issues. Experiential learning activities support students in developing an understanding of themselves and others by examining events and the world from different points of view (Provenzo et al., 2008). Students develop self-understanding by reflecting on their own beliefs and actions when engaged in the experiential learning activities. Students develop an understanding of others through paradigm shifting by experiencing events through the lens of others which help build an understanding and acceptance of different points of view.

Experiential learning activities are an effective way to teach about social justice because they provide opportunities to build trust and a sense of community within the classroom (Carver, 1996; Obenchain & Ives, 2006). Additionally, the self-reflection element of experiential learning aligns with the goals of social justice education which require students to examine and understand their own beliefs to better understand the viewpoints of others (Cochran-Smith et al., 2009).

Furthermore, experiential learning positively impacts attitudes about disability. Wozencroft and colleagues (2015) note that this learning strategy can increase student engagement, promote relationship building, and create a safe learning environment. Researchers from this study administered the Scale of Attitudes Toward Disabled Persons (SADP) as a pre- and post-assessment. This scale asks participants to rank 24 items on a 6-point scale (*I disagree very much* to *I agree very much*). Between these administrations, students received 12 weeks of instruction about disabilities. Results indicate a significant change in attitudes between the pre- and post- assessment. Researchers note the importance of education and people's attitudes towards students with disabilities.

Practical and Engaging Strategies

Virtual reality experiences are an effective pedagogical tool for students to engage in experiential learning activities without the need to leave the classroom (Asad et al., 2021). For example, students can engage in virtual reality experiences that allow them to visit national monuments and geographic landforms. Students can virtually engage in government processes or viewing key historical events.

The Virtual History Museum (VHM) is a free experiential learning web-based tool that integrates the principles of Universal Design for Learning (UDL) into a social studies curriculum (Bouck et al., 2009). The teacher acts as the museum curator by selecting the exhibits for the students to explore. Exhibits can include artifacts and texts related to historical figures or select global events. Teachers can alter the museum texts or create their own texts to align with the students' reading level, interests, and curricular focus. VHM integrates the UDL principle of multiple means of representation through the variety of materials provided. For example, exhibits may include text, images, videos, audio, and physical artifacts. VHM integrates the UDL principle of multiple means of expression by offering students multiple modalities to demonstrate learning. For example, students can engage in writing activities such as essays, letters to historical figures, newspaper articles, and diaries. Students can also demonstrate their learning by creating charts and maps of geographical locations. VHM integrates the UDL principle of multiple means of engagement by allowing students to work independently, in groups, or as a whole class. This allows teachers to vary the pace of learning for all students based on the individual supports needed. VHM is an effective tool to use both in general education and special education settings and can be modified to meet the individual needs and interests of all students. A sampling of museums that offer extensive virtual experiences are outlined in Table 8.1.

In-person engagement strategies include field trips, guest speakers, and service-learning opportunities. Social studies teachers can plan field trips to local historical sites, museums, and government facilities. Guest speakers from local sites or agencies can also visit social studies classrooms to share knowledge and expertise. Additionally, teachers can provide service learning opportunities which increases engagement and benefits students both with and without disabilities (Wozencroft, et al., 2015).

Implementation and Suggestions for the Future

According to Kolb and Kolb (2017), there are four common roles teachers play in experiential learning activities: facilitator, subject expert, standard-setter/evaluator, and coach. Teachers should adopt all four roles during experiential learning activities. When in the facilitator role, teachers

TABLE 8.1 Virtual Experiences Resources

Title	Website
Smithsonian Museum of American History	https://americanhistory.si.edu/exhibitions/online
National Women's History Museum	https://www.womenshistory.org/womens-history/online-exhibits
Anne Frank House	https://www.annefrank.org/en/
British Museum	https://www.britishmuseum.org/
Franklin D. Roosevelt Presidential Library & Museum	http://www.fdrlibraryvirtualtour.org/index.asp

assist students with reflecting on their experiences in the activity through discussions and relationship building. As the subject expert, teachers help students make connections between their experience in the activity and the social studies content. This is often facilitated by teacher modeling, lectures, readings, and supporting students' critical thinking related to the content. As the standard setter/evaluator, teachers evaluate students' learning based on standards related to content and performance expectations. While in the coaching role, teachers work collaboratively with students to help them apply their learning to real life contexts.

It is important to note that teacher feedback is a crucial element supporting student learning during experiential learning activities (Burch et al, 2019). It is necessary for teachers to provide specific feedback both during and immediately following the experiential learning activity. Teacher's provide feedback to support student meaning-making by reflecting upon the experience and connecting the experience to prior knowledge and experiences.

Challenges to implementing experiential learning activities into instructional practices include diminished teacher self-efficacy for implementing the strategies due to the additional time and support needed to implement the strategies (Speicher, 2021). Therefore, it would be beneficial for practicing teachers to create planning and support teams of teachers when implementing experiential learning activities. Teachers can work together to plan activities, debrief after implementation, and provide collaborative feedback to enhance the experiential learning activities. A second challenge to implementing experiential learning activities is the associated cost. While access to virtual reality technology may serve as a barrier due to the financial restraints of schools, it may serve as a viable option for remote rural school districts with limited opportunities for their students to engage in real world in-person experiential learning contexts.

ROLE PLAY

Role play in social studies is an instructional technique that increases student engagement (Bonwell & Eison, 1991) by having students assume the role of historical characters or acting out associated historical events. Yardley-Matwiejczuk (1997) describes role play in terms of "as-if" scenarios in which the students are performing "as if" they are the character they are portraying. Role play typically follows a three phase process. During phase one, the teacher provides the students with content knowledge related to their character and the historical event in question. During phase two, the students engage in the role play by acting out the event. Phase three is the reflection phase where students reflect on their experience by making connections to their prior learning experiences and analyzing the characters' actions as compared to their own beliefs and understandings.

Yardley-Matwiejczuk (1997) categorizes role play activities as being either passive or active. During passive role play, students act "as if" they are the character in order to mimic his/her exact experiences. For example, a student engaged in passive role play may read a speech written or follow a detailed script that is an exact replica of their character's actions. In active role play, students are given more freedom to develop their character's actions and spoken language. In active role play, students act as if they are the character by developing their own scripts and actions based on what they have learned about the character's beliefs and past actions.

Role play provides students with opportunities to explore different perspectives (Lo, 2018). Incorporating role play into social studies classrooms supports student understanding of diversity, equity, and inclusion (Wright-Maley, 2015b). Students engaged in role play develop cross-cultural awareness and understanding when the scenarios depict varying beliefs and practices. Such scenarios aid in reducing intolerance and stereotypes particularly when the student's role (character perspective) is different from their own (Shannon, 2019).

Role play activities provide opportunities to explore controversial issues by students assuming roles with contrasting views. This allows students to examine issues from the point of view of others and deepen their understanding through reflection (Lo, 2018). Additionally, when students take on various roles they are, ostensibly, provided new-found "gateways to multiple perspectives—avenues that help students see (and even understand) the differences among us, but also the shared beliefs that ultimately bring us together" (Lo, 2018, p. 333).

Practical and Engaging Strategies

Examples of role play activities for the social studies classroom are described below:

1. The Arts-Integrated Academic Club described by Anderson and Valero (2020) is a role play approach that incorporates multisensory (visual, auditory, tactile, and kinesthetic) activities to help students retain and recall social studies content in a socially and emotionally supportive academic setting. The club includes four main components: (a) collaborative membership, (b) classroom structure and personalization, (c) multisensory learning activities, and (d) authentic assessment. The collaborative membership component an integrated, inclusive classroom model where all stu-

dents are welcomed and encouraged to participate. The classroom structure and personalization components of the club include entering routines such as secret handshakes, dramatic role play for the teacher and students, agreed upon club norms for behavior, costumes for teacher and students, props, and room decorations. The multisensory learning activities component includes visual arts, performing or drama, music, and dance or movement art forms. For example, students can engage in a role play where they learn about a historical figure and then reenact a critical event in the life of the figure selected. Students prepare for the role play by researching the historical figure, writing a script, creating costumes, designing props, and selecting or creating music to accompany the performance. The authentic assessment component allows students to be assessed for their overall participation and engagement and individualized skill outcomes related to language, cognition, and social/emotional, goals.
2. Role play examples (Lo, 2018) include Imperialism and the beginnings of globalization where students assume the role of a delegate to a seventeenth-century global summit. A second example, related to early tool evolution and migration patterns, has students taking on the role of a member of a prehistoric tribe. Students can also assume the role of merchant or trader as they role play the origins of early trading systems.
3. An example of passive role play (Teachers' Curriculum Institute's, 1998) focuses on the French Revolution activity. Here, students are assigned roles based on the three French Estates. Students act out their designated role related to the overthrow of King Louis XVI and the Reign of Terror. This is an example of a passive role play as students must accurately adhere to the historical record of the events led to the French Revolution.
4. Alvarez (2008) describes an active role play that reenacts the development of the Declaration of Independence and Constitution. In this activity, students assume the roles of notable philosophers and leading political figures. As an example of an active role play, students are given the freedom to interpret—and speak for—their chosen character as they deem fit.
5. Morch et al. (2019) describe a role play that uses Minecraft to address social studies content. The teacher initially presents students with content background and knowledge (e.g., colonial agitation for independence). Using Minecraft, students construct replicas of building and/or scenes relevant to the content (e.g., the Pennsylvania State House). Students then role play by using their Minecraft

creations as historical backdrops (e.g., portray members of the Constitutional Convention).
6. Social process role play activities allow students to focus on human interaction and communication (Uzun & Uygun, 2022). For example, a social process activity relevant to the social studies classroom can related to power, difference, and social class. These constructs can be manifest through ice-breakers, team building activities, and kinesthetic-based scenarios. Simply, students are experiencing relevant dynamics evidenced throughout history by experiencing—and reflecting upon—them in the social studies classroom.

Implementation and Suggestions for the Future

When teachers consider which roles to select for students to play, Lo (2018) cautions to avoid those that are "derogatory, inauthentic, or portray a skewed sense of history that may induce trauma" (p. 331). Lo (2018) recommends selecting figures that are, if not familiar, at least relevant to the lives and experiences of students. This provides a connection between the past (as evidenced through the historical figure) and the present. Additionally, assigning roles that differ from the perspectives of students facilitates tolerance and the recognition of difference. This may be initially challenging for some students but, at its core, it facilitates and develops an understanding and acceptance of other perspectives.

A note of caution for teachers to consider is that role playing may result in the unintended trivialization of tragic historical events and may facilitate and support misconceptions for students (Dack et al., 2016). Teachers can mitigate this by modeling both respect for and sensitivity towards the event in question. Teachers should also ensure fidelity to both the event and the figures being represented. Teachers also need to be mindful that role playing controversial topics may upset some students and parents (Lo, 2018). The concern of upsetting students is addressed through the first and third phases of the role-playing activity. During the first stage, students develop foundational knowledge of the issues and points of view of their assigned role. This development of accurate, contextual knowledge is crucial in addressing and preventing biases and stereotypes. During the third stage, students make personal connections (or points of contrast) between their assigned role and their own beliefs. Additionally, this stage allows students to reflect upon how they perspectives may have shifted by assuming a particular role. Teachers can address parental concerns by being both proactive and transparent. Communicate to parents the purpose, goals, and learning outcomes of the activity and stress that, in no way, is the activity meant to undermine or dismiss established beliefs.

COGNITIVE STRATEGY INSTRUCTION

A common strategy to provide students with explicit instruction is cognitive strategy instruction (CSI). CSI helps students, including those with disabilities, generalize and transfer knowledge and skills to other content areas via real-word applications. Specifically, CSI "embeds metacognitive or self-regulation strategies in structured cognitive routines that help students monitor and evaluate" their own learning (Krawec & Montague, n.d., p. 1). Pfannenstiel and colleagues (2015) noted that the implementation of metacognitive strategies not only helps students plan and monitor their own strategy use, but also assists students in modifying or adapting their strategy use to improve learning. This is critical for students with disabilities. Often students can use a strategy in a controlled, often "contextualized" setting. That is, students may use a math strategy to solve word problems but have difficulty realizing that they may use this same strategy within another content area or setting. Therefore, CSI may help students generalize and transfer skills and knowledge.

CSI has proven effective for students with disabilities, specifically in reading, writing, and writing (Krawec & Montague, n.d.). Because good social studies instruction often integrates concepts from other content areas, it is logical that the use of CSI may be warranted and effective.

Practical and Engaging Strategies

Teachers can use CSI when presenting complex content to students with and without disabilities. CSI consists of six steps: (a) activating background knowledge; (b) introducing the new strategy including providing a rationale; (c) modeling how to use the new strategy; (d) memorizing the strategy; (e) practicing the strategy (to promote fluency); and (f) using the new strategy independently with no prompting (Krawec & Montague, n.d.). Because this process is complex, students may need several practice sessions (Step 5) to become fluent and, ultimately, to use it with little support or prompting.

Implementation and Strategies for Future Use

This strategy provides the needed information to activate students' background knowledge and sufficient ("enough") practice opportunities before independent utilization.

In social studies, teachers could use CSI when teaching about the Civil War. Learning about war (or any conflict) can be complicated and complex for some students as it requires an understanding of people, places, time, and events. There is a sequential aspect to this as well – origin, events, conclusion, impact. Teachers can "set the stage" by connecting the event (the Civil War) to the lives and experiences of students (dispute with a sibling or a neighbor). Next, teachers introduce the timeline and emphasize how important it will be to understanding sequence of events. Students are asked to memorize this strategy (the use of timelines). Next, teachers model this new strategy by producing a timeline of, say, student birthdays. This makes the strategy relevant and accessible to students. The strategy is then used throughout instruction by both teacher and student whereby, ultimately, the student can (and does) create their own timelines relevant to the Civil War.

CSI can be combined with other strategies described in this chapter including PBL. Outlined below is a description about how to implement CSI using a PBL activity.

1. Students analyze and evaluate the impact of school rezoning. Background knowledge is initially activated by teaching key vocabulary and providing key historical, economic, political and geography content (context). Next, teachers should introduce a strategy linked to analysis and evaluation. Teachers would demonstrate (model) how to use this strategy within different contexts and from different perspectives. Students will memorize and practice the strategies with the teacher and peers. Finally, after sufficient practice, students can independently use the strategy to analyze and evaluate and the rezoning of schools.

CONCLUSION

This chapter described PBL, simulations, kinesthetic learning, experiential learning, and role play as higher-level strategies that can be implemented in social studies classrooms to assist all students. These strategies address the NCSS standards for K–12 content knowledge learning (NCSS, 2022).

When preparing to integrate higher level strategy instruction into social studies lessons, it is important that teachers offer scaffolded supports to all students as they learn and apply new skills and gain new competence. This begins with pre-assessing students to determine if they need direct instruction to develop the needed background knowledge in order to fully participate in the activities (Martin et al., 2021). Students need to have an adequate level of social studies content knowledge in order to make connections between their background knowledge and the activity being used. These connections will result in deeper understanding and application of the content. If the preassessment indicates that some students are lacking the requisite background knowledge required for the activity, direct and explicit instruction is needed to adequately prepare the students for the activity. The direct and explicit instruction should follow the steps of cognitive strategy instruction (CSI) described in this chapter.

REFERENCES

Abrahamson, D. (2013). Building educational activities for understanding: An elaboration on the embodied-design framework and its epistemic grounds. *International Journal of Child–Computer Interaction, 2*(1), 1–16.

Alvarez, P. (2008). Students play the notables: Testing a simulation exercise. *History Teacher, 41*(2), 179–197.

Anderson, A., & Valero, L. (2020). Supporting academic vocabulary and social emotional skills of students with learning disabilities through an arts-integrated social studies approach. *Teaching Exceptional Children, 53*(2), 150–162.

Ayala, N. A. R., Mendívil, E. G., Salinas, P., & Rios, H. (2013). Kinesthetic learning applied to mathematics using Kinect. *Procedia Computer Science, 25*, 131–135.

Asad, M. M., Naz, A., Churi, P., & Tahanzadeh, M. M. (2021). Virtual reality as pedagogical tool to enhance experiential learning: A systematic literature review. *Education Research International*, 1–17.

Bonwell, C. C., & Eison, J. A. (1991). *Active learning: Creating excitement in the classroom.* (ASHE-ERIC Higher Education Report). School of Education and Human Development, George Washington University.

Bouck, E. C., Courtad, C. A., Heutsche, A., Okolo, C. M., & Englert, C. S. (2009). The virtual history museum a universally designed approach to social studies instruction. *Teaching Exceptional Children, 42*(2), 14–20.

Brooks, P., & Rock, T. C. (2018). Using social studies to lead project-based learning: An innovative teacher's story. *Social Studies and the Young Learner, 31*(2), 4–10.

Burch, G. F., Giambatista, R., Batchelor, J. H., Burch, J. J., Hoover, D., & Heller, N. A. (2019). A meta-analysis of the relationship between experiential learning and learning outcomes. *Decision Sciences Journal of Innovative Education, 17*(3), 239–273.

Carver, R. (1996). Theory for practice: A framework for thinking about experiential education. *Journal of Experiential Education, 19*, 8–13.

Cassar, A., & Jang, E. (2010). Investigating the effects of a game-based approach in teaching word recognition and spelling to students with reading disabilities and attention deficits. *Australian Journal of Learning Difficulties, 15*(2), 193–211.

Cochran-Smith, M., Shakman, K., Jong, C., Terrell, D., Barnatt, J., & McQuillan, P. (2009). Good and just teaching: The case for social justice in teacher education. *American Journal of Education, 115*(3), 347–377.

Dack, H., van Hover, S., & Hicks, D. (2016). "Try not to giggle if you can help it": The implementation of experiential instructional techniques in social studies classrooms. *The Journal of Social Studies Research, 40*(1), 39–52.

Duke, N. K., Halvorsen, A.-L., Strachan, S. L., Kim, J., & Konstantopoulos. (2021). Putting PBL to the test: The impact of project-based learning on second graders' social studies and literacy learning and motivation in low-SES school settings. *American Educational Research Journal, 58*(1), 160–200.

Foglia, L., & Wilson, R. A. (2013). Embodied cognition. *Wiley Interdisciplinary Reviews: Cognitive Science, 4*(3), 319–325.

Gravett, E. O. (2018). Response to "quick fix: Get up! Five ways to energize a classroom with physically active learning." *College Teaching, 66*(4), 211–212.

Hall, R., & Nemirovsky, R. (2012). Introduction to the special issue: Modalities of body engagement in mathematical activity and learning. *Journal of the Learning Sciences, 21*(2), 207–215.

Jabonetea, J. D., Mejarito, C. L. (2021). Integration of kinesthetic approaches in the core academic subjects: A compendium. *International Journal of Research Publications, 80*(1), 1–23.

Kellman, P. J., & Massey, C. M. (2013). Perceptual learning, cognition, and expertise. *The Psychology of Learning and Motivation, 58,* 117–165.

Kingston, S. (2018). Project based learning and student achievement: What does the research tell us? *PBL Evidence Matters, 1*(1), 1–11.

Kolb, D. A. (1984). *Experiential learning.* Prentice-Hall.

Kolb, A. Y., & Kolb, D. A. (2017). Experiential learning theory as a guide for experiential educators in higher education. *Experiential Learning & Teaching in Higher Education, 1*(1), 7–44.

Kosmas, P., Ioannou, A., & Retalis, S. (2018). Moving bodies to moving minds: A study of the use of motion-based games in special education. *TechTrends, 62,* 594–601.

Krawec, J., & Montague, M. (n.d.). *What is cognitive strategy instruction?* Current Practice Alerts on Teaching LD. https://s3.amazonaws.com/cmi-teaching-ld/alerts/21/uploaded_files/original_Alert19.pdf?1331403099

Lo, J. C. (2017). Adolescents developing civic identities: Sociocultural perspectives on simulations and role-play in a civic classroom. *Theory & Research in Social Education, 45*(2), 189–217.

Lo, J. C. (2018). "Can we do this every day?" Engaging students in controversial issues through role-play. *Social Education, 82*(6), 330–335.

Martin, M., Lintner, T., & Minarik, D. (2021). Kinesthetic social studies for students with exceptionalities. *Journal for the Liberal Arts and Sciences, 24*(2), 26–36.

McCarthy, M. (2016). Experiential learning theory: From theory to practice. *Journal of Business & Economics Research, 14*(3), 91–99.

Minarik, D., & Lintner, T. (2016). *Social studies & exceptional learners.* National Council for the Social Studies.

Morch, A. I., Mifsud, L., & Eie, S. (2019). Developing a model of collaborative learning with Minecraft for social studies classrooms using role-play theory and practice. In *Computer Supported Collaborative Learning Conference Proceedings* (pp. 272–279). International Society of the Learning Sciences. https://repository.isls.org/handle/1/1578

National Council for Social Studies. (2022, October 31). *National curriculum standards for social studies: A framework for teaching, learning, and assessment.* https://www.socialstudies.org/standards/national-curriculum-standards-social-studies

Obenchain, K., & Ives, B. (2006). Experiential education in the classroom and academic outcomes: For those who want it all. *Journal of Experiential Education, 29*(1), 61–77.

Pfannenstiel, K. H., Bryant, D. P., Bryant, B. R., & Porterfield, J. A. (2015). Cognitive strategy instruction for teaching word problems to primary-level struggling students. *Intervention in School and Clinic, 50*(5), 291–296.

Provenzo, E. F., Butin, D. W., & Angelini, A. (2008). *100 experiential learning activities for social studies, literature, and the arts, grades 5–12.* Corwin Press.

Richards, T. (2012). Using kinesthetic activities to teach Ptolemaic and Copernican retrograde motion. *Science and Education, 21*(6), 899–910.

Shannon, V. P. (2019). Role-play simulations and changing perceptions of the other: Model UN, model Arab league, and student views of the Muslim world. *International Studies Perspectives, 21,* 219–239.

Sibley, B., & Etnier, J. (2003). The relationship between physical activity and cognition in children: A meta-analysis. *Pediatric Exercise Science, 15*(3), 243–256.

Speicher, S. (2021). Building community using experiential education with elementary preservice teachers in a social studies methodology course. *Journal of Global Education and Research, 5*(2), 111–120.

Strean, W. B. (2011). Creating student engagement? HMM: Teaching and learning with humor, music, and movement. *Creative Education, 2*(3), 189–192.

Teachers' Curriculum Institute. (1998). Exploring the fervor of the French Revolution. In *History alive! World history program: Western Europe in the modern world* (pp. 45–88). Teachers' Curriculum Institute.

Uzun, C., & Uygun, K. (2022). The effect of simulation-based experiential learning applications on problem solving skills in social studies education. *International Journal of Contemporary Educational Research, 9*(1), 28–38.

Wozencroft, A. J., Pate, J. R., Griffiths, H. K. (2015). Experiential learning and its impact on students' attitudes toward youth with disabilities. *Journal of Experiential Education, 38*(2), 129–143.

Wright-Maley, C. (2015a). Beyond the "babel-problem": Defining simulations for the social studies. *The Journal of Social Studies Research, 39,* 63–77.

Wright-Maley, C. (2015b). What every social studies teacher should know about simulations. *Canadian Social Studies, 48*(1), 8–23.

Wright-Maley, C. (2015c). On "stepping back and letting go": The role of control in the success or failure of social studies simulations. *Theory & Research in Social Education, 43*(2), 206–243.

Yardley-Matwiejczuk, K. M. (1997). *Role play: Theory and practice.* SAGE Publications.

CHAPTER 9

SOCIAL STUDIES LITERACY

Daniel Wissinger
Indiana University of Pennsylvania

Susan De La Paz
University of Maryland

What was the Civil Rights Movement, and when did it begin? In addition, what role did youth in the African American community and their nonviolent protests play in helping to shape unjust segregation and discrimination laws for the entire nation? These types of questions are central to the study of United States History and state and national standards that require students to consider how continuity and change have influenced history (see, e.g., Pennsylvania Department of Education [PDE], 2002). The novice might address these questions by reading a textbook such as the *United States History: The Twentieth Century* (Lapsansky-Werner et al., 2019), and providing a factual answer (e.g., "The civil rights movement was a political movement against racial segregation and discrimination that started in 1954."). Rather than considering multiple textual accounts or points of view, the novice views information about the past as factual and something that might be retrieved from a textbook, which they view as an authority (van Drie & van Boxtel, 2008).

Creating an Inclusive Social Studies Classroom for Exceptional Learners, pages 175–196
Copyright © 2024 by Information Age Publishing
www.infoagepub.com
All rights of reproduction in any form reserved.

By contrast, despite ongoing debates about starting points (i.e., see Cassimere [1977] and opposition to *Plessy v. Ferguson* in 1896), the historian (or expert) recognizes that movements like those for civil rights are not simply a series of isolated events that occur in a single space in time. Rather, such events are situated in specific places in southern states in America and involved multiple causes and consequences. To understand both the successes and tragedies of the civil rights movement (and the influence of historical actors and groups such as youth), the historian sifts through the available historical evidence (e.g., letters, speeches, diaries, newspapers, and public records; Seixas & Mortan, 2013).

Historians who study the civil rights movement look beyond the "Montgomery to Memphis" timeframe (i.e., 1955 to 1968) and even historic icons such as Dr. Martin Luther King Jr., Rosa Parks, and James Baldwin. For example, civil rights scholar Harvard Sitkoff (1978) argued that the "seeds that would later bear fruit" in the civil rights movement were planted during the Great Depression and in the late 1930s when there were increasing protests in major American cities like Chicago and Baltimore, and a growing struggle to overthrow segregation and institutionalized racism. By the 1940s, the social structure of Black America continued to change (Gates et al., 2022). More than a half million African American workers joined the Congress of Industrialized Organizations (CIO) union, and membership in the NAACP increased from 50,000 to 450,000 members. Following the Supreme Court's landmark decision in *Smith v. Allright* (1944), African American voter registration increased by nearly 800,000 in 1948 and evolved into more expansive participation in political organizations in the 1950s.

Youth and young adults in the African American community also played a critical role in helping to shape unjust segregation and discrimination laws in the 1960s. Documents from the Martin Luther King Jr. Papers Project (King Research and Educational Institute, Stanford University) describe how Birmingham, Alabama became a "do-or-die" battleground for the civil rights movement in the Spring of 1963. Aware that support and participation in protests were beginning to lose traction, members of the Southern Christian Leadership Conference (SCLC) canvassed local schools for volunteers and began training them to use tactics of nonviolent protests (Welch, 2007). Using word-of-mouth and non-discrete forms of communication, more than 4,000 school children "ditched" class to march for justice on May 2–3, 1963. With the jails filled to capacity and the number of marchers growing, Birmingham authorities grew desperate. In *Witness to Freedom, Young People Who Fought for Civil Rights*, Rochelle (1993) reports first-hand accounts from Birmingham's "youngest freedom fighters." The fire department was ordered to use firehoses and police dogs were dispersed to contain and intimidate youth demonstrators. Members of the media and photographers watched in horror as police clubbed women, dogs attacked young children, and high-pressure water hoses pummeled young bodies to the ground. Though the media had largely ignored events coming out of Birmingham, the images and stories of police brutality and the mass jailing of American children became front page news in major outlets across the globe. On May 7th President John F. Kennedy held a press conference and, within days, a new federal bill outlawing segregation was introduced in the House of Congress (Rochelle, 1993).

Taken together, earlier movements to attain political rights evolved into a movement to exercise those rights (see Fairclough, 1990). While certain figures and events played more prominent roles (i.e., Dr. Martin Luther King Jr., and the Montgomery Bus Sit-in), the civil rights movement expanded across several decades, and was influenced by many elements including workers unions to youth and young adults within the African American community.

As demonstrated above and, similarly, reported in Wineburg's (1991) seminal work, the differences between novices and experts results from a difference in knowledge about historical facts or topics, as well as from a difference in knowledge about how to think about historical evidence. Learning these skills is an important aspect of social studies literacy and a part of the modern instructional landscape for all students, including those who are at risk and identified with disabilities (Bulgren et al., 2013). Perhaps more important, developing more advanced literacies in the social studies is an entry point for helping youth and young adults become more informed citizens who are active and engaged in public life (National Council of the Social Studies [NCSS], 2013).

In this chapter, we will discuss theoretical underpinnings and what it means to teach towards historical expertise. Next, we highlight practical strategies from the research literature that can be used by teachers to facilitate the development of both domain-general and more sophisticated social studies literacies. The final section of this chapter provides recommendations for how teachers and school professionals can get started and concludes with suggestions for future research.

PART 1: THEORETICAL UNDERPINNINGS AND TEACHING TOWARD EXPERTISE

Over the past two decades, extensive reforms in social studies education have changed the way students with disabilities are educated in the classroom. In part, these shifts have been shaped by changes in standards (Common Core State Standards; National Governors Association Center for Best Practices & Council of Chief State School Officers, 2010; *College, Career, & Civic Life [C3] Framework* [NCSS, 2013]) and calls for the integration of disciplinary literacy instruction in subject matter classrooms (Monte-Sano et al., 2017). Current standards, like those provided by the NCSS (2013), have mapped out key themes (e.g., culture, time, and continuity and change) and what students need to learn across grade-levels to foster the development of expertise. These expectations are consistent with models used in cognitive research and assert that mastery evolves from domain-general declarative knowledge to discipline-specific procedural knowledge (Alexander 2003, 2005).

Dimensions of Developing Expertise in Social Studies

One of the most respected models used to explain how expertise is developed is Alexander's (2003) model of domain learning, which consists of five dimensions: (a) topic knowledge [concrete first-order knowledge], (b) domain knowledge [both abstract first-order knowledge and second-order knowledge], (c) deep-level strategies [procedural knowledge how to transform knowledge in a domain], (d) epistemological beliefs [ideas about the nature and source of knowledge in the domain), and (e) situational interest [students can connect new topics to prior knowledge and the broader domain].

When applied to social studies, topic knowledge (which is sometimes called first-order knowledge) refers to specific, factual knowledge about historical dates, figures, or events. Domain knowledge is more enduring and includes both *first-order knowledge* and *second-order knowledge*, which are characterized as conceptual knowledge about elements of domain thinking such as cause and using evidence to construct narratives about the past. The third dimension involves deep-level strategies and active knowledge construction. The use of deep-level strategies is accompanied by a reduction in generic, surface-level strategies (e.g., rereading, comprehension, and paraphrasing) and an increase in strategy knowledge that informs how to construct history (e.g., asking questions, constructing interpretations, and evaluating historical evidence). Alexander's (2003) model proposes that, after students have progressed through the first three dimensions, their beliefs about knowledge shift and they begin to view domain knowledge as something that can be constructed (i.e., they develop epistemological beliefs). More advanced learners are likely to view the domain as more engaging, which facilitates greater interest and the capacity to generalize domain-specific thinking and knowledge to other topics and subjects (Alexander, 2003, 2005).

Bridging Theory on Expertise to the Extant Literature

In addition to explaining the dimensions of domain learning, Alexander's (2003) model can be used to organize the extant literature on social studies literacy. For example, a meta-analysis synthesizing more than 40 years of research with students with learning disabilities in the social studies revealed effective interventions for developing students' learning and knowledge in all five dimensions (Ciullo et al., 2020). While most of the studies have targeted students' topic and domain knowledge, a corpus of more recent studies reveals several promising strategies and forms of instruction that teachers can use to facilitate the use of deep-level strategies and changes in epistemological beliefs.

PART II: STRATEGIES FOR SOCIAL STUDIES LITERACY

To help teachers differentiate between more general strategies and instructional approaches, and those designed to scaffold the construction of knowledge, we have organized the next part of this chapter into two subsections: (a) domain-general strategies and instruction and (b) discipline-specific strategies and instruction. Our rationale for using these two categories is to acknowledge that there are critical differences between types of instruction targeting topic and domain knowledge and interventions that target deep-level strategies that help to shape epistemological beliefs and situational interest.

Domain-General Strategies and Instruction

In this section of the chapter, we highlight several practical and engaging practices that teachers can use to help students who are at risk or identified with disabilities develop important topic and domain general knowledge, which provides a foundation for more complex social studies literacies and thinking (National Research Council, 2000). These studies are organized around two themes: (a) general literacy and (b) writing.

General Literacy
Based on other reviews targeting intervention research with students with learning disabilities (LD; see Ciullo et al., 2020), we have summarized a select group of studies that target general literacy strategies and outcomes in the social studies, including questioning, the acquisition of vocabulary, and reading for comprehension.

Questioning. Strategies for questioning text can lead to more active processing of information, self-monitoring, and retention of topic and domain knowledge (Okolo & Ferretti, 2014). A study by Bulgren and colleagues (2011) investigated the effectiveness of a question-exploration routine (QER) on middle school students who were learning about modern warfare and the use of biological and chemical weapons. Students learned the QER in three instructional phases: "cue," "do," and "review." In the "do" phase, students learned the acronym ANSWER, which prompted them to:

1. *Ask* a critical question.
2. *Note* and explore key terms and basic knowledge needed to answer the critical questions.
3. *Search* for supporting questions and answer those questions.
4. *Work* out or formulate a clear, concise main-idea answer to the critical question.
5. *Explore* the main-idea answer in a related area.
6. *Relate* the main idea to today's real world.

Students used a graphic organizer while learning note-taking strategies, formed main-idea statements to answer critical and supporting questions, and were prompted to relate main ideas to the real world. Students with LD who learned the QER strategies increased their performance on multiple-choice, matching, and short-answer questions more than students who were exposed to lecture and discussion.

Vocabulary. Given the increased use of handhelds, phones, and other smart devices in the classroom, research findings with technologies and multimedia are critical (Wissinger & Ciullo, 2018). Kennedy and colleagues provide an example for how to use multi-media technologies (i.e., content acquisition podcasts [CAPs]) to provide vocabulary instruction to students in high school (Kennedy et al., 2015). Using cognitive theories on multi-media and instructional design, Kennedy and his colleagues blended the best features of podcasts with research-based instructional principals to develop a series of CAPS. Each CAP was between 6 to 9 minutes long and contained a narrated presentation on vocabulary terms that were paired with distinct images. In one study, the students were assigned to one of four types of multimedia-based vignettes: (a) CAPs containing explicit strategy instruction (EI), (b) CAPs with the keyword mnemonic strategy (KMS), (c) CAPs containing explicit instruction and keyword mnemonic strategy (EI + KMS), and (d) instructional videos with the same audio narration as student in the EI group. Students in each of the four conditions watched 10 CAPs per class period over three consecutive days. Outcomes included a 30-item multiple-choice assessment of vocabulary definitions and world history concepts (e.g., imperialism), and an application task that required students to write synonyms, antonyms, and any additional information that they knew about each term. The findings indicated that the combination of effective design principles (i.e., multimedia materials with redundancy, signaling, images and video) and mnemonic strategies were most effective for teaching vocabulary to adolescents with LD in secondary social studies classrooms.

Comprehension. Intervention research using text structures and content-enhancement strategies to enhance students' ability to read for understanding from social studies text has been expansive over the past four decades (Ciullo et al., 2020). We now review two especially relevant multicomponent interventions (using a combination of several evidence-based strategies) with students with disabilities in the social studies (O'Connor et al., 2017; Vaughn et al., 2013; Swanson et al., 2015).

Swanson and colleagues (2015) reported on the effectiveness of the Promoting Acceleration of Comprehension and Content Through Text (PACT) intervention with eighth grade students with disabilities. Over a period of 10 weeks, students acquired background knowledge and improved content reading comprehension. In this intervention, researchers provided lessons with an overarching question for the instructional unit with a motivational springboard (short video, photo, or map). This is referred to as a comprehension canopy. Students learned 4–5 vocabulary words each day and reviewed previously learned words in subsequent lessons. Next, students read and discussed informational texts in small teams. Teachers provided constructive feedback and encouraged students to offer text evidence and justification for answers to the comprehension canopy question. Eighth grade students with disabilities who were in the PACT condition outperformed comparison peers with disabilities on content knowledge and reading comprehension measures demonstrating PACT's effectiveness.

In O'Connor and colleagues' (2017) BRIDGES (building reading interventions designed for general education subjects) work, teachers taught students with disabilities reading comprehension strategies and a strategy for decoding multisyllabic words as they read expository texts. Teachers followed scripted lesson plans that included: 5 minutes of decoding practice using multisyllabic words pulled from the text; 5 minutes of academic word instruction; and 10–15 minutes of a comprehension strategy (main idea, compare and contrast, or cause and effect relationships) for reading brief history passages taken from textbooks, primary sources, or history websites that were modified to a lower reading level. Outcomes included multiple-choice vocabulary tests and researcher-designed comprehension measures that required students to express their understanding in writing. Students also completed a multiple choice and short answer content assessment that was based on the participating teachers' bank of content items. Students in the intervention condition made strong gains in reading and outperformed peers with disabilities in the control condition on all measures but did not improve on a standardized reading comprehension measure.

Writing

Explicit instruction (EI) is a direct, structured, and systematic approach for teaching academic skills, and it is an evidence-based approach to teaching students with disabilities. The underlying principles of EI include review, presenting new content in manageable steps, guided practice, corrective feedback, and opportunities for independent practice (Archer & Hughes, 2011). In the social studies literature, these principles can be found in a vast number of studies with students with LD (see Ciullo et al., 2020). One of the most effective examples is using Self-Regulated Strategy Development (SRSD) to teach expository writing (Harris et al., 2008). The SRSD approach incorporates a process by which students gradually take ownership of learning by (a) moving from teacher modeling to collaborative (group) practice to independent execution of specific academic and self-regulation strategies and (b) fading procedural scaffolds such as the use of graphics or other prompts that contain strategy steps (De La Paz, 2005).

Collins and colleagues (2021) examined the effectiveness of SRSD to improve third grade students' ability to read and summarize information from social studies texts in expository essays. Before implementing SRSD instruction with students, teachers completed 12 hours of practice-based professional development and received an hour of coaching each week (or two 30-min. sessions) across the 16 weeks of the study. Teachers provided SRSD strategy instruction to students using the heuristic, TIDE (topic sentence, important details, explain details, ending), for close reading, planning, and writing essays using social studies text. After instruction, SRSD students included more genre elements in their expository essays and improved the holistic quality of their writing. Students in the SRSD condition also included more genre elements when writing about an expository topic they remembered learning, and outperformed control students on a norm-referenced writing measure.

Summary

Evidence from the research literature shows there are several evidence-based strategies and instructional practices that teachers can use to enhance general literacies in the social studies. Using critical questions, embedded within graphic organizers, can help students learn key terms and vocabulary, identify main ideas in text, and make connections to real-world issues like how biological and chemical weapons have been used in war (and the long-term implications of such practices; Bulgren et al., 2011). Creating and using CAPs is another effective method for providing engaging vocabulary instruction using modern multimedia and tools that can be accessed on a standard cell phone (Kennedy et al., 2015). While programs like BRIDGES and PACT (O'Connor et al., 2017; Vaughn et al., 2013) are more resource and labor intensive, both approaches feature multiple evidence-based approaches (i.e., building background knowledge, vocabulary instruction, decoding strategies, discussion, and timely teacher feedback) that have been shown to increase reading comprehension. Last, based on the principals of SRSD, teaching strategies for close reading, planning, and providing text structures is an effective way to improve students with disabilities' expository writing (Collins et al., 2021).

Discipline-Specific Strategies and Instruction

Requirements for all students to become more proficient readers of evidence in support of the production of writing that is valued in the social studies community is a major challenge. However, promising lines of research have emerged and provide several evidence-based practices for how teachers can help their students develop more sophisticated social studies literacies. In this section, we discuss practical strategies and scaffolds that can be used to enhance students' historical reading and writing, as well as how group dialogue and discussion can be used to promote deep-level strategies and changes in epistemological beliefs.

Historical Reading and Writing

Research shows that experts in each discipline use distinct practices to read and think about text. In Wineburg's (1991) seminal work, he discovered that historical experts rely on three specific practices: sourcing, corroboration, and contextualization. For example, historians view the reading of source documents, artifacts, photographs, and artwork as detective work. Their goal is to move beyond the literal meaning of text and address underlying questions about the time, place, and circumstances in which the document was created. Moreover, the historian wants to understand who created the historical source, and whether they are trying to persuade their audience for some purpose (i.e., sourcing). The perspectives and facts given by one author are weighed against those of others (i.e., corroboration), and the historican thinks about information about the authors and their ideas in connection with information about the time and place that the events occurred (i.e., contextualization). Together, these ways of reading set the historian apart from novices and help them develop a more authentic understanding about the past (Wineburg, 1991).

How experts think about and read historical evidence also guides their production of text (Seixas & Morton, 2013). Learning strategies for historical reading and thinking helps students become more sophisticated writers (Wissinger & De La Paz, 2016). At the same time, crafting historical essays helps students read more critically and with greater levels of understanding (Stoe et al., 2017).

Cognitive Apprenticeship Framework

One of the more promising approaches for teaching students strategy-driven analytic skills is through the cognitive apprenticeship (CA) framework (Collins et al., 1991). For example, in two studies, De La Paz and colleagues (2014; De La Paz et al., 2017) implemented the heuristic *IREAD* to guide learners in reading and making annotations about historical evidence. Students first learned *IR* ("*identify* the author's purpose" and "*read* each paragraph and ask about the author's main ideas") to prompt them to determine the authors' point of view and to summarize important ideas in each document. Next, to teach students how to make judgments about the evidence they were reading (i.e., to source and contextualize text), they were provided instruction on the *EA* portion of the mnemonic ("*evaluate* the author's reliability" and "*assess* the influence of context"). The final component of the strategy was presented through the letter *D* ("*determine* the quality of the author's facts and examples"). Together, *IREAD* prompted students to analyze and critique text while making detailed notes to use later for planning essays. To help facilitate the historical reading process, students were provided a foldable cardstock that featured the *IREAD* mnemonic. Each flap on the cardstock provided prompts to make specific notations for each of the five steps in the process.

De La Paz and colleagues (also created the *H2W* (or "how to write") strategy to teach students a text structure for writing historical arguments, and embedded essential components (i.e., quote or evidence, explanation of evidence, and a judgment about the author's role, context, or use of facts) in an argumentative essay. Teachers also engaged students in reflection after writing, and students learned to analyze and improve previously written essays and to set goals for future historical investigations which reinforced important aspects of historical and general argument writing.

Consistent with SRSD (Harris et al., 2008), teachers first modeled how to use heuristics in ways that were visible, thinking aloud and making annotations on document cameras. In these sessions, teachers visually demonstrated how to *identify* the author's purpose, *read* and identify main ideas, *evaluate* the author's reliability, *assess* the influence of context, and *determine* the quality of the author's facts and examples as well as how to develop an essay using H2W. Perhaps more importantly, teachers showed students how to coordinate multiple cognitive processes for historical reading, discussing and writing. As students progressed into historical investigations four through six, teachers focused on students' application of strategies, with increasing emphasis on how they were to manage reading and writing processes on their own.

Building on De La Paz's earlier work, Wissinger and De La Paz (2020; Wissinger et al., 2021) evaluated the benefits of a CA for teaching historical reading and writing with fourth–sixth graders who had writing difficulties (WD). Each historical investigation was taught in 5 days, which allowed teachers to provide background information, model, facilitate guided practice, and hold discussions. Each lesson also included expansive resources and materials, such as digital images, audio, and video media due to the elementary students limited background knowledge on the topics.

Students learned to read historical evidence using a simplified heuristic, I3C, which prompted them to (a) *identify* the author's stance; (b) highlight *3* facts, ideas, or reasons supporting the author's stance; and (c) *check* for limitations in the author's argument, by considering reliability issues and problems related to drawing inferences from perspectives in a single source. Instruction in "check for limitations" also helped students compare perspectives across sources and explore the actions and intentions of historical authors across other sources.

Teachers provided instruction on text structure for writing historical arguments by first explaining a heuristic called PROVE IT! The prompt guided students to (a) *provide* background information, by describing the historical problem; (b) report—or state—your interpretation; (c) *offer* three reasons by including evidence from the documents; (d) *voice* the other side's interpretation; (e) *establish* a rebuttal, then consider; (f) *is* the argument convincing; and (g) *total* up what you know by adding a sentence that concludes your essay.

Consistent with earlier work by De La Paz and colleagues (2014, 2017), teachers actively taught the elementary students historical reading and writing heuristics and modeled them by thinking aloud (Collins et al., 1991). As students progressed through each historical investigation, teachers gradually released more responsibility to students who applied the heuristics with decreasing levels of scaffolding. The findings showed that elementary students in the I3C/PROVE IT! classes performed more than one-half of a standard deviation higher on historical essays than their peers who were exposed to a traditional form of instruction.

Group Dialogue and Discussion

The field now has ample support for the use of discussion as a tool for enhancing students' historical reading, writing, and thinking (De La Paz & Wissinger, 2017; Del Favero et al., 2007; Monte-Sano et al., 2021). Yet, helping students bridge the gap between spoken and written language does not happen naturally (Nussbaum & Edwards, 2011). Researchers have highlighted the connection between strategy-driven analytic skills developed through explicit heuristic instruction and scaffolded dialogue, and the retrieval and organization of information when it is time to write (Chin & Osborne, 2010; Yore et al., 2002).

For example, De La Paz and Wissinger (2017) examined the impact of teaching schemes and critical questions (see Walton et al., 2008) sixth- and seventh-grade students in general education social studies classrooms. General instructional procedures focused on a series of activities that featured: (a) examining controversial topics in U.S. history, (b) reading from conflicting source documents, (c) small group discussion, and (d) constructing argumentative essays. Students were also taught a modified version of De La Paz and Graham's (1997) DARE (*develop* a stance about the controversy, *add* evidence from the documents to support your stance, *rebut* arguments from the other side, and *end* by restating your stance) as a heuristic for including important elements in their historical writing. As a side note, instruction with DARE was provided because prior research indicated that students in elementary (Reznitskaya et al., 2007) and middle school (Nussbaum & Edwards, 2011) had difficulties transferring new ideas from discussions to their writing.

Discussion groups contained between 5 to 8 students of varying academic abilities. Teachers used two historically-related argument schemes (e.g., argument from expert opinion, and argument from consequences) and five critical questions from Walton et al.'s (2008) dialectical framework to engage students in dialogue and analyses of conflicting perspectives presented in historical controversies. Questions for the argument from expert opinion were: (a) "Is the author an expert on the historical topic?"; (b) "Is he/she a reliable source?"; and, (c) "Is what the author is stating based on sound evidence (are their statements based on first-hand or second-hand accounts)?" Critical questions for the argument from consequences were: (a) "What are the good/positive consequences in following through with this decision?"; and (b) "What are the bad/negative consequences?"

Teachers in a comparison condition used a traditional set of comprehension questions borrowed from the school's English language arts textbook to facilitate dialogue and document analyses among students. These questions prompted students to identify the historical actors, determine the author's purpose and position, identify main or big ideas, and record details that supported main or big ideas: (a) "What happened?"; (b) "When did it happen?"; (c) "Who were the major persons involved?"; (d) "Why did the author present his or her message?"; and (e) "Where did the author stand on the historical controversy?"

Students with and at-risk for LD who were taught to use argumentation schemes and critical questions wrote essays that contained greater levels of substantiation, perspective recognition, and more sophisticated rebuttals. Delayed writing prompts administered two-months after the study showed that students who engaged in disciplinary discussions continued to write essays that contained more sophisticated levels of historical thinking.

Summary

A promising and practical approach for teaching discipline-specific strategies for reading, critical reasoning, and writing with historical evidence is through the CA framework. The CA emphasizes an explicit teacher-directed instruction routine that embeds modeling, guided support, extensive corrective feedback, opportunities for independent practice, and the fading of instructional support until the student is able to reason and write historical arguments independently (De La Paz, Felton, et al., 2014, De La Paz, Monte-Sano, et al., 2017; De La Paz & Wissinger, 2017). Another effective practice for facilitating the development of social studies literacies is by using group dialogue and discussion. When paired with schema-based instruction or critical questions and structured scaffolds, group discussion has been shown to increase historical reasoning, and helps bridge ideas that surface in dialogue with peers to writing (De La Paz & Wissinger, 2017; Wissinger & De La Paz, 2016).

PART III: GETTING STARTED IN THE CLASSROOM AND FUTURE RESEARCH

The final section of this chapter provides guidance for educators about how to get started with implementing both domain-general and discipline-specific strategies and instruction. We conclude by outlining several recommendations for future research topics.

Getting Started: Resources and Recommendations

While new initiatives will require teachers to get involved in additional professional development opportunities, integrating activities that enhance students' historical reading, writing, and thinking will not require an entire overhaul of the curriculum (see De La Paz, Monte-Sano, et al., 2017; De La Paz & Wissinger, 2017). In fact, most of the studies in this line of work have reported favorable outcomes among groups of academically diverse learners with as little as 3 weeks of intensive instruction across the school year. Given the already exhaustive demands placed on teachers, even 3 weeks may seem unrealistic (Walker, 2022). However, meeting students at their current levels and raising their skills to the levels necessary to meet requirements (see CCSS, 2010; NCSS, 2013) will require more intensive, discipline-specific teaching, especially when targeting schools serving high concentrations of students who are disadvantaged and those with or at-risk for LDs (Farbman et al., 2014).

A second concern voiced by teachers has been the lack of access to resources and curricular materials that offer rich supplies of historical evidence such as primary and secondary source documents, historical maps, artwork, and historical cartoons. Put differently, while teachers may want to embrace requirements to integrate discipline-specific forms of literacy instruction in their classrooms, they do not have the time to seek out materials needed to create authentic historical learning environments. Fortunately, social studies teachers and special education teachers do not have to spend hours surfing the internet to locate instructional materials that align with modern state and national standards. In the past several years, experts have developed teacher-friendly websites, textbooks, and accompanying materials designed with struggling learners in mind (see Table 9.1). These resources provide valuable tools for facilitating authentic reading and writing skills in the disciplines. Moreover, they allow social studies teachers and their colleagues to focus on what they do best—teaching students.

Conclusions and Future Research

Similar to the heroes and iconic figures of the civil rights movement, such as Dr. Martin Luther King Jr. and Rosa Parks, Wade Blank (a Presbyterian minister from Ohio), and other members of the Atlantis[1] community protested the absence of wheelchair-accessible buses by laying in the streets and surrounding buses with wheelchairs for two days in July of 1975 (Rudolph, 2015). The protests shed light on the many discriminations and abuses faced by members of the disabled community and, ultimately, was a part of a movement that led to bipartisan legislation to address systematic discrimination against people with disabilities (see Americans With Disabilities Act, 1990).

Throughout both U.S. and world history, individuals with disabilities have mobilized to become a powerful conduit for advancing their rights (see Fleischer & Zames, 2011). However, current trends show that the participation of adolescents and young adults with disabilities in electoral politics (i.e., writing to a public official, distributing information on candidates, or working a political campaign) and the civic affairs of their communities have decreased over the past several decades (Ho et al., 2020). This lack of involvement can lead to less inclusive and responsive forms of democracy where people with disabilities hold disproportionately little social, economic, and political power in the decision-making process. While there is

Social Studies Literacy • 189

TABLE 9.1 Resources for Social Studies Teachers

Materials	Descriptions
Preparing Content Acquisition Podcasts (CAPs) Website: https://journals.sagepub.com/doi/10.1177/1053451214542046#fig1-1053451214542046	Step-by-step directions for how teachers can develop CAPs. Links to a library of sample CAPS are also embedded within the publication.
Promoting Adolescents' Comprehension of Text Website: http://admin.meadowscenter.org/projects/detail/promoting-adolescents-comprehension-of-text-pact	The site offers research literature and a practitioner-based overview on the Promoting Adolescents' Comprehension of Text (PACT) intervention. Teachers can also download lesson plans, instructional materials, and videos on key features of PACT instruction (i.e., essential words, comprehension canopy, critical reading, and the team-based learning comprehension check).
Reading, Thinking, and Writing About History: Teaching Arguments Writing to Diverse Learners in the Common Core Classroom, Grades 6–12. Monte-Sano, C., De La Paz, S., & Felton, M. (2014)	Textbook provides classroom-ready materials on six, 3-day historical investigations that target historical reading and argumentative writing for teachers who have little time to locate their own resources (e.g., source documents, a central historical question, and accompanying resources to teach historical strategies for reading, writing, and thinking).
Reading Like a Historian: Teaching Literacy in Middle & High School History Classrooms. Wineburg, S., Martin, D., & Monte-Sano, C. (2013).	Textbook demonstrates a practical approach for teaching students in middle and high school how to read and evaluate historical evidence more critically. Investigations range from exploring Pocahontas to John F. Kennedy and the Cuban Missile Crisis. Materials include a total of eight historical investigations with accompanying historical evidence, and strategies for understanding how to read and think about source documents.
Website	
Stanford History Education Group (SHEG) https://sheg.stanford.edu/	SHEG offers 91 lessons in the U.S. curriculum, 41 lessons of the world curriculum, and the 5 lessons in the introduction to historical thinking unit which can be taught in succession. Lessons are designed to stand alone and supplement what teachers are already doing in their classrooms, with most lessons requiring a full class period. The U.S. and world history lessons follow a three-part structure emphasizing: (a) developing background knowledge, (b) working from historical evidence, and (c) whole class discussion.

some debate about what influences civic and community engagement, the academic experiences of an individual are highly relevant to the formation of civic identities (Syvertsen et al., 2012). For students with and at risk for disabilities, these experiences have been marked by numerous challenges, including the demands of high-stakes testing. Yet, over the last four decades, researchers have uncovered a growing corpus of promising practices that can be used to help students become more literate and engaged thinkers who can construct their own interpretations and views about the past (and, perhaps, about the present). In this chapter, we highlighted strategies and instructional approaches that teachers can use to facilitate the development of both general and more sophisticated social studies literacies.

Future Research

Despite an increased number of intervention studies with students with disabilities in the social studies, most of the literature has targeted domain general skills such as instruction to promote reading comprehension, strategies to support the learning of vocabulary or declarative knowledge, and modifications to traditional text to enhance content knowledge. Far fewer studies have addressed the development of discipline-specific literacies with this group of learners (Ciullo et al., 2020).

The results from the small corpus of intervention studies targeting discipline-specific interventions reveal that students as young as fourth grade can be taught to engage in sourcing and to write interpretations when tasks are structured for younger students (Williams et al., 2007). To be sure, older students are more capable of understanding the goals of historical inquiry.

Though the topic of disciplinary literacies with students with developmental disabilities has not been studied widely in the literature, several studies have shown that explicit strategy instruction and structured inquiry-based instruction, paired with repeated practice, enhanced their understanding of science text, and led to improvements in recall memory (Roberts et al., 2019; Ryan et al., 2019). A recent meta-analysis also revealed that strategy instruction (and SRSD studies especially) with students with intellectual and developmental disabilities yielded large effects in different domains of writing, including the construction of informational, narrative, and persuasive essays (Rodgers & Loveall, 2022). Given the effectiveness of the CA framework with multiple types of learners in elementary, middle, and high school and its similarities with SRSD (see De La Paz, 2005), future researchers may consider how the model could be further adapted to meet the individual needs of students with developmental disabilities and help them develop literacies that are authentic in the social studies.

Moreover, important differences between novices and historians will always be evident because historians possess richer conceptual and factual knowledge than students, and because true historical inquiry requires independent research, which is not feasible in school settings. Moreover, the type of cognitive strategies that they engage in depends on their specialization (Nokes & Kesler-Lund, 2019). However, with that caveat in mind, a growing body of literature shows that students with disabilities can learn to engage in disciplinary reasoning through a combination of explicit instruction, metacognitive modeling, differentiated tools and instructional feedback, all of which are provided through CAs.

In addition to recommendations for more discipline-specific research, studies in other disciplines of the social studies (e.g., economics, geography, and civics and government) are nearly absent from the literature. Many people see history classrooms as the best place to prepare young people for civic engagement. Civic engagement demands many of the strategies of historical reading, thinking, and writing. For instance, Kuhn et al. (1994) found great overlap between historical reasoning and juror reasoning. Both the historian and juror reconstructed an event, piecing it together from incomplete, biased, and positioned stories of varying credibility. Both processes required sourcing, corroboration, and mild skepticism. Still, questions remain about whether nurturing historical strategies prepares young people for a life of researching issues, making an appeal to government representatives, voting, or serving on a jury.

Ongoing studies identify other strategies that historians use that may have applications for civic engagement. The manner through which historians explore plausible alternatives, even those that do not fit their interpretation at the moment, before arriving at a conclusion, may be useful in civic engagement as citizens work together and with elected officials to find mutually beneficial solutions. Moreover, the disciplinary reading skills developed in historical inquiry may have applications in civic online reading because similarities exist between literacies needed to read, think, and write with historical evidence and to research unsubstantiated outlets of information on the Internet. Future intervention work might study the effects of having teachers describe and model for students the importance of using sourcing when conducting online research by showing students how to identify the source of a webpage and use that source information to engage in lateral reading (McGrew et al., 2018). If we are to achieve the goal set forth by the NCSS (1992, 2013) and ensure that all students, especially those with and at risk for LD, are provided opportunities to become more informed citizens who are active and engaged in public life, those in the research community must explore how to teach students to apply their social studies literacies in ways that promote civic engagement.

NOTE

1. The Atlantis Community was formed by Wade Blank in 1975 to provide free, individualized care to those in need of housing, meals, in-home care, and job training (Rudolph, 2015).

REFERENCES

Alexander, P. A. (2003). The development of expertise: The journey from acclimation to proficiency. *Educational Researcher, 32*(8), 10–14.

Alexander, P. A. (2005). Teaching towards expertise. In P. Tomlinson, J. Dockrell, & P. Winne (Eds.), *Pedagogy—Teaching for learning* (pp. 29–45). British Psychological Society.

Americans With Disabilities Act of 1990, 42 U.S.C. § 12101 *et seq.* (1990). https://www.ada.gov/pubs/adastatute08.htm

Archer, A. L., & Hughes, C. A. (2011). *Explicit instruction: Effective and efficient teaching.* Guilford.

Bulgren, J. A., Graner, P. S., & Deshler, D. D. (2013). Literacy challenges and opportunities for students with learning disabilities in social studies and history. *Learning Disabilities Research & Practice, 28*(1), 17–27.

Bulgren, J. A., Marquis, J. G., Lenz, B. K., Deshler, D. D., & Schumaker, J. B. (2011). The effectiveness of a question-exploration routine for enhancing the content learning of secondary students. *Journal of Educational Psychology, 103*(3), 578–593.

Cassimere, R. (1977). Equalizing teachers' pay in Louisiana. *Integrated Education, 15*(4) 3–8.

Chin, C., & Osborne, J. (2010). Students' questions and discursive interaction: Their impact on argumentation during collaborative group discussions in science. *Journal of Research in Science Teaching, 47*(7), 883–908.

Ciullo, S., Collins, A., Wissinger, D., McKenna, J., Lo, S., & Osman, D. (2020). Students with learning disabilities in the social studies: A meta-analysis of intervention research. *Exceptional Children, 86*(4), 393–412.

Collins, A., Brown, J. S., & Holum, A. (1991). Cognitive apprenticeship: Making thinking visible. *American Educator, 15*(3), 6–11, 38–46.

Collins, A., Ciullo, S., Graham, S., Sigafoos, L., Guerra, S., David, M., & Judd, L. (2021). Writing expository essays from social studies texts: A self-regulated strategy development study. *Reading and Writing: An Interdisciplinary Journal, 34,* 1623–1651.

Common Core State Standards Initiative. (2010). *Common core state standards for English language arts & literacy in history/social studies, science, and technical subjects.* https://eric.ed.gov/?id=ED522008

De La Paz, S. (2005). Effects of historical reasoning instruction and writing strategy mastery in culturally and academically diverse middle school classrooms. *Journal of Educational Psychology, 97*(2), 139–156.

De La Paz, S., Felton, M., Monte-Sano, C., Croninger, R., Jackson, C., Deogracias, J. S., & Hoffman, B. P. (2014). Developing historical reading and writing with adolescent readers: effects on student learning. *Theory & Research in Social Education, 42*(2), 228–274.

De La Paz, S., & Graham, S. (1997). Strategy instruction in planning: Effects on the writing performance and behavior of students with learning disabilities. *Exceptional Children, 63*(2), 167–181.

De La Paz, S., Monte-Sano, C., Felton, M., Croninger, R., Jackson, C., & Piantedosi, K. W. (2017). A historical writing apprenticeship for adolescents: Integrating disciplinary learning with cognitive strategies. *Reading Research Quarterly, 52*(1), 31–52.

De La Paz, S., & Wissinger, D. (2017). Improving the historical knowledge and writing of students with or at-risk for LD. *Journal of Learning Disabilities, 50*(6), 658–671.

Del Favero, L. D., Boscolo, P., Vidotto, G., & Vicentini, M. (2007). Classroom discussion and individual problem-solving in the teaching of history: Do different instructional approaches affect interest in different ways? *Learning and Instruction, 17*(6), 635–657.

Fairclough, A. (1990). Historians and the civil rights movement. *Journal of American Studies, 24*(3), 387–398.

Farbman, D., Goldberg, D., & Miller, T. (2014). *Redesigning and expanding school time to support common core implementation*. Center for American Progress: National Center on Time & Learning. https://www.americanprogress.org/article/redesigning-and-expanding-school-time-to-support-common-core-implementation/

Fleischer, D., & Zames, Z. (2011). *The disability rights movement: From charity to confrontation* (Updated ed.). Temple University Press.

Gates, H. L. (Writer), Burk, K. (Producer), & Harris, S. (Director). (2022). *Making Black America: Through the Grapevine* [Film]. McGee Media, Inkwell Media, and Washington Educational Telecommunications Association.

Harris, K. R., Graham, S., Mason, L., & Friedlander, B. (2008). *Powerful writing strategies for all students*. Brooks.

Ho, S., Eaton, S., & Mitra, M. (2020). *Civic engagement with people with disabilities: A way forward through cross-movement building*. Lurie Institute for Disability Policy, Brandeis University. https://heller.brandeis.edu/lurie/pdfs/civic-engagement-report.pdf

Kennedy, M. J., Deshler, D. D., & Lloyd, J. W. (2015). Effects of multimedia vocabulary instruction on adolescents with learning disabilities. *Journal of Learning Disabilities, 48*(1), 22–38.

Kuhn, D., Weinstock, M., & Flaton, R. (1994). How well do jurors reason? Competence dimensions of individual variation in a juror reasoning task. *Psychological Science, 5*(5), 289–296.

Lapsansky-Werner, E. J., Levy, P. L., Roberts, R., & Taylor, A. (2019). *United states history: The twentieth century*. Pearson Education.

McGrew, S., Breakstone, J., Ortega, T., Smith, M., & Wineburg, S. (2018). Can students evaluate online sources? Learning from assessments of civic online reasoning. *Theory & Research in Social Education, 46*(2), 165–193.

Monte-Sano, C., De La Paz, S., & Felton, M. (2014). *Reading, thinking and writing about history: Teaching argument writing to diverse learners in the common core classroom, Grades 6–12*. Teachers College Press.

Monte-Sano, C., De La Paz, S., Felton, M., Worland, K., Yee, L. S., & Carey, R. L. (2017). Learning to teach disciplinary literacy across diverse eighth-grade history classrooms within a district–university partnership. *Teacher Education Quarterly, 44*(4), 98–124.

Monte-Sano, C., Schleppegrell, M., Sun, S., Wu, J., & Kabat, J. (2021). Discussion in diverse middle school social studies classrooms: Promoting all students' participation in the disciplinary work of inquiry. *Teachers College Record, 123*(10), 142–184.

National Council for the Social Studies. (1992). *National curriculum standards for social studies: Executive summary.*

National Council for the Social Studies. (2013). *College, career, and civic life (C3) framework for social studies state standards: Guidance for enhancing the rigor of K–12 civics, economics, geography, and history.* Retrieved from http://www.socialstudies.org/c3

National Research Council. (2000). *How people learn: Brain, mind, experience, and school* (Expanded ed.). National Academy Press. https://doi.org/10.17226/9853

Nokes, J. D., & Kesler-Lund, A. (2019). Historians' social literacies: How historians collaborate and write during a document-based activity. *The History Teacher, 52*(3), 369–410.

Nussbaum, E. M., & Edwards, O. V. (2011). Critical questions and argument stratagems: A framework for enhancing and analyzing students' reasoning practices. *The Journal of the Learning Sciences, 20*(3), 443–488.

O'Connor, R. E., Sanchez, V., Beach, K., & Bocian, K. (2017). Special education teachers integrating reading with eighth grade U.S. history content. *Learning Disabilities Research & Practice, 32*(2), 99–111.

Okolo, C. M., & Ferretti, R. (2014). History instruction for students with learning disabilities. In L. Swanson, K. Harris, & S. Graham (Eds.), *Handbook of learning disabilities* (pp. 463–486). The Gilford Press.

Pennsylvania Department of Education. (2002). *Academic standards for history.* Retrieved from https://www.stateboard.education.pa.gov/Documents/Regulations%20and%20Statements/State%20Academic%20Standards/E%20HISTORY%20web03.pdf

Reznitskaya, A., Anderson, R. C., & Kuo, L. (2007). Teaching and learning argumentation. *The Elementary School Journal, 107*(5), 449–472.

Roberts, C. A., Kim, S., Tandy, J., & Meyer, N. (2019). Using content area literacy strategies during shared reading to increase comprehension of high school students with moderate intellectual disability on adapted science text. *Education and training in autism and developmental disabilities, 54*(2), 147–160.

Rochelle, B. (1993). *Witness to freedom, young people who fought for civil rights.* Penguin Random House.

Rodgers, D. B., & Loveall, S. J. (2022). Writing interventions for students with intellectual and developmental disabilities: A meta-analysis. *Remedial and Special Education, 44*(3), 239–252.

Rudolph, K. (2015, May 18). "We will ride!" The origin of the disability rights movement in Denver. Blair-Caldwell African American Research Library Newsletter. https://history.denverlibrary.org/news/we-will-ride-origin-disability-rights-movement-denver-0

Ryan, J., Jameson, J. M., Coleman, O. F., Eichelberger, C., Bowman, J. A., Conradi, L. A., Johnston, S. S., & McDonnell, J. (2019). Inclusive social studies content instruction for students with significant intellectual disability using structured inquiry-based instruction. *Education and Training in Autism and Developmental Disabilities, 54*(4), 420–436.

Seixas, D. P., & Morton, T. (2013). *The big six historical thinking concepts.* Nelson Education.

Sitkoff, H. (1978). *A new deal for Blacks: The emergence of civil rights as a national issue.* Oxford University Press.

Stoel, G. L., van Drie, J. P., & van Boxtel, C. A. (2017). The effects of explicit teaching of strategies, second-order concepts, and epistemological underpinnings on students' ability to reason causally in history. *Journal of Educational Psychology, 109*(3), 321.

Swanson, E., Wanzek, J., Vaughn, S., Roberts, G, & Fall, A. (2015). Improving reading comprehension and social studies knowledge among middle school students with disabilities. *Exceptional Children, 81*(4), 11–24.

Syvertsen, A., Wray-Lake, L., Flanagan, C., Osgood, D., & Briddell, L. (2012). Thirty-year trends in U.S. adolescents' civic engagement: A story of changing participation and educational differences. *Journal of Research on Adolescents, 21*(3), 586–594.

Van Drie, J., & Van Boxtel, C. (2008). Historical reasoning: Towards a framework for analyzing students' reasoning about the past. *Educational Psychology Review, 20,* 87–110.

Vaughn, S., Swanson, E. A., Roberts, G., Wanzek, J., Stillman-Spisak, S., Solis, M., & Simmons, D. (2013). Improving reading comprehension and social studies knowledge in middle school. *Reading Research Quarterly, 48*(1), 77–93.

Walker, T. (2022, February 1). *Survey: Alarming numbers of educators may soon leave the profession.* neaToday. https://www.nea.org/advocating-for-change/new-from-nea/survey-alarming-number-educators-may-soon-leave-profession

Walton, D., Reed, C., & Macagno, F. (2008). *Argumentation schemes.* Cambridge University Press.

Welch, S. E. (2007). *Soldiers of Martin Luther King Jr: A memoir from the trenches of the CRM.* RoseDog Books.

Williams, J. P., Nubla-Kung, A., Pollini, S., Stafford, K. B., Garcia, A., & Snyder, A. E. (2007). Teaching cause–effect text structure through social studies content to at-risk second graders. *Journal of Learning Disabilities, 40*(2), 111–120.

Wineburg, S. S. (1991). Historical problem solving: A study of the cognitive processes used in the evaluation of documentary and pictorial evidence. *Journal of Educational Psychology, 83*(1), 73–87.

Wissinger, D. R., & Ciullo, S. (2018). History literacy research for students with or at risk for learning disabilities: A systematic review. *Learning Disabilities Research & Practice, 33,* 237–249.

Wissinger, D. R., & De La Paz, S. (2016). Effects of critical discussions on middle school students' written historical arguments. *Journal of Educational Psychology, 108*(1), 43–59.

Wissinger, D. R., & De La Paz, S. (2020). Effects of discipline-specific strategy instruction on historical writing growth of students with writing difficulties. *Journal of Learning Disabilities, 53*(3), 199–212.
Wissinger, D. R., De La Paz, S., & Jackson, C. (2021). The effects of historical reading and writing strategy instruction with fourth- through sixth-grade students. *Journal of Educational Psychology, 113*(1), 49–67.
Yore, L. D., Hand, B. M., & Prain, V. (2002). Scientists as writers. *Science Education, 86*(5), 672–692.

ABOUT THE EDITORS

Darren Minarik is a professor in secondary social studies and special education and is co-director for the Virginia Inclusive Practices Center at Radford University. Darren's research and presentations address inclusive educational practices, self-determination, disability history, and civic engagement.

Timothy Lintner is Carolina Trustee Professor of Education at the University of South Carolina Aiken. He teaches the middle level/secondary social studies methods course at USC Aiken. His research explores the intersection between social studies and special education.

ABOUT THE CONTRIBUTORS

Liz Altieri is professor of special education and co-director of the Virginia Inclusive Practices Center at Radford University. Her practice and research with inclusive practices that support children and youth with significant disabilities dates back to 1983. She has a particular interest in the skills needed by general and special educators in supporting the academic and social success of students with disabilities in the general education classroom.

Leah Bueso is an assistant professor of urban education at the University of Illinois Springfield. Her research examines the role of race/ethnicity, socioeconomic status, and disability in education law and policy, special education, English language arts, and social studies with a focus on civic engagement.

Janis Bulgren is a research professor at the University of Kansas Center for Research on Learning where she serves as director of the Institute for Content Area Learning and Teaching. Her research has focused on developing and validating instructional procedures to help teachers and students engage in higher order thinking and reasoning across different content areas based on rigorous standards.

Rich Cairn is history, civics and social studies inclusion specialist and founder of the Emerging America program at the Collaborative for Educational Services in Massachusetts. His work focuses on teaching disability history and on engaging all learners in civic engagement.

Stephen Ciullo is an associate professor of special education at Texas State University. He teaches courses that focus on literacy instruction and intervention for students with learning disabilities. Stephen's research addresses content-area literacy, writing instruction, and professional development for special education teachers.

Susan De La Paz is a professor in the Department of Counseling, Higher Education, and Special Education at the University of Maryland, College Park. Her research program focuses on adolescent literacy for students with and without learning disabilities (LD). Her work intersects special education, history education and science education through the study of written argumentation.

Karen Douglas is professor and co-director of the Virginia Inclusive Practices Center at Radford University. Her research focuses on enhancing inclusive practices in schools to support the academic and social/emotional skills of all students but especially students with disabilities.

Justin Garwood is a professor of special education at the University of Vermont, where he is director of the PhD in Social-Emotional-Behavioral Health and Inclusive Education program. His research is focused on relationship-based approaches to inclusive education for youth with emotional and behavioral disorders.

Timothy Lintner is Carolina Trustee Professor of Education at the University of South Carolina Aiken. He teaches the middle level/secondary social studies methods course at USC Aiken. His research explores the intersection between social studies and special education.

Melissa Lisanti is an associate professor in elementary education at Radford University. With experience teaching social studies in K–12 inclusive classrooms, she now works in collaborative teacher preparation focusing on Universal Design for Learning, multi-tiered systems of support, and high-leverage teaching practices.

Melissa Martin is an associate professor in special education at the University of South Carolina Aiken. She teaches special education methods courses to preservice teachers. She also serves as the director of Pacer LIFE, a postsecondary program for college students with intellectual and developmental disabilities.

Darren Minarik is a professor in secondary social studies and special education and is co-director for the Virginia Inclusive Practices Center at Radford University. Darren's research and presentations address inclusive educational practices, self-determination, disability history, and civic engagement.

About the Contributors

Kari A. Muente is a professor of social studies education and the middle and secondary division chair at Martin Luther College. She teaches K–12 social studies methods courses and several social studies content courses. Her scholarship focuses on implementing Universal Design for Learning (UDL), culturally responsive pedagogy, and inclusive practices in the social studies classroom.

Alison Puliatte is an associate professor in childhood education at SUNY Plattsburgh and co-regional director for the North Country region of the NYS Master Teacher program. She teaches courses in elementary and special education and educational leadership. Her research explores relationships between teacher content knowledge, self-efficacy, and student achievement.

Dan Wissinger is a professor in the Department of Professional Studies in Education (PSE) at Indiana University of Pennsylvania (IUP). Before joining the faculty at IUP, he was a special education teacher for over ten years and earned his PhD at the University of Maryland. His research focuses on writing interventions for struggling readers and writers in content area classrooms.